CALL TO ACTION

CALL TO ACTION

Handbook for Ecology, Peace and Justice

EDITED BY BRAD ERICKSON

Sierra Club Books
SAN FRANCISCO

The Sierra Club, founded in 1892 by John Muir, has devoted itself to the study and protection of the earth's scenic and ecological resources—mountains, wetlands, woodlands, wild shores and rivers, deserts and plains. The publishing program of the Sierra Club offers books to the public as a nonprofit educational service in the hope that they may enlarge the public's understanding of the Club's basic concerns. The point of view expressed in each book, however, does not necessarily represent that of the Club. The Sierra Club has some sixty chapters coast to coast, in Canada, Hawaii, and Alaska. For information about how you may participate in its programs to preserve wilderness and the quality of life, please address inquiries to Sierra Club, 730 Polk Street, San Francisco, CA 94109.

Copyright © 1990 by Environmental Project on Central America

Library of Congress Cataloging in Publication Data
Call to action: handbook for ecology, peace, and justice / edited by Brad Erickson.
    p.   cm.
  Includes bibliographical references.
    ISBN 0-87156-611-7
    1. Policy sciences. 2. Environmental policy. 3. International relations. 4. Peace. 5. Social justice. 6. Social action. 7. Social movements.
H97.C35 1990
361.2—dc20

        89-29296
        CIP

Editor: Brad Erickson
Picture Editor: Rebecca Solnit
Editorial Advisors: David Brower, Florence Gardner, Claire Greensfelder, Richard Grossman, Jane McAlevey, Donna Shore, Lauren Webster and Beth Weinberger.
Research: John Cothran, Karl Erb, Todd Steiner, Lisa Tweten, Denise Voelker.

Cover design by Paul Bacon
Book design by Paula Schlosser
Production by Susan Ristow
Printed in the United States of America on recycled paper.

10   9   8   7   6   5   4   3   2   1

Dedication

I express my deep respect for the courage of the people of El Salvador for whom the connection between ecology, peace and justice is no abstraction but an everyday reality in the struggle to feed one's family, and in the hope for land, justice and dignity.

I dedicate this book to the Salvadoran people, and to people everywhere who struggle for a better world for themselves, their families and their descendants; and to the memory of those who have died in struggle who will never taste the fruit of their actions. Let us not forget what others have sacrificed. Let their lives be our inspiration.

Contents

Acknowledgments

I am deeply indebted to the contributors, advisors and sponsors that made this book possible. Writers, editors, activists, artists, photographers and researchers donated time, knowledge, material and talent to help produce it. The credit for much of the diversity and creativity contained in this book goes to this team. All errors or omissions, however, are entirely my responsibility. Additionally, although the advisors and many of the authors were integrally involved throughout the book's progress, they should not be assumed to unanimously approve all editorial decisions.

I want to express my appreciation and love for the generous help, support and encouragement from all the contributors and collaborators named, and also to Harriet Barlow, Robert Borosage, Cal Broomhead, China Brotsky, Terrie Brown, Nilo Cayuqueo, David Cross, Kevin Danaher, Bill Devall, Mark Dubois, Michael Gemignani, Angela Gennino, Karen Gosling, Dave Henson, Ivan Illich, Sarah James, Tyler Johnson, Joe Kane, Josh Karlinger, Joe Karten, Sam Kitner, John Knox, Winona La Duke, James Lee, Ellen Manchester, Wangari Maathai, Palesa Makhale, Dora Miranda, Marie Miranda, Juana Alicia Montoya, Danny Moses, Susan McGovern, Greg Nacco, Jennie Oppenheimer, Moringe Parkipuny, Laura Peterson, Jonathon Puth, Mary Gail Snyder, John Steere, Carrie Stewart, Nick Soter, Nick Wilton, Mark Windsor, Hazel Wolf and the staff of the Earth Island Institute.

—Brad Erickson

The Hole in the Ozone Layer is excerpted from Parade Magazine, September 11, 1988. Copyright ©1988 by Carl Sagan. Reprinted by permission of the author. All rigths reserved.

Embracing Diversity: Building Multicultural Alliances Copyright March, 1989. Tools for Change.

Rethinking Population is excerpted with permission of Betsy Hartmann from *Reproductive Rights and Wrongs: The Global Politics of Population Control and Contraceptive Choice.* 1987. New York: Harper & Row. Reprinted by permission of Harper & Row Publishers, Inc.

Third World Debt is excerpted with the author's permission from the final chapter of forthcoming, fifth printing of *A Fate Worse Than Debt.* Food First Books/ Grove Press. New York. 1988. United Kingdom and Commonwealth including Canada, Penguin Books. London. 1988.

Share the Wealth was originally published as "Why is Money Like Manure? You've Got To Spread It Around," *Mother Jones,* May, 1988. Excerpted with permission of the authors.

Addressing the Nuclear Threat is adapted from a speech by Helen Caldicott to the American Humanist Association. It originally appeared in the September/ October 1982 issue of *The Humanist* and is reprinted by permission of Helen Caldicott.

Oceans originally appeared in US News and World Report, June 24, 1985 as "Conversation with Jacques Cousteau." Reprinted by permission. Copyright 1985, US News and World Report.

Preface

REV. JESSE L. JACKSON

THE OLD ORDER is dying; a new one struggles to be born. Across the world, we are witnessing the dawn of a new enlightenment. People are realizing that environmental protection is no longer a rich man's preserve but everyone's preservation and that arms spending contributes not to national security but to international insecurity. We must learn new ways of thinking and new ways of acting. This *Call to Action* provides a guidebook for that effort.

In the past thirty years, even the mainstream has come to understand the fragility of nature. During the Industrial Revolution—in all ideologies from capitalist to communist—nature was a mysterious and infinite storehouse of wealth to be stormed and plundered. The very idea of progress—in science, in culture, in civilization—was identified with conquering nature, bending its powers and riches to our will.

The transformation of our consciousness began slowly. Nuclear weapons suddenly gave humans the God-like power to destroy human civilization. Pictures from outer space allowed us to see our fragile planet against the fathomless universe. Global communications brought evidence of human interconnection into our living rooms.

Today a new enlightenment is spreading across the world even as our environment continues to deteriorate. The major elements of the environmental crisis are well known: the greenhouse effect, acid rain, weakening of the ozone layer, spreading of deserts, fouling of land, waters, and air, even of oceans once thought to be a bottomless disposal.

Our security is also threatened by war and poverty. Despite improvements in US/ Soviet relations, the threat of nuclear war will be ever-present until we disarm. Regional wars waste precious resources and turn civilians into refugees. Paper democracies are wearing thin and we are starting to see the faces of the impoverished and homeless who now refuse to remain invisible. We see ourselves participating in the building of our future, no longer content to have decisions made for us by leaders who lack the vision to work for the common good.

With a new way of seeing comes the ability to change how we think and how we act. It requires a monumental struggle about values, priorities, knowledge. This book provides a guide for thinking and acting. Its authors speak on many subjects, but some principles are held in common.

We must make fundamental changes in the way we live, and particularly in our system of production. Science can and must offer us new inventions to conserve energy, recycle and reduce wastes, and recover from disasters. But technology alone is not the solution. For too long, environmental effects have been an "externality" to corporations, a free good that went unpriced in the search for profit and growth. It is only in the past twenty years that some countries—primarily those in the industrialized North—have begun to make corporations pay at least some of the costs of their use of nature's wealth. One byproduct has been the export of destructive goods and industries to Third World countries too desperate for jobs and capital to object.

No one can be free of the threat to the environment until everyone is free. Multinationals may export destructive production and poisonous products to the Third World, but when they do, we import global despoliation. When export agriculture drives peasants off their land to chop down forests and overwhelm marginal lands, the resulting deserts threaten us all. When multinationals raze the rainforests to raise cattle we are all threatened. Air pollution, whether produced in Mexico City or in Pittsburgh, equally threatens the ozone layer and contributes to global warming and acid rain.

Ecological security requires economic justice. Over the past decade, inequality has grown across the world. The disparity between the rich and poor nations, between the rich and poor people in this nation is greater than ever. Although the rich and poor may live in separate worlds, they share the same globe. Humankind cannot survive one-third wealthy and two-thirds destitute. In the short term, of course, there is profit

and pleasure for the lucky. The North can make Africa a dumping ground for toxic waste and distance itself from its poisons. We can continue to transform Latin America into a vast corporate plantation for the export of foods and resources for our enjoyment. But we are trading short-term profit for long-term pain. The supplanting of food crops for export crops creates the very overcrowding and desperation that has produced the desertification of the Sahel, the leveling of 11 million hectares a year of rain forests in the Amazon, and now poses a growing threat to the existence of all. As the United Nations' Brundtland Commission concluded, protection of the environment requires equitable development.

We must change our priorities to meet this new challenge. Since World War II, the United States has spent over 3 trillion dollars on the military, seeking security from external attack. Now our very existence is threatened by an environmental crisis that our weapons cannot protect us from. Yet we continue to spend 300 billion dollars a year on the military—much of it on weapons we cannot use and do not need—while ignoring necessary measures to protect against a real security threat. We can save some of that money and invest it to preserve a world for our children to inherit.

We must change the way we think to address our real security challenges. We have spent 10 billion dollars fighting popular movements in Central America in the name of anti-communism. But we are not threatened by these small, impoverished, environmentally degraded nations composed mostly of subsistence farmers struggling to survive. We are threatened by the accelerating destruction of rainforests in Central America and deepening hunger and poverty, which our current policies only exacerbate or ignore. We should be sending environmental aid, not military aid.

Global security requires empowerment.

The Earth will not be saved by powerful savants issuing edicts from afar. The environment will not be saved by corporations whose mandate is to maximize profit, nor by bureaucracies whose mandate is to manage people. The new enlightenment requires that people be empowered to change the way institutions act. Only popular mobilization can create the political force necessary for the transformation—of the laws that determine how corporations produce, the priorities that governments will pursue, the practices that people adopt.

When the people act, the powers that be must respond. But this requires organization at the local level, mobilization at the regional and national level, communication and coordination at the international level. On this fragile globe, we are truly our brother's and our sister's keeper.

In this volume, Brad Erickson has put together a feast for citizens hungry for inspiration, empowerment, tools and tactics. But is more than that. It is a call to conscience, a call to commitment, a call to action. We can usher in a new enlightenment to the benefit of generations to come. But the crisis brooks little delay; the time for action is now. Join us and help keep hope alive.

CALL TO ACTION

Forward on All Fronts

BRAD ERICKSON

"Injustice anywhere is a threat to justice everywhere. We are caught in an inescapable network of mutuality, tied in a single garment of destiny."
—MARTIN LUTHER KING, JR.

T HE WORD *JUSTICE* IS used with the universal agreement that it is something everyone should have. Many people fight injustice, sometimes winning, sometimes losing, always on uncertain ground. Why doesn't everyone oppose ecological destruction all the time? Where is our anger at toxic dumping, military intervention, and government indifference to racism, unemployment and homelessness? Because we still pass injustice everyday in the street, we need to ask what is it we haven't done and what we need to do differently.

No one claims to support injustice and yet many surely do. Exxon poisons a vast expanse of our common natural heritage in Alaska and claims that responsibility for clean-up is an undue hardship while their profits are hardly touched. Union Carbide commits mass negligent homicide in Bhopal, India and considers $1,000 per human life a generous compensation. Congress funnels millions of dollars per day to violently repressive governments such as El Salvador's while perhaps 3 million homeless suffer within our own borders. The justice that is talked about is not the same as the justice we get.

It is easy for decisionmakers to pay lip service to justice and democracy while catering to an elite minority who prosper via *in*justice. For the victim, it is easy to complain about unjust conditions without changing them. It is more difficult for a determined group of people to identify and confront the root of injustice, demand an end to it, and if need be, directly intervene to prevent its continuation. But so far, that is the only approach that works. And that is what this book is about. As Frederick Douglass said:

"Those who profess to favor freedom and yet depreciate agitation, are people who want crops without ploughing the ground; they want rain without thunder and lightning; they want the ocean without the roaring of its many waters. The struggle may be a moral one, or it may be a physical one, or it may be both. But it must be a struggle. Power concedes nothing without a demand; it never has and it never will. People may not get all they pay for in this world, but they most certainly pay for all they get."

Throughout history, many have fought injustice. The successes of the labor movement and the civil rights movement in the US include many rights we now take for granted. Popular opposition to the war in Vietnam prevented the US from "winning" the war by dropping a nuclear warhead. Everywhere, people met the challenges of injustice, violence and hunger, as individuals, groups, and movements.

Our strengths and accomplishments are encouraging, but our efforts and our movements haven't yet done enough. The spread of war and poverty, and the destruction of the Earth point depressingly to our failure to create a society of equality and peace, or to develop intelligent plans for our continued existence on and with the planet. Popular opinion polls in the US suggest that most people favor strict environmental regulations, full employment, and peaceful solutions to international conflict. So why doesn't our government provide this? Does our democracy represent us? Our voices are barely discernable in policy discussions; decisions are made by and for an elite; are we participating in our governance or standing by as objects? If we are to move beyond simply suffering and reacting to crises, and actually begin building a better world, we must not only fight for specific changes but also insist on full democratic participation in our governance.

Individual lifestyle changes, such as recycling or boycotting irresponsible corporations, allow us to practice what we preach; but only through challenging and restructuring unequal power relationships can we achieve the changes this book is talking about. Creating alternative institutions and practices is part of the change, but can't replace confronting exploiters, warmakers and poisoners.

The fate of the Earth is a common responsibility; each of us can play a part in creating a better world. But that is not to say that workers and owners, consumers and manufacturers, or students and politicians are equally to blame for environmental destruction, war or social inequality. We may each be a thread in the fabric but we did not all design the garment, nor are we equally warmed by it. To say that we all have an equal responsibility is to deny the patterns of power operating in our society. David Rockefeller and a coal miner do not share the same responsibility or an equal capacity for action. The coal miner has no choice but to struggle for fair wages, safe working conditions and adequate healthcare—in short, to survive. In contrast, Rockefeller has the influence, the opportunity and the luxury of choice to change economic policies that ravish the Earth and deepen poverty while enriching those who pump poisons, pillage nature, bust unions and build weapons. He chooses not to do so. So let us take responsibility for our shared problems but blame the instigator, not the victim.

In order to grow as a movement to meet the challenges we face we will have to be self critical—to give ourselves clarity about our objectives, and to make ourselves stronger and more effective. We have seen the results of *not* working for justice: slavery and its hangover of systemic racial inequality, an economic order that enriches a few while creating poverty for the world's majority, the specter of nuclear holocaust, the tragedy of history's genocides, the poisoning of the

Spontaneous demonstration in support of human-rights advocate Bishop Camus following Mass in south-central Chilean town of Linares. STEVEN RUBIN, 1987, IMPACT VISUALS

Earth for short-term economic gain, the oppression and extermination of native peoples, and the extinction of thousands of species that we and future generations will never see again. We've also seen the results of lobbyists and moderate organizations who work *for* justice—but with narrow and compromising vision, limited allies, and without high aspirations. Many of us recognize the threat of apathy, compromise, or ineffective action. Many are outraged by the system of injustice, destruction and exploitation that we have inherited, but why don't all of us do something?

Busy with our day-to-day survival, we find it easy to forget or deny the destruction of the Earth and the oppression of its inhabitants and trust that Government or Science will fix it. But sadly, our government and industry's "progress" are the instruments of this injustice. We know how to feed and clothe all of humanity and we already have

numerous alternatives to destructive technologies such as nuclear power and fossil fuels but our government lacks the political will to implement this knowledge for our benefit.

Government and industry seemingly do whatever they want, with or without the consent of the people who elect and charter them, but not without our cooperation. Gandhi said that it is our active duty not to cooperate with evil: that if we do not resist wrongdoing, we are equally responsible for the outcome. You and I didn't vote to send the $3 billion to El Salvador that have purchased 70,000 deaths there since 1980. But if we don't oppose and resist our government's policy of war by proxy, the torture, assasinations, civilian bombing and ecological devastation will continue or even increase.

As isolated individuals we have little effect on great evils, but working in organized groups we have the potential to restructure nondemocratic, destructive institutions and create equitable and sustainable ones. For example, co-ops and collectives already incorporate democratic practice into economic relationships. In education, active parent participation can revitalize schools and make educational administrators accountable to the real needs of youth, insuring that each child receives an education that prepares them to enter society with confidence as a full participant. Neighborhoods can cooperate to provide services such as affordable childcare, healthcare and legal services. And to dream on a larger scale: what would happen if, in noncooperation with the military-industrial complex, we stopped paying war taxes? Nuclear warheads could not be built and military aid could not be used to escalate international conflict. Even though the CIA could continue to finance covert intervention through narcotics trafficking, if we didn't buy their cocaine, the warmaking would eventually have to stop.

Dependence on a healthy planet for our survival unites us all in common cause for halting the destruction of the environment. Yet environmentalists on their own are only marginally effective, often labelled just another special-interest group in Congress and regularly defeated by industry's demand for economic expansion. The largest corporations justify their pollution, their tax exemptions and other special privileges with the argument that their success will "trickle down" to the rest of the population. If the billions in profits these corporations amass *are* trickling down, many are still waiting for the first drop.

Against the might and momentum of government controlled by industry, isolated single issue groups fight for reforms that fall far short of their aims. We cannot trust politicians or lobbyists to halt the destruction of the Earth for us. If the US *is* a democra-

cy—*of the people, for the people and by the people*—why can't we take hold of our government and demand that it be accountable to the needs of *all* of its population? The environmental movement will continue to be marginal as long as it limits itself to "environmental" issues. Until our movements address, challenge and change exploitive power relationships to change the way decisions are made, we are in fact policing ourselves on behalf of the destroyers. We might save a forest here or a species there, but we're just putting out fires while we let the arsonists go scot-free.

When we open our hearts we know that the liberation struggles of women, working people, people of color, the elderly, the disabled, the landless, and the impoverished are just. The *blame the victim* rhetoric of policymakers must be confronted and exposed as fallacy: the impoverished are not "lazy"; many have full-time jobs and still live in poverty. Children, senior citizens, and single mothers are not a "burden" on society; we all depend on one another. The developing nations are not a bottomless begging bowl, dependent on our benevolence and generosity. In fact, with only 6 percent of the world's population, the US consumes close to one-half of global resources. Through the current-day colonization of international lending, the developing nations are now paying over $100 billion net every year to the industrial nations. Who's subsidizing whom?

Inequality is universal—but why have we let it go so far? The US is one of the wealthiest nations on Earth yet unemployment and homelessness are at an all time high; of all industrialized nations, we have the highest rate of homicide and teenage drug abuse; we are still the only industrial nation, save South Africa, without national health insurance; and, next to South Africa and the Soviet Union, we imprison a larger percentage of our population than any other nation on Earth.

In each case, people confront these outrageous conditions, yet as individuals or even as independent, single issue groups, we are often vulnerable and ineffective against industry and the politicians they help elect. Too often we allow polluters and exploiters to define what changes in their actions are *possible at this time* when what they're really determining is that their activities be *profitable at all times*. In the limited debate that follows, we hear and sometimes even believe arguments such as "If we have to stop dumping dioxin in the river, it'll put us out of business and that'll put good people out of work. Do you want to see families go hungry?" Environment is pitted against the workforce, as if jobs which destroy the environment are the only and the best jobs that we can create.

The deaths of tens of thousands of us on the job and the birth defects of our children; whether from pesticide poisoning, asbestoses, or radiation; show that jobs that poison the Earth are equally lethal to workers and their families. In the face of this poisoning we have to ask how environmentalists and labor activists can work together to compel the industrial economy to serve the needs of society as a whole.

Cesar Chavez and the United Farm Workers have united community anti-toxics groups with exploited and poisoned farm workers. Jesse Jackson's Rainbow Coalition has brought together people of color, labor, the economically disenfranchised, women, peace activists, environmentalists, religious leaders, gays and lesbians, senior citizens and youth. The Green movement and the progressive wing of the international environmental movement link issues of environment, peace, indigenous rights, social justice and feminism. National liberation movements in the Third World and activists

in the US work in solidarity to fight foreign domination and intervention, mutually inspiring and supporting each other. This kind of coalition-building is an opportunity for all movements to transcend special interest status and develop the popular support that is needed to achieve real and lasting change. By learning about the histories and current issues of each others' struggles and vocally expressing our support and solidarity we can build the bridges to lasting alliances.

Solidarity comes naturally. One doesn't need a Ph.D. to see that the political and economic system that destroys the Earth is the same system that exploits workers, that excludes women and people of color from the corridors of power, that makes a fiefdom of the "Third World," and that fuels the profoundly obscene weapons industry while 40,000 people, mostly children, die of hunger each day.

We can't solve any problem without revealing fundamental power imbalances and changing them. Banning pesticides without challenging unjust First World/Third World relations leads to pesticide dumping in the poorer nations. Winning environmental regulations in the US without controlling the movement of capital leads to the relocation of industry to the developing nations where corporations avoid paying equitable wages and are able to keep environmental and labor movements at arm's length. And civil rights victories in the absence of the redistribution of wealth and economic power do not prevent widespread poverty: there is now an African-American "underclass" living in worse economic conditions than those during Dr. King's lifetime.

Coalitions between individuals, neighborhood groups, peace activists, ecologists, workers, feminists, and anti-racists have the potential to achieve, in solidarity, what none of us can achieve alone. Margaret

Mead said that "the Earth is an island": we are a family who share the same fate, and we must learn to cooperate for our shared well-being. An active, progressive coalition within each community could provide the model of cooperation that we will need in order to survive together into the next century. We are united not only by our common, intertwined fate but by humanity's most hopeful redeeming qualities: our compassion for one another and our collective will to fight for justice.

The time for compromising on justice and survival and taking a *wait-and-see* attitude is over. We don't need to wait for another Bhopal or Chernobyl before halting production of lasting, lethal poisons. We don't need to starve another 14 million people to death again this year before we start to change the way we produce and distribute food.

There are no easy answers to the problems we face. To build a new world or even to improve this one, we must know what we want. This requires study, debate, planning and determined action. As Peter Kropotkin, the Russian prince turned revolutionist, advised: "Find out what kind of world you want to live in, what you are good at, and what to work at to build that world."

The contributions to this Handbook describe ways that we can work to insure that justice is a practice and not just a good idea. The final answers are not in, but we are offering a starting point for informed, effective action. No one person can pursue all the issues in all the ways. However, with effort, each person can have an effect on the issues they care about, and with an inspired commitment, we *can* change the world.

This *Call to Action: Handbook for Ecology, Peace and Justice* presents crucial steps to sustaining the rich diversity of life on the planet and protecting ourselves from injustice in its many interrelated forms.

These goals cannot be met without effort nor without confronting powerful forces, whether their name is Exxon, Dole, World Bank, General Electric, CIA, President, Landlord or Boss. What we've done in the past has been good but it hasn't been enough. We have to find new, more effective, more insistent ways of presenting and attaining our aims. How can we most strongly resist injustice? How do we strengthen democratic participation to insure the broadest and most equal administration of justice? As we become global citizens, we will find that we must struggle on many fronts to attain global justice. Let us do what we can to regain control over our world by gaining control over the institutions which hold the Earth's fate in their hands.

I began my activism in 1980, as a student. I helped organize a students' congress at the New College of California to insist on direct input to policies that shaped our education. For me, it was a positive action to take in response to a lack of power. It instilled in me a strong sense of the need for participation in decision-making affecting conditions in one's own community. Even though, in this instance, we did not reach our aim, I achieved a sense of camaraderie, of teamwork directed toward a common goal, and I remain firmly convinced that we each have a right to share in determining the conditions in which we live. In continuing to work for change I find constant support and stimulation in the activist community. Despite the serious nature of activist work, the spirit of celebration manifests itself in cultural events, parties and in the carnival atmosphere of marches and demonstrations. In creating cultures of celebration we affirm our resistance to fossilized institutions which suppress creativity, generosity and the human will.

This book gathers the experiences of several generations of committed activists.

The younger generation, my generation, stands at the edge of the next millennium, facing dangers and challenges no other generation has faced. We may be the last generation—or we may be the generation that resists injustice and destruction so strongly that we seize control from the narrowly self-interested institutions that lead us toward destruction, violence and oppression. We may be the generation that thinks more of what kind of world we will pass on to future generations than of short-term financial gain, the generation that builds institutions founded on our collective survival and well-being. That is my hope and my determination.

Our generation is not alone. We have the support and encouragement of generations of activists. We can learn with them from past victories and mistakes to forge new goals and strategies. Time runs short. We need new blood, fresh courage and new actions to vigorously resist and transform unjust and destructive institutions. We may make mistakes in our rush to action, but it will be a far greater mistake if we act slowly or not at all.

Some of us had the fire of activism lit under us by directly experiencing destruction and oppression. Some of us are motivated by our compassion for others. Some of us react intellectually to the senseless and needless waste of life and human potential. Many are motivated by witnessing the positive and creative actions of others who are fighting for their beliefs. And some are just scared to death of what will happen if they *don't* do something. Whatever that spark is for you, I hope that you will build it into a fire that burns through despair and discouragement, penetrating obstacles so that we may spare the planet for future generations and reach our goals of peace, justice and equality—and that the flame of your action leaves a warmth that inspires others to act for generations to come.

"One has to speak out and stand up for one's convictions. Inaction at a time of conflagration is inexcusable."

—MOHANDAS GANDHI

Creating Cultures of Resistance
RICHARD GROSSMAN

DESTRUCTION AROUND US is becoming obvious to more and more people.

Sources of destruction are not so obvious. Neither is it clear how to dismantle the destroyers, care for victims, salvage the planet and change the ways countries do business.

The press reports mostly symptoms, ignoring history and connection. Our country still thinks and talks the language of the destroyers.

Environmental and conservation organizations act as if they prefer the respect of the poisoners and the destroyers to that of the poisoned and destroyed.

Isolated people who *see* the sources, who viscerally grasp the magnitude of the destruction, have difficulty believing societies can rearrange production, distribution, work and wealth in harmony with ecological and social justice imperatives. Institutions that dominate our culture, after all, have been educating us on this score for centuries.

So what are people committed to action and change to do? As we plan and act, as we build cultures of resistance all over the world, I suggest we pay attention to common principles, solidarity, political literacy and strategy.

I. Identifying Common Principles

What do we want?

Today, people are calling for major changes in order to protect the planet. This book calls for energetic activism.

To what end? What do we have in mind regarding relationships between producers and consumers? Owners and workers? Investors and investment neighbors?

Can we imagine different ways the country can choose what to produce and how to produce it? What do we think about money? Private property? The democratic process?

Richard Grossman is the publisher of the *Wrenching Debate Gazette* based in Washington, DC. He was a founder of Environmentalists for Full Employment and the author of *Fear at Work*.

Who should be accountable to whom? Whose criteria should we use? How should the burdens of transition be shared? Who would be responsible for reparations and succor?

Labor organizer and pacifist A. J. Muste said that the challenge in building an effective movement "is to bring the state and other institutions of the world to adjust themselves to our demands . . ."

How will we plan to meet that challenge when the men and women who direct the institutions of the world labor lavishly to:

- limit even talk of reforms

- keep the burden of proof on critics and victims

- keep governments beholden to them

- sanctify their institutions (and themselves) as the only credible agents for progress, jobs, freedom, national security

- manipulate our culture so that millions and millions of people regard them, in the words of historian Lawrence Goodwyn, as "venerable repositories of good sense when they are, in fact, merely powerful . . . "?

Can we change these institutions without marginalizing ourselves as whining victims or irrational fanatics? Can we plan their evolution into cooperatives controlled by communities, or into the oblivion where some belong?

What will we have them do with their offal?

How can we help one another understand the extent of historical conflicts between these institutions and masses of people? Between these institutions and the Earth?

Why, after 20 years of citizen activism and education and legislation, are energy

and chemical corporations richer, more powerful, more destructive? How did we allow the US government to become the biggest poisoner in the world, and such an effective buffer between corporate poisoners and the public?

We need to act, but we need reflection too. We need to test our experiences against one another. We need to talk about power and authority, democratic processes, building trust.

We need to agree on our goals and bottom lines to plan our actions from A to Z.

II. Building Solidarity

Of course, people of all classes, races and regions should join to stop poisoners and destroyers, aid victims, restore the Earth.

So why isn't there not only unity but also good old-fashioned thick-and-thin solidarity?

Why is there more solidarity among the poisoners than among the poisoned? The way nuclear governments practice solidarity with each other makes me green with envy.

Why have we let the institutions that dominate production, consumption and culture define our economy and our ecology for us? Why do we let them tell us what "efficiency," "acceptable," and "possible" are, and create influential "progress" indexes that hide the harm they do?

I think Americans do not know enough about pivotal moments in history when destroyers took fateful steps to consolidate their power; when they beat down workers and communities and then were able to establish Earth-harming production processes. We need to know more about struggles over money, production, resources and sweat that have been going on for centuries. We need to know that these struggles continue today, in every community where men

Zimbabweans at an election rally. CASON/
FLESHMAN, IMPACT VISUALS

and women work in mines, fields, factories
and offices; where people are neighbors to
poisoners and destroyers; where people live
in squalor and hopelessness; where people
see their taxes and their labor supporting
destruction and terror around and off the
globe.

All America needs to see these struggles.
You need to help make these struggles visible. You need to be part of these struggles.

These people and communities have
been dealing daily with the producers and
poisoners, who also happen to be their em-
ployers. Shouldn't you cherish their experience, seek out their wisdom?

But if you go to them, will they be interested in the conservationist, the bioregional,
the environmental, the Deep Ecology vision? Why should they believe they would
have more opportunity to shape their communities' and the nation's fate if one of
these visions becomes reality? After all, they

know well that in every transition, people at
the production end have been chewed up,
have suffered what the poisoners and their
apologists have blessed as "creative destruction." Why should they expect the next
transition—even one in the name of "saving
the Earth"—to be any different?

How do we make it different?

How do we build solidarity into
thought, plans and activism? Where do we
have to go? Who do we have to talk to? Listen to? Stand beside?

How do we build international solidarity—not with multilateral investment institutions and global polluters and supergov-
ernments or globe-trotting politicians, but
rather with the people in communities
across the globe who know that the world
can withstand neither the sales obsessions
of the productively aberrant nor the desperate foraging of the poor.

III. Creating Political, Ecological and Economic Literacy

The Earth is oppressed. The Earth's oppres-
sors have not only disrupted natural balances, harmed its inhabitants and misdirect-
ed its peoples' labor. They have also stolen
our language and our histories.

They have made us illiterate.

The Brazilian teacher Paulo Freire
writes that a person is literate "to the extent
he or she is able to use language for social
and political reconstruction . . . . To be literate is to be present and active in the struggle for reclaiming one's voice, history,
future. . . . Literacy is the precondition for
engaging in struggle around the relations to
meaning and relations to power."

We need to be literate to understand the
symptoms we experience, to trace them to

their sources. We need to be literate to believe our own senses, to develop ambitions equal to saving our communities.

We should not believe that masses of people are now ready to mobilize to save the planet, or even to save their communities. It is easy to think otherwise, especially when environmental news dominates front pages, when business leaders and politicians "become" environmentalists.

We need to see that neither "news" nor catastrophe nor instantaneous conversion organizes people to bring about the changes that we need.

Our immediate task, then, is to foster cultures of resistance among people *who already see,* who are already committed to change. These cultures of resistance can become beacons of education and encouragement and leadership, can help transform symptoms and "news" of symptoms into strategies for institutional and political change into a political movement with values and clout.

We build cultures of resistance by doing many things simultaneously. People need to be strategizing together about acting, thinking, planning, educating, organizing; about supporting spontaneous resistance, directing sieges and other long-term creative efforts; about building commitments to one another and to the Earth.

Call To Action, which you hold in your hands, is just a book. It describes problems but it calls upon *you* to provide the action.

Maybe, as people like you who already see join together around common principles, you will be able to legitimize people's experiences and intensify aspirations for economic justice and ecological harmony.

Maybe, as the afflicted stand together at the sources of destruction, more and more people will stand together.

Maybe, as we make ourselves literate, more people will come to learn with us.

And maybe, as we strategize together to withdraw support from institutions of poison and destruction, we will be able to assist devastated people and places and create relationships between producers and users, owners and workers, factories and communities, which dignify life and respect the Earth.

Grassroots Organizing for Everyone

CLAIRE GREENSFELDER AND MIKE ROSELLE

"Never doubt that a small, highly committed group of individuals can change the world; indeed, it is the only thing that ever has."

—MARGARET MEAD

GRASSROOTS ORGANIZING IS a personal, hands-on approach to gathering people together in your community to take direct action on issues that affect your shared future. It is most effective, exciting and rewarding when done person to person, neighborhood by neighborhood and friend to friend.

In these days of high technology, grassroots organizing is enhanced by the speed of communication. For those who have resources, phone and increasingly, electronic mail and fax machines facilitate up to the minute information on key issues. New communication and travel technologies have made it possible to organize national and global "neighborhoods" of mutual interest. Whatever your means of communication, the bottom line is the same—the basis of good organizing is person to person contact.

Organizing is not a static concept, but a dynamic process that is constantly adapting to changing conditions while relying on a few basic principles:

1. You are not alone. There are others who feel the way that you do on issues that concern you.

2. Outreach. By reaching out to others

Claire Greensfelder is the Director of the 3220 Gallery in San Francisco, a community center focusing on US/Soviet relations. Previously Outreach Director for the California Nuclear Weapons Freeze Campaign (Proposition 12), and a wilderness leader and Co-Chair of the Sierra Club's Inner City Outings Program, she was a Jesse Jackson delegate to the 1988 Democratic National Platform Committee.

Mike Roselle is the Director of the Tropical Timber Campaign of the Rainforest Action Network, and a Co-Founder of Earth First!. Formerly the Direct Action Coordinator of Greenpeace USA, he has played a key role in wilderness, anti-toxic and anti-nuclear campaigns.

who are of like mind you can organize a coordinated group to take action, whether a local petition drive to save a neighborhood creek or to remove a toxic dump, or a national campaign of non-violent direct action against nuclear testing.

3. **Power in numbers.** Through working together, people can and will exercise power over their own lives, and use that power to confront a system or institution that is repressing or limiting their rights as individuals and as a community.

Working in groups is the key to grassroots organizing. One person may be able to call the community's attention to a problem or injustice, but real change comes only when a critical mass of citizens in the community are convinced that direct action needs to be taken.

While there will always be some cases of individuals single-handedly mounting successful campaigns to make change, such as an attorney winning a legal battle, most successful and long lasting campaigns involve many individuals working together in organizations.

Here are some questions to ask in planning your campaign:

1. What do you want to change? (goal) Is it realistic? Is it winnable?

2. What and who will it require to get it done? (resources) List what resources you already have and list what resources you will need to accomplish your goal. For example:

   People resources—volunteers, committees, staff

   Financial and physical resources— money, telephone, office

3. Who else in your community is affected? Who are your allies and constituents? How can you get them involved?

4. Are there others who have worked on this problem already? Can they help you develop your strategy?

5. Who has the power to give you what you want or solve the problem? Which individuals/organizations/corporations/or elected officials do you want to target for results?

6. What needs to be done? What tactics can you use? How will you communicate your plan? Petitions, fliers, posters, brochures, press, free speech messages?
   Who creates opinion in this area? (press, civic leaders, politicians) (For examples see *Tools, Terms and Tactics A-Z*)

7. How long will it take? Developing a *timeline* is an essential ingredient.

8. How will you know when you have succeeded? (evaluation)

9. How will you make decisions in your key group? (process) Consensus, vote, leadership caucus?

10. What will you do after your success/ failure? (analysis, defining issues, next steps) It is critically important to have next steps, or a new campaign planned to overlap with the end of one campaign in order to maintain momentum and interest.

Ideas on Outreach

Many people are concerned about issues, but are hesitant to take action until someone asks them directly and gives them the

Guerrilla Theater. Earth First! demonstrators protest against Maxxam Corp. and California Dept. of Forestry's plan to destroy one of the last remaining stands of old-growth redwoods. DAVID CROSS, 1987

opportunity to get involved. Remember how we began this chapter, "grassroots organizing is a hands-on approach to social change, most effectively done person to person." Many first-time (and sadly, some long-time) organizers forget that not everyone shares their zeal for a particular issue at first glance.

All too often, an organizer writes a wonderful flier, designs it beautifully, prints it and distributes it throughout the neighborhood, yet only 3 people show up for the meeting (s/he'd put out 50 chairs and had a lot of stale doughnuts on his/her hands). What happened?

People today have very busy, often stressful lives with many considerations and competing interests for their time. Work, family, health issues, education, not to mention lack of all of those and the increasing

elimination of institutional community support puts everyone on the run. The key difference in getting people active is frequently a personal one.

Ask a group at a meeting why they came for the first time and more often than not they will say "my friend invited me to come," or, "a public official said we should come," or "my teacher suggested we get involved," "my neighbor told me about it," or "I received a flier *and* a phone call." A follow up phone call from you or a member of your organization significantly increases the likelihood that an individual will feel valued and needed for the campaign. Personal contact can be *the* element that makes the difference in thinking about joining up, and actually attending a meeting.

Another key way to reach people is through other organizations. People come together for many reasons in our society—political, spiritual, social, professional, geographic, ethnic, etc. Use existing networks to reach new people. You don't have to reinvent the wheel. If you can get a local labor union or a religious organization to print the announcement of your meeting in their newsletter, or to endorse its purpose, it makes it more likely that a member will support you or come to your event. You may also want to ask if you or another member of your organization can attend their meeting and make an announcement for your event.

If you hold an event in a hall that the people you are inviting are familiar with, it is more likely they will come. If you break down some of the barriers of unfamiliarity, then the newness of the issue or the cause, or the fear of being in a room full of people that you don't know is diminished.

People want to feel that they can make a difference and most need validation from other people that coming to a meeting or volunteering for a cause will make a difference. Be fearless in seeking new people to help with your cause!

People are ready to hear what you have to say about your issue, if you are ready to listen to what they think about it themselves. But don't stop there.

Don't just ask them their opinion, or get their endorsement on a petition. *Ask* them to do something to show their commitment to the issue. Increasing individual levels of commitment is the secret to good organizing.

One of the real arts of working with others is to develop an individual's interest to the maximum point of their potential leadership and commitment. You can ask, will you . . .

sign a petition?
donate $5?

write a postcard?
come to a meeting?
join a committee?
bring two friends?
write for our newsletter?
chair a committee?
be on our steering committee?
speak publicly for our cause?
organize an event?

The notion of increasing commitment is especially important as you try to build an organization and avoid "burning out" your volunteers and members. Burnout is much easier to avoid than to cure. New members should be encouraged to get involved at many levels from the very beginning, so that they may quickly learn the ropes. It not only increases their sense of ownership and commitment, but also spreads out the responsibility and the workload.

Sharing the workload is especially critical in a new, small organization with big plans. Always be on the lookout for a volunteer or staff member that is over-committing themselves and attempt to intervene with increased volunteer support to their work. Learn how to delegate!

Establish a Group Decision-Making Process

Grassroots organizations depend on democratic and decentralized decision making to avoid problems that can arise during a campaign. Open meetings and an atmosphere of trust are essential. Clandestine groups or committees that are not responsive to all members of an organization can often discourage new supporters and can actually impede the progress of a cause by creating isolated communities of non-trusting individuals.

Involving People and Organizations in the Planning Stages

People and organizations are more likely to become involved, to turn out their members for your events, to speak out on your issues if their input and participation is engaged in the planning stages. It is critical that you don't just invite people to your agenda, but that you invite them to join in building a common agenda.

It may take longer to plan a conference or a mobilization with many people involved, but the extra time is critical if you wish to see genuine participation on the part of individuals and groups. People really want to share their ideas and to use their own networks and skills to help in the work. Furthermore, you will probably not think of everything by yourself. The project may not look exactly as you imagined it would if you let others help you plan it, but isn't it wonderful to know that you didn't have to do all the work alone!

Building Coalitions for Social Change

We mostly have discussed working with individuals, however, a key way to organize for certain goals is to build a coalition to get the job done. Working with coalitions is similar to working with individuals—the main difference is rather than dealing with a group of people, you are dealing with a group of organizations and their representative. Many of the principles remain the same:

Banner-hanging at St. Louis Union Station National Historic Monument at 1989 Ralston Purina Annual Stockholders Meeting. ORIN LANGELLE, 1988

- define decision making
- involve folks early in the planning stages
- define tasks clearly
- increase levels of commitment and participation
- define common goals

One key difference is that organizations, more so than people, have their own structures and agendas, and it may take longer to come to agreement on goals and plans than with a group of individuals that are only accountable to themselves. However, the increased impact of the sheer numbers of people involved gives a coalition an immediate power that new, smaller organizations do not have.

Some groups rarely work in coalitions because they do not wish to compromise their goals or their agendas in any way. They have taken too long to come to agreement just within themselves, or perhaps they just wish to retain a narrower focus. Other groups work frequently in coalitions because they wish to have a broader focus than their own constituency and they wish to reach out beyond their own agenda.

Coalitions can be especially effective in organizing large rallies and demonstrations, turning out individuals to vote or public opinion campaigns where large numbers are required for maximum impact. One caution about coalitions: a good coalition is put together to accomplish a specific goal, a rally, a campaign, a fundraising drive. After the goal has been completed, the coalition will sometimes take on a life of its own and decide to stay together to carry out more collective work. This only works if the coalition has a clearly defined new task to accomplish. Many old coalitions languish on with no clear agenda finding it difficult to

agree on something that everyone wants to do and without the organizational excitement that caused everyone to come together in the first place.

Coalitions are most effective when they come together out of an immediate need, shared agenda, and mutual self-interest (solidarity). After that need has been met, inevitably, the agendas of the member organizations and the agenda of the coalition may come into conflict. Be brave! Admit it when your coalition has done its job well, and let it be set aside with a victory behind it. Bring it back together only when it has a job to do.

Keeping Communication Open/Staying in Touch

As you build an organization, it is important to stay in touch with your members, supporters and volunteers. Don't just send out mailings, or put up posters in the community and expect people to turn out to work with you. Contact your members as if they were first time recruits to your cause. Get direct commitments beyond dues. Invariably, a hard-working core group will develop, but members want to be involved too. Their financial contribution should be as respected as the volunteer time others are giving. (But not more respected, either, as can sometimes be the case.)

Organize regular meetings and volunteer nights. If your organization can afford to provide food and drink, it's a good way of thanking people and makes it easier for them to attend. Let people know how to reach you. Don't make it difficult for your supporters to be involved and to know what's going on. There are often hidden resources among your members that are going untapped merely because they were never asked.

It is important to look for ways that individuals and organizations can use their own special skills to help your campaigns. Business people and lawyers can help with financial plans and incorporation, journalists can help with your literature, teachers can teach public speaking, social workers can share their skills in group process, everyone can enlist the help of the other organizations they belong to. And, don't cubbyhole people into one professional niche. Many folks have multiple talents that are waiting to be used.

A true story with a moral: In one campaign office, a college professor had been assigned to do research and administrative work and was never asked to help on the phone—it was seen as not up to his skills. One night he volunteered on a phonebank (much to everyone's surprise) and raised over $500 in the first half-hour. It turned out that he had worked his way through college selling Bibles on the telephone!

Moral: get to know your volunteers! Take the time to interview them and find out what they want to learn to do, and *why* they have joined your cause. It can be humbling and enlightening. Spending quality time with your volunteers always furthers the work.

Continue your outreach! Methods of community outreach include canvassing, phone calls, public events, press conferences, media events, direct action, leafletting, information tables (or ironing boards) and special events. Many organizations and campaigns have detailed organizing manuals describing community outreach that they will send you. Take a look at the glossary, *Tools, Terms and Tactics A-Z*, at the back of this book for descriptions of these and other methods of getting the word out.

Appreciation, Motivation and Perseverence

Thanking donors and supporters, congratulating one another on jobs well done, throwing parties, giving rousing speeches and inspiring presentations, organizing empowering demonstrations and successful actions all serve to encourage and motivate us. Celebrating your victories and going on from your defeats are cornerstones of sustained activism. Even when you are not successful it's important to give yourself credit for the work you put in. Evaluate what you did well, acknowledge the strengths and weaknesses of your campaign, and use it as a learning experience. With all this knowledge, you will be ready for your next campaign as a citizen activist!

Act Locally: Using the Powers of City Government to Effect Social Change

NANCY SKINNER

Introduction

We in the activist community are well versed in the use of boycotts, direct action, petitions, and education campaigns to effect change. These tactics are most often directed at multinational corporations, the federal government or international organizations, all decisionmakers who are well out of our immediate reach. Though we're familiar with the adage "Think globally but act locally," we often don't realize the opportunities for significant change right at our doorsteps.

Cities and local government provide a gold mine of opportunity for effecting social change. Using the powers of investment, contracting, purchasing, zoning, and legislation cities can take action that benefits the local community and creates far reaching impacts, nationally and internationally.

Contrary to popular myth, you don't have to be in elected office to get local government to act! Most local governments are still very accessible to citizens and have many formal and informal mechanisms for citizen influence and participation.

Some of the City of Berkeley's most significant public policies were developed by citizens using the tools of initiative campaigns, proposing to the City Council resolutions and/or legislation, or simply requesting Mayoral proclamations. Berkeley's rent control law, the 50% recycling goal, the styrofoam ban, and the AIDS non-discrimination law were all developed, proposed or passed by activists and citizen groups. These measures, backed with the formal support of local government, resulted not only in tangible, structural change for the Berkeley community; many have served as catalysts for change in much larger arenas.

Nancy Skinner has been a Berkeley City Councilmember for the past five years. She has been recently known for her sponsorship of Berkeley's law banning styrofoam and her initiation of the national Stop Styro/Clearinghouse for Plastics and Packaging Reduction. Councilmember Skinner began her career in politics as an activist in garbage issues. Faced with a proposal to build an incinerator on Berkeley's waterfront, she joined with other concerned citizens and wrote an initiative to ban garbage burning in the City of Berkeley. The Measure passed overwhelmingly. In 1984, Nancy Skinner co-authored a second successful initiative mandating that Berkeley endorse a goal of recycling of 50% of its waste and develop a plan to meet that goal by 1990.

The following are examples of Berkeley citizens' use of city government to make their city humane, just and environmentally sound and an inspiration for activists around the world.

Styrofoam Ban

By demonstrating how the use of a certain product or material threatens the public good, cities have the power to enact bans. In Berkeley, we began talking about banning styrofoam to express our opposition to ozone-damaging CFC's as early as 1986. The ban was first recommended by our citizen Solid Waste Management Commission. Community groups like the Ecology Center, the Greens, other environmentalists and businesses joined the effort and presented the issue to the City Council. Simply discussing the ban attracted national press. Shortly after, other organizations began targeting McDonald's as a major user of CFC styrofoam, again receiving widespread press. Within six months McDonald's Corporation announced their decision to eliminate CFC styrofoam in all of their operations nationwide.

By the time Berkeley passed the styrofoam ban in 1988, CFC's were no longer the primary issue. Instead styrofoam became the symbol of wasteful, environmentally damaging packaging and a major representation of the United State's phenomenal garbage crisis. Berkeley's law not only bans styrofoam but also requires food businesses to reduce their non-recyclable, non-biodegradable packaging and to provide recycling bins for their customers' use. Cities across the country began following suit and laws quickly passed in Portland, Oregon; Minneapolis; Newark, New Jersey; and the State of Florida.

After receiving requests for information from across the country, my City Council office and the Ecology Center began the "Stop Styro Clearinghouse for Plastics and Packaging Reduction" to assist local government groups and citizens in these efforts. Now over 75 local governments have passed similar laws, some even stronger and more comprehensive than Berkeley's, and the plastics industry is scrambling to develop and promote recyclable plastics.

Recycling Policy Initiative. In 1984, long before any cities or states were talking about the need for recycling or setting recycling goals, the citizens of Berkeley through a grassroots effort collected signatures and put an initiative on the ballot mandating Berkeley to recycle 50% of its garbage. Sponsored by Berkeley Friends of Recycling, this initiative passed overwhelmingly. Using the initiative process, this same group also made Berkeley the first city to ban garbage incinerators/waste-to-energy plants. Both of these efforts received wide acclaim and have served as models for citizen groups across the country fighting garbage incineration and working to promote recycling.

Sister City Relationships. Grassroots groups in Berkeley have effectively used the sister city concept with Leon, Nicaragua and San Antonio Los Ranchos, El Salvador to communicate the people of Berkeley's opposition to US policies in Central America. Although the Berkeley City Council formally adopted these relationships, no city funds are allocated. Community-based groups fundraise, collect material aid and send delegations to our two sister cities. To date, the Leon Sister City Organization has collected donations and material aid to benefit the people of Leon in an amount equal to the amount of Berkeley tax dollars that the federal government has contributed to the Contras. With close communication and watchdogging, the San Antonio Los Ranchos sister city group has been successful in obtaining the release of San Antonio community leaders who were jailed by the Salvadoran government.

Socially Responsible Investment Policies. Cities are big business. Berkeley, with a population of 112,000, has a city budget of $147 million. How we spend and invest that money can have a big impact tangibly and symbolically. Citizen groups in Berkeley have passed two responsible investment initiatives. The 1979 Responsible Investments Ordinance made Berkeley the first city to remove its funds from South Africa. Berkeley's Nuclear Free Zone Initiative divested city funds from nuclear power and nuclear weapons producers and banned the transport of nuclear materials within city limits. These policies also included purchasing clauses that restricted the city's purchase of products made by companies who either do business with South Africa or produce nuclear weapons.

Mayors Central America Peace Initiative. In 1987, locally-based Central American support groups approached Berkeley Mayor Loni Hancock with an idea to put United States mayors on record opposing aid to the Contras. Congress was scheduled to vote on yet another Contra aid package shortly after the Mayors' gathering. Focusing on the loss of federal funds to cities and the desperate need for fighting "battles at home" such as homelessness, poverty and drug abuse, the Mayor's Peace Initiative advocated that Congress should fund the cities, not the Contras. Over 40 mayors from cities like Atlanta, Boston, Chicago, San Francisco, Los Angeles, Detroit and, of course, Berkeley signed the initiative and held a press conference to communicate their views. The resulting press coverage on ABC World News, CBS Evening News, and many major papers made the connection between the overriding economic problems of cities and the federal government's misplaced financial policies. The Congressional vote on Contra funding occurred two weeks later and failed.

Conclusion. Using the power of local government offers a true and effective expression of grassroots democracy. I hope these simple examples inspire you and your community to carry on the challenge and take similar actions!

Resources. *Building Municipal Foreign Policies, An Action Handbook for Citizens and Local Elected Officials* by Michael H. Shuman, published by the Center for Innovative Diplomacy, Irvine, CA.

"Stop Styro Clearinghouse for Plastics and Packaging Reduction," Councilmember Nancy Skinner, 2180 Milvia Street, Berkeley, CA 94704.

PART ONE
ATMOSPHERE

The Hole in the Ozone Layer

CARL SAGAN

IT WAS ALL DONE responsibly, carefully, with concern for the environment. The problem was to find a material that would do no harm. You want to sell, say, a deodorant in a can—press the button, out it comes in a fine spray mist, and your customer is ready for the big date. You need a safe propellant to carry the deodorant out of the can. Or you're manufacturing a refrigerator and you need a coolant, liquid under the right conditions, that will circulate inside the refrigerator but won't hurt anything if the refrigerator leaks or is converted to scrap metal. The industrial chemists worked hard and developed a class of molecules called chlorofluorocarbons (CFCs), made up of one or more carbon atoms to which are attached some chlorine and/or fluorine atoms. They're used in air-conditioning, refrigeration, spray cans, insulating, foams and plastics, and industrial solvents. Safe as safe could be, everyone figured. That's why,

these days, a surprising amount of what we take for granted depends on CFCs.

A CFC molecule in the atmosphere survives for a century before giving up its chlorine. Chlorine is a catalyst that destroys ozone molecules but is not destroyed itself. It takes a couple of years before the chlorine is carried back into the lower atmosphere and washed out in rainwater. In that time, a chlorine atom may preside over the destruction of 100,000 ozone molecules.

Ozone is our shield against ultraviolet light from the Sun. If all the ozone in the upper air were brought down to the temperature and pressure around you at this moment, the layer would be only 3 millimeters thick. It's not very much ozone. But that ozone is all that stands between us and the fierce and searing long-wave u.v. from the sun.

The u.v. danger we often hear about is skin cancer. But increased skin cancer, while a direct consequence of enhanced u.v. and

---

Carl Sagan is the David Duncan Professor of Astronomy and Space Sciences and Director of the Laboratory for Planetary Studies at Cornell University. He has played a leading role in the Mariner, Viking and Voyager expeditions and is a recent co-recipient of the Leo Szilard Award for Physics in the Public Interest for his contributions to the theory of nuclear winter. His television series *Cosmos* has now been seen in 60 countries by more than 250 million people.

Carl Sagan being booked after his arrest at an action protesting the February 1987 nuclear bomb test that broke the Soviet moratorium. DAVID CROSS

threatening millions of deaths, is not the worst of it. Probably more serious is the fact that u.v. injures the immune system—the body's machinery for fighting disease. Yet, as serious as *this* seems, the real danger lies elsewhere.

Experiments by Sayed El-Sayed of Texas A&M University show that even a moderate increase in u.v. harms the one-celled plants common in the Antarctic Ocean and elsewhere. Larger increases can be expected to cause profound distress and, eventually, massive deaths. But if increasing u.v. falls on the oceans, the damage is not restricted to these little plants—because they are the food of one-celled animals, who are eaten in turn by little shrimplike crustaceans, who are eaten by small fish, who are eaten by large fish, who are eaten by dolphins, whales, and people. The destruction of the

little plants at the base of the food chain would cause the entire chain to collapse. There are many such food chains, on land as in water, and all seem vulnerable to disruption by u.v.

For years, the British Antarctic Survey, a team of scientists stationed at Halley Bay in the southernmost continent, had been measuring the ozone layer high overhead. In 1985 they announced the disconcerting news that the springtime ozone had diminished to nearly half what they had measured a few years before. Two-thirds of the springtime ozone over Antarctica is now missing. There is a hole in the antarctic ozone layer. It has shown up every spring since the late 1970s. While it heals itself in winter, the hole seems to last longer each spring. No scientist had predicted it.

Naturally, the hole led to more calls for a ban on CFCs, as did the discovery that CFCs add to global warming caused by the carbon dioxide greenhouse effect. But industry officials seemed to have difficulty focusing on the nature of the problem. Richard C. Bennet, Chairman of the Alliance for a Responsible CFC Policy—formed by CFC manufacturers—complained: "The rapid, complete shutdown of CFCs that some people are calling for would have horrendous consequences. Some industries would have to shut down because they cannot get alternative products—the cure would kill the patient." But the patient is not "some industries"; the patient is life on Earth.

Berkeley, California has banned the white CFC-blown foam insulation used to keep fast foods warm. McDonald's has pledged replacement of the most damaging CFCs in its packaging. Facing the threat of government regulations and consumer boycotts, Du Pont finally announced in 1988 that it would phase out the manufacture of CFCs—but not to be completed until the year 2000. Other American manufacturers have not even promised that. But the United States accounts for only 30 percent of worldwide CFC production. Clearly, since the long-term threat to the ozone layer is global and the manufacture and use of CFCs is global, the solution must be global as well.

In September 1987, many of the nations that produce and use CFCs met in Montreal to consider a possible agreement to limit CFC use. At first, Britain, Italy and France, influenced by their powerful chemical industries, participated in the discussions only reluctantly, and such nations as South Korea were altogether absent. The Chinese delegation did not sign the treaty. Interior Secretary Donald Hodel, a conservative averse to government controls, reportedly suggested that, instead of limiting CFC production, we all wear sunglasses and hats. This option is unavailable to the microorganisms at the base of the food chains that sustain life on Earth, and the US signed the Montreal Protocol despite Hodel's advice.

Now 37 nations, including the Soviet Union, have agreed to a schedule of cutbacks in CFC production, so that by 1989 production reverts to 1986 levels, and by 1999 to about 50 percent of that. The trouble is we will have to stop producing all CFCs and then wait a century or two before the atmosphere cleans itself. The longer we dawdle, the greater the danger.

Clearly, the problem will be solved if a cheap and effective CFC substitute can be found that does not injure us or the environment. But what if there is no such substitute? What if the best substitute is more expensive? Who pays for the research, and who makes up the price difference—the consumer, the government, or the chemical industry that got us into this mess?

The Montreal Protocol is important not for the magnitude or speed of the changes agreed to but for their direction. The Montreal conference was sponsored by the United Nations Environment Programme, whose director, Mostafa K. Tolba, described it as "the first truly global treaty that offers protection to every single human being." But not enough protection. What is needed is a worldwide ban on CFCs as rapidly as possible, greatly enhanced research to find safe substitutes and monitoring of the ozone layer all over the globe. If we must make a mistake, let it be in the cause of the human species.

We must begin to think and act not merely in terms of our nation and generation (much less the profits of a particular industry) but in terms of the entire vulnerable planet Earth and the generations of children to come.

The hole in the ozone layer is a kind of skywriting. Does it spell out a newly evolving ability to work together on behalf of our species, or our continuing complacency before a witch's brew of deadly perils?

ACTION

1. **Join and support a complete global ban of CFCs by 1992.** Environmental activists and many in the scientific community are supporting this call. Join and support the numerous international actions, campaigns and demonstrations.

2. **Establish your community as a "Styro Free Zone,"** requiring all merchants to find alternatives to disposable styrofoam containers.

3. **Boycott all products and companies that produce CFCs.** Write to them and tell them that you'll continue the boycott until their CFC production stops. This includes most styrofoam and foam products, air conditioners, refrigeration systems and producers of industrial solvents and electronic components such as IBM and Du Pont. Remind them that alternatives to CFCs already exist.

4. **Campaign:** Assess the damage to the atmosphere in trillions of dollars and apportion a financial penalty between IBM, Union Carbide, McDonald's, Du Pont and the other CFC producers. Include the costs of gathering all the CFCs from existing systems and putting them into dumps. Make an example of the offenders, sending a clear message that endangering life on the planet is a grievous crime, and will not be tolerated. The poisoners will argue that the penalties will put them out of business; we must insist that the existence of a few corporations is of inestimably smaller consequence than the existence of life on Earth. Join with the employees who work at these plants to focus attention on in-plant and community health problems. Take political action to force the firms to find substitutes. Workers need to have a democratic role in the direction of their labor. Don't make the workers the enemy, or victims in changes of policy. We should talk about transitions like salaries for life if they are laid off because of the introduction of new products or processes. How about a "Superfund" for workers? Many politicians claim that they are tough on crime. Let's require them to prove it by also going after these mega-criminals who threaten not just individuals or communities but all of life. While we're at it, let's look at the military-industry contribution to ozone depletion.

5. **Tactic: Print millions of "ozone holes"** and hang them around the necks of corporate and public officials. We need to make ozone holes visible here on Earth. Draw ozone holes around offending factories. Drive trucks through ozone holes. Push a piano through an ozone hole.

6. **Consider alternatives.** Some suggestions are:

   - Alternatives to air conditioning in your home:
     Insulate to keep out heat.

     Install an effective fan-cooling system.

     Plant trees on the side of your house with southern exposure to provide shade. (Deciduous trees will allow sunlight in colder months.)

   - Avoid using aerosol sprays. (CFC propellants are already banned in some countries, including the US.)

*Action section by Brad Erickson and Bill Prescott

- Avoid buying products packaged in polystyrene foam containers, and voice your concern to retailers. (If you don't know which packaging foam is made with CFCs, it doesn't hurt to avoid all styrofoam.)

- Purchase a fire extinguisher that is halon-free.

- If you already own a car with air conditioning, check it periodically for leaks and make sure the CFCs are recycled before the car is scrapped. When purchasing a car, consider one without air conditioning. A light colored model with a white interior and tinted windows can help keep temperatures down in hotter climates.

- Install a CFC-efficient refrigerator and repair any leaks immediately. (The CFCs should eventually be recycled.)

Remember to check all products before purchase to make sure they don't contain ozone-damaging chemicals. These include CFC-11, CFC-12, CFC-113, CFC-114, CFC-115, Halon-1211, Halon-1301 and Halon-2402.

Global Warming

BILL PRESCOTT

"For two hundred years we've been conquering nature. Now we're beating it to death."

—TOM MCMILLAN, CANADIAN ENVIRONMENTAL MINISTER

I T'S FINALLY HAPPENED. Over decades of population growth, economic expansion and surging industrial development, we've pumped a disastrous excess of carbon dioxide (CO_2) and other greenhouse gases into the atmosphere. Now the whole Earth is responding. Our planet is warming up.

The culprits are chemicals: carbon dioxide, nitrogen oxide, methane, tropospheric ozone, and CFCs, all of which are spewed into the air by human activities, and all of which trap some of the Earth's heat that would normally radiate out into space. And so the Earth slowly warms. As it warms, the global systems that generate climate will change ever so slightly. And with that slight change—a few degrees of warming worldwide, a few feet of sea level rise, a little difference in rainfall patterns—comes the most horrendous list of ecological disasters in human history.

We can expect severe heat waves, more droughts, floods, forest fires, and crop failures, as well as melting glaciers and icecaps, rising sea levels inundating coastal areas, low-lying deltas, and marshlands, along with saltwater intrusion into fresh water supplies, changes in ocean currents, displaced monsoons and agricultural zones, increased desertification, difficulty with photosynthesis in plants, the death of forests and coral reefs, disruption of the food chain in the oceans, death of many species as habitat disappears, and more frequent and worsening storms, with winds up to 225 miles per hour.

Unchecked, the global climate crisis

Bill Prescott is the Director of Public Information of the Climate Protection Institute. He has also served as the Global Education Director for Planet Earth Foundation and the Director of the Seattle-based Campaign to End World Hunger.

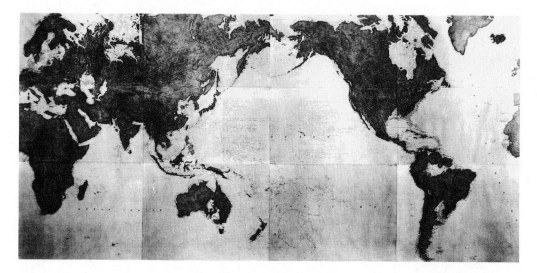

From The Lagoon Cycle: The Seventh Lagoon. *"How the Lands Would Shrink as the Oceans Grew." Artists' map speculating on the effect of massive global warming—continent contours after seas rise 300 feet.* HELEN MAYER AND NEWTON HARRISON

will profoundly affect nearly all ecological as well as human systems. The likely social consequences include social disruption and disintegration as more and more sustainability barriers are breached; mass unemployment and poverty as economic structures deteriorate; hundreds of millions of environmental refugees as sea levels rise and desertification forces populations from their homes; chronic undernourishment and famine as food stocks plummet while overpopulation continues; health crises as water supplies are depleted and contaminated, while insect pests, bacteria, and viruses increase with the warmer weather; and finally, civil strife, resource wars, and the decline of democracy as democratic infrastructures strain to cope with the deepening crisis.

Global climate change is inevitable. But the difference between disaster and manageable change is a matter of what we do in the next ten years. We can still mitigate the problem enough to survive. But citizen activists, governments, and industry must make basic changes *now*.

So where do we start? We need to get rid of chlorofluorocarbons first. They are the most pernicious greenhouse gases: they destroy the ozone layer on which the entire biosphere depends, while they are 10,000 to 20,000 times more effective at trapping heat than carbon dioxide. Unfortunately, chemical substitutes currently proposed by industry are still highly dangerous as greenhouse gases, even though they may not destroy the stratospheric ozone. We need more benign substitutes, and we need them rapidly, or we may have to resort to a global ban.

Next we need to cut down on our addiction to fossil fuels. National energy policies must change in favor of renewable energy sources and soft energy paths, much more fuel efficient cars and public transportation. In this endeavor we may be able to emphasize natural gas as a "bridge" fuel to more sustainable practices, but there is no excuse to continue burning coal, which is pouring carbon dioxide into the air as well as the sulphur that becomes acid rain. And there's no excuse for reconsidering nuclear energy. Even if it were cheap (which it's not) and safe (which it's not), waste disposal will always be a problem, and though the nuclear industry claims no carbon dioxide is produced in nuclear generation of electricity, huge amounts of coal are used for the enrichment of the necessary uranium.

The short-term key to a climate-sensitive energy policy is conservation. The United States produces a staggering 25 percent of global carbon dioxide emissions, a figure which we could easily cut in half through conservation of energy, using a wide range of easily instituted practices that can save us literally hundreds of billions of much-needed dollars.

Next we need to stop deforestation, especially tropical deforestation, since we need the trees to absorb carbon being released. The burning of rainforests to clear land for cattle and agriculture contributes 25 percent to 50 percent of all the carbon dioxide released each year. There were 170,000 tropical forest fires in one state in Brazil last year, each of them pouring smoke filled with carbon dioxide and other greenhouse gases into the atmosphere. At the same time that we work to halt deforestation, we need to begin major reforestation campaigns worldwide, planting literally billions of trees, in order to slow the pace of global warming.

Methane is the second-largest contributor to global warming after carbon dioxide, but its control will perhaps prove even more difficult. Methane, a highly effective heat-trapping gas, is formed in rice paddies and in the bellies of sheep and cattle, as well as in garbage dumps. As a result, we may have to seek alternatives to some agricultural, livestock, and garbage disposal practices. And since a great deal of our nitrous oxide problems come from petrochemical fertilizers, alternative practices must be sought.

In the long run, more than "alternative practices" will be needed. Investment criteria and the way we "do business" will have to change towards sustainability and community-oriented democratic processes, if the civilization is to survive. Since unprecedented change will inevitably occur, it is up to each one of us to make sure this change takes the shape of a sustainable global culture, instead of a mishmash of reactive policies, technological fixes, and societal denial, which can only lead to unalterable breakdown.

ACTION*

One citizen activist can make a difference. Needed actions fall into five broad categories: become politically active; conserve as much energy as possible; recycle; plant trees; support organizations that are really confronting, rather than accommodating, industry on the issue.

1. **Become politically active.** The single most powerful step you can take is to become politically active. The urgency

of this problem requires immediate national policy change and and an unprecedented level of international cooperation, both of which need massive citizen involvement the world over to generate the necessary political will. Even though the future of the planet hangs in the balance, it is still true that politicians will not take needed actions unless we adamantly insist that they do so. And it is more true than ever that

*Action Section by Bill Prescott and Brad Erickson

the industries causing most of the damage will not voluntarily stop unless we force them into responsible practices or out of business if need be. People have to become informed, not only about the problems, but about the politics of reform. We need bans on the production of scores of chemicals that contribute to global atmospheric poisoning.

- The best thing to do is to join with other citizen activists. Become a part of a lobbying organization, such as Greenhouse Action. Or find out how to start your own lobbying group by writing the Earth Island Action Group. You can also start study groups, legal action groups, community recycling programs, and boycotts of energy-wasteful products, especially gas-guzzling autos.

- There are a number of bills in Congress that deserve support, from Congresswoman Claudine Schneider (R-R.I.), Senator Timothy Wirth (D-Co.), and Senator Al Gore (D-Tenn.), among others. These bills may take years to be passed. Individuals can write and call their elected representatives and request that they actively support the changes outlined in this chapter. Call and write your Congressperson, and ask for a reply. Remember that one letter is the equivalent of the voices of hundreds of constituents, since so few people bother to write. Ask your Representative if these bills really go far enough, if they really set the highest standards, and if they address ownership and decision-making questions. If this is going to be a long struggle, let's not fight for reforms that are "realistic" according

to industry, but realistic in terms of attaining the deep structural changes necessary for long-term survival and proportional to effective political organizing. How do we scare politicians into waking up and becoming "educable"?

2. **Conserve as much energy as possible.** The vast majority of our energy is produced by burning fossil fuels, and that has to stop. We need to move towards non-polluting energy sources such as solar, wind, and even hydrogen power. This transition requires structural changes that go to the heart of capital and government power. Don't get caught in blaming the victim, the consumer. But there are individual lifestyle changes that embody the principles of energy efficiency. Start by saving as much electricity as possible: turn down the air conditioner and the heater, turn off all the lights and appliances you aren't using. While you're at it, buy only the most energy-efficient appliances you can find, including some of the new fluorescent lightbulbs that can save 70 percent to 90 percent on lighting bills. And make sure that your house or apartment is properly insulated.

- Use as little gasoline as possible. Drive less; use public transportation. If you don't have access to public transportation, insist that your local government develop a plan for expanded service. The average American petropig car emits its weight in carbon each year. It's time that consumers demanded much more fuel-efficient cars from Detroit. If you must drive, buy the car with the best gas mileage you can find, and then keep it well-tuned and running efficiently. Organize carpools and consolidate your errands. Fight to make cities hospitable to pedestrians and bicyclists.

3. **Recycle everything you can.** Demand a ban on non-recyclable products. Recycle all the paper, glass, and metal you use, both at home and on the job, and you'll be saving a lot of the energy that goes into manufacturing these products. You can demand that the CFCs in your refrigerators and air conditioners are recycled when these appliances are serviced, sold, or junked. And make sure those appliances have no leaks. These chemicals are incredibly dangerous to life on this planet, and they ought to be about as legal as Agent Orange.

4. **Plant trees.** We need government policy on the federal, state and local level to plant billions of trees in cleared forest areas, on marginalized cropland, and in urban areas. The trees need to be diverse, not just pines, but hardwoods and the full range of trees indigenous to each region. With enough trees as carbon sinks, we should be able to slow down the rate of global warming enough to allow the other major policy and lifestyle changes to be implemented. There are some five billion of us; if we each planted and nurtured a tree, that would be a good start. Planting trees is particularly advantageous in cities and suburbs, since trees in urban areas absorb more carbon than trees in forests, and since planting shade trees around houses can significantly cut down on summer electricity bills. Demand that lumber companies end clearcutting and foot the bill for reforestation. It's time that the profits they've made by shortsighted, devastat-

ing exploitation of our forests be paid back to repair the damage they've done. Anyone who cuts a tree down must plant and nurture five. We need a special fund for trees, perhaps derived from a gas tax or check-offs on income tax forms.

5. **Support organizations that are working on the issue.** There are hundreds of groups working on different aspects of the issue, from those that promote energy efficiency, like the Rocky Mountain Institute, to organizations working to save the rainforests, like the Rainforest Action Network, and groups working on urban reforestation, like Tree People. Many major environmental groups have campaigns to mitigate global warming through education, policy formation, and lobbying. These include Earth Island Institute, Environmental Defense Fund, Environmental Policy Institute, Greenpeace, Natural Resources Defense Council, Sierra Club and World Resources Institute. They deserve your help and your input. The United Nations Environmental Programme, whose work is supported in part by the Friends of UNEP, has the difficult diplomatic task of organizing an international protocol to limit the emission of greenhouse gases. The addresses of these groups appear in the resource list at the end of this section of the book.

6. **Insist that private automobiles be banned in urban centers** and that the automotive industry pay for expanding public transportation. Frequent and inexpensive civic light rail services can be run on renewable energy sources that do not poison the atmosphere. A percentage of car registration fees and of auto manufacturers' and petroleum

companies' gross income should be used to subsidize public transport, bringing the cost down for all users. For decades, road and highway building and maintenance and police traffic patrol have been subsidized for the auto industry and private car owners by the rest of the tax-paying public. It's time for the poisoners to pay the bill to counteract the harm they've done. Why not nationalize the oil industry or at least suggest different ideas of ownership and control?

7. **Encourage non-payment of taxes that go to global/community poisoning.** Your community could withhold 10 percent of its taxes and invest the money in a community tree fund. We need more ideas that empower people and challenge traditional decision-makers through communal acts.

Space as Wilderness

GAR SMITH

"Things learned on Earth we shall practice in heaven."
—ROBERT BROWNING

FORTY YEARS AFTER the dawn of the Space Age, the once-mysterious realm of space has become commonplace. Satellite dishes dot the urban landscape; space stations glide across the sky; we've been to the Moon. It is becoming increasingly apparent, however, that our planet's "space environment" is now threatened by the same forces that have destroyed the quality of life on Earth—pollution, commercialization and militarization.

It is no coincidence that space has been popularly portrayed as the "last frontier," complete with "challenges to be overcome," "new worlds to conquer" and places waiting to be "colonized." The vocabulary used to inspire today's spacefaring dreams is the same that was used in the past to justify the desecration of mountains, rivers, forests and indigenous peoples. It is the rhetoric of unregulated, exponential growth.

Our Earth Island is surrounded by a vast ocean of space—a seemingly limitless resource. But in the regions of "near space" which surround our water planet, large portions of Earth's last and greatest wilderness have been turned into an orbital dump. Despite the vast sums of tax dollars consumed by the US space program, decisions about our role in space and the consequences of space technology have been made without public debate or the attention of most environmentalists.

Pollution in Space

Since the beginning of the Space Age in the 1950's, more than 15,000 detectable items of space debris have accumulated in planetary orbit—spent payloads, rocket bodies, clamps, fragments of exploded satellites,

Gar Smith is editor of *Earth Island Journal*, a quarterly international environmental newsmagazine that links environmental, peace and justice issues.

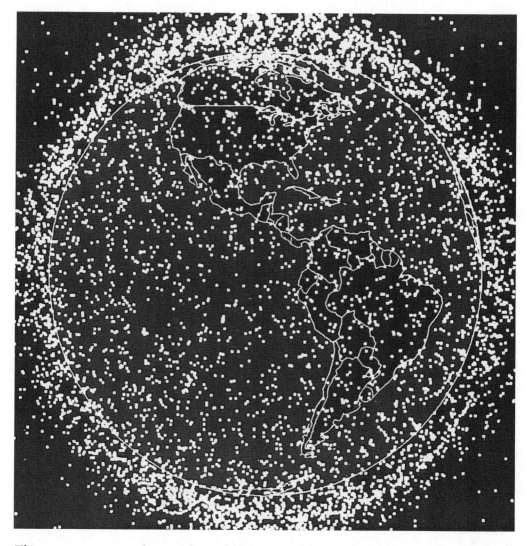

This computer-generated image shows the locations of thousands of satellites, spent rocket stages and break-up debris in low Earth orbit. NASA

lost wrenches and lumps of frozen human waste. More than 80 satellites are known to have broken apart in orbit. (Space junk is believed to have knocked Russia's COS-MOS 954 out of the sky; a brush with a speeding chip of paint nearly caused a disaster when it cratered the window of a US space shuttle.)

Orbiting debris has been growing at a rate of 13 percent per year, according to the Aerospace Corporation's Vladimir Chobo-tov, who warns that in the next 15 years nearly 10 percent of the larger satellites risk damage from space junk, triggering a growing chain reaction of further collisions.

Chobotov has called for the design of "non-littering" space systems with reusable and retrievable parts and equipped with "bumpers to resist collision damage." Chobotov also stresses the need for international agreements on procedures for "space debris collection" and suggests that the US, as a major user (and polluter) of space, set an example of "good housekeeping" for the rest of the world's spacefaring nations.

Profiteering in Space

Some of this "pollution debt" could be borne by the hundreds of corporations that are now heavily invested in space, thanks, in large part, to more than $200 billion in government contracts and NASA's decision to defer millions of dollars in launch costs to make space safe for US business.

One of these privately owned beneficiaries is Space Services of Houston, which not only plans to orbit a $250-$500 million space factory, but also won permission from NASA, the Pentagon and former Transportation Secretary Elizabeth Dole, to make a fast buck by launching cremated human remains into Earth orbit. Working with a team of former NASA engineers and Florida morticians, Space Services proposed charging up to $3,000 each to shoot the ashes of 5,000 pioneering cadavers into an eternal, 1900-mile-high resting place.

Reactors in Space

The US space program, like the nuclear power industry, has been portrayed as a peaceful, civilian program. In fact, both operations have been integrally tied to military needs from the beginning. Both programs came together in 1958 when the US became the first and only nation to explode atomic and hydrogen weapons in space (in a series of military experiments that caused serious damage to the protective electromagnetic fields surrounding the planet).

Every nuclear reactor placed in orbit or currently planned, has been, is, or will be a military reactor. Today all nuclear-powered reactors in orbit are Soviet but that may change. The military-nuclear-industrial complex recognizes that the only way it can keep its grip on its great share of the federal budget is to see that the arms race (and its nuclear component) is moved into space. Hence the "Star Wars" system, originally sold as a defense from nuclear weapons, now requires using the space shuttle to orbit as many as 100 military reactors (These 6,000-pound SP-100 reactors would have to be replaced every ten years.) While some Soviet scientists have called for a ban on future reactors in space, the US and Japan are planning to place nuclear reactors into the increasingly debris-strewn and dangerous flyways around the Earth.

Of the 60 or so nuclear-powered space missions undertaken so far, one-fifth have met with failure. The potential for a "Chernobyl in the Sky" became a reality on January 24, 1978 when the COSMOS 954 crashed into northern Canada, spreading radioactive debris over 40,000 square miles. The clean-up took six months and cost $14 million. (Following that disaster, leftover Soviet space reactors have been routinely separated and kicked up into a designated "nuclear dump site" 600 miles above the Earth.)

Environmental Laws for Space

Near and Outer Space are more than just a "High Frontier" to be expropriated for the convenience of the fittest Earth-based entrepreneur. These regions are the "High Commons" of our planet and, like any other wilderness, they require protection and preservation.

Several existing bodies of law suggest ways to protect the "high seas" of space and the celestial islands of the cosmos. The 1967 Outer Space Treaty includes a number of "wilderness provisions" including freedom of scientific investigation, public access, a ban on "nuclear weapons or any other weapons of mass destruction," noncontamination of celestial environments and the internationalization of space as "the province of all mankind." Article 7 of the 1979 Moon Treaty forbids "disruption of the existing balance of [the Moon's] environment." (The US has refused to ratify this treaty because of Article 11, which proclaims the satellite to be the "common heritage" of all Earthlings.) And, most recently, Senator Tom Harkin introduced the Outer Space Protection Act before the 101st Congress in early 1989.

Faced with mounting evidence that human exploitation of the planet's resources is finally approaching limits, there is a tendency to look to space as a convenient "escape hatch." This "disposable planet mentality" (which holds that humanity has simply outgrown the Earth and is destined to find new worlds to colonize on the Moon, Venus or Mars) only serves to take the pressure off the industrial polluters and warmakers who are the proper targets for action.

It is unlikely that the human race could survive aboard small, self-contained interplanetary spaceships when we have not yet mastered the ability to survive successfully within the larger limits of Spaceship Earth. Before novice pilots are allowed to take off into the sky, they must first graduate from Ground School and from all evidence at hand, it would appear the human race has not yet even learned to taxi safely.

As we prepare to face the wilderness of space, we should take care that we are not simply turning our backs on the planet Earth. A march to the stars could really be nothing more than fleeing our responsibilities as dwellers upon the Earth to solve the critical problems of our age—pollution, waste, militarism, and social injustice. Problems that will surely be carried with us into the far reaches of space, if they remain unaddressed and unsolved here on Earth.

ACTION*

1. **Boycotts.** Boycott companies that are profiteering off plans to turn tax dollars into space weapons—e.g., General Electric and Martin-Marietta. Withhold alumnus contributions from campuses doing space weapons research—e.g., Pittsburgh's Carnegie Mellon University and the University of California. Inform students at these universities and encourage protest and rebellion. Contact INFACT for information about the GE boycott and contact the Boycott Newsletter, 6506 28th Avenue NE, Seattle, WA 98115, (206) 526-7295.

2. **Letter Writing Campaigns.** Oppose the militarization of the US space program, plans to launch US nuclear reactors in Earth orbit, the military "takeover" of space shuttle missions and plans to spend billions of tax dollars on space weapons. Tell elected representatives that they'll be out on their ears at the next election if they don't oppose the militarization of space.

*Action section by Gar Smith

3. **Demand an end to the federal hand-outs** that have given corporations a free ride into space. No more waivers of the $70 million-plus launch costs to private sector users.

4. **Demand a reallocation of the military space budget** to fund a "Mission to the Earth"—use space technology to aid global environmental protection programs.

5. **Generate Popular Support.** What can communities do? Communities need money which now goes to military and space programs. One goal could be prying loose, say $50 billion, for communities. How about an "Adopt a Planet, Moon or Asteroid" sister city program that opposes the militarization of space?

- Host video screenings of *Star Wars: A Search for Security* (narrated by Ed Begley, Jr.) and related films available from the Educational Film and Video Project. Call (415) 655-9050.

- Request the "Action Pack for Peace in Space," by *Earth Island Journal*, a collection of *Journal* articles, a guide to treaties on the peaceful uses of space and a report on pending legislation. Available from Earth Island for $2.

––––––––––––––– *RESOURCES* –––––––––––––––

Organizations

Citizens for Peace in Space
P.O. Box 915
Colorado Springs, CO 80901
(719) 389-0644

Coordinates local actions to educate the public on the dangers of Star Wars spending and organizes protests at the site of the new Star Wars research center at Colorado's Falcon Air Force Base.

Computer Professionals for Social Responsibility
P.O. Box 717
Palo Alto, CA 94301
(415) 322-3778
IN WASHINGTON, DC:
(202) 775-1588

Works to educate the public about the dangers of accidental nuclear war. Waged a historic lawsuit battle claiming "launch on warning" computer defense systems were an unconstitutional delegation of war-making power from the President to a machine.

Earth Island Institute
300 Broadway, Suite 28
San Francisco, CA 94133
(415) 788-3666

Initiates and supports internationally oriented action projects for the protection and restoration of the environment. Earth Island's projects include the Climate Protection Institute. A $25 membership includes the quarterly Earth Island Journal. Earth Island addresses global warming and air pollution through its commitment to making explicit the ties between politics, economics, justice and environmental ecology.

Environmental Defense Fund
257 Park Avenue South
New York, NY 10010
(212) 505-2100

An advocacy organization of scientists, economists and attorneys who maintain that the greenhouse effect is the environmental equivalent of nuclear war. They recommend dismantling the patchwork of subsidies that distort energy production and use decisions. Their monthly EDF *Letter alerts readers to atmospheric and other global threats and presents actions and alternatives.*

Florida Coalition for Peace and Justice
P.O. Box 2486
Orlando, FL 32802
(407) 422-3479

Has led peaceful protests at the Kennedy Space Center calling for the demilitarization of the US space program and a ban on nuclear fuel for orbital and deep space missions.

Greenpeace USA
1436 U Street NW
Washington, DC 20009
(202) 462-1177

An international non-profit organization, with over a million members in 23 countries, dedicated to protecting the environment and to nuclear disarmament. Major current emphasis includes atmospheric issues: Greenpeace lobbies for clean air legislation, and economic policies and industrial standards that would help alleviate global warming.

Institute for Security and Cooperation in Outer Space
#8 Logan Circle
Washington, DC 20005
(202) 462-8886

A non-profit, non-partisan research and education organization providing information to the public and decision-makers regarding the benefits of international cooperation in a non-weapons space environment. Their monthly newsletter, Spaceline, *is available for $25/year.*

Institute for Space and Security Studies
7720 Mary Cassatt Drive
Potomac, MD 20854

Headed by former USAF Lt. Col. Robert M. Bowman, ISSS analyzes the costs and technological pitfalls of plans to militarize space.

National Clean Air Coalition
503 7th Street SE
Washington, DC 20003
(202) 797-5436

NCAC is a network of thousands of individuals and state and local organizations concerned with the protection of the environment, health, labor, parks and other resources threatened by air pollutants. The coalition includes 36 member organizations and works primarily on education and lobbying campaigns.

Natural Resources Defense Council
40 West 20th Street
New York, NY 10011
(212) 727-2700

Working to protect natural resources and improve the quality of the human environment, NRDC combines legal action, scientific research and citizen education. Major current project is the Atmospheric Protection Initiative.

The Planetary Society
65 North Catalina Avenue
Pasadena, CA 91106
(818) 793-5100

One of the most respectable space-interest organizations, the 100,000-strong Planetary Society is chaired by Dr. Carl Sagan. Membership includes subscription to the magazine The Planetary Report.

Progressive Space Forum
1724 Sacramento Street #9
San Francisco, CA 94109
(415) 822-3221

The leading critical, progressive voice on the militarization of space. PSF sounded the first alarms about arming the heavens three years before the President's "Star Wars" speech. PSF sponsored the "Action Forum Against Star Wars" in San Francisco in January 1986. Members receive monthly newsletter Space for People.

Rocky Mountain Institute
1739 Snowmass Creek Road
Old Snowmass, CO 81654
(302) 927-3128

A non-profit research, education and public advocacy organization fostering the efficient and sustainable use of energy resources as a path to global security. Major emphasis on energy efficiency. RMI has published magazine articles on energy sources and the greenhouse effect. They have also published Greenhouse Warming, *a comparative analysis of two abatement strategies.*

Sierra Club
730 Polk Street
San Francisco, CA 94109
(415) 776-2211

Promotes conservation of the natural environment by influencing public policy decisions—legislative, administrative, legal and electoral. Works to practice and promote the responsible use of the earth's ecosystems and resources; to educate and enlist humanity to protect and restore the quality of the natural and human environment. Current emphasis includes global warming. A $33 membership includes Sierra *magazine.*

Tree People
12601 Mulholland Drive
Beverly Hills, CA 90210
(818) 769-2663

Works to retard global warming by developing the planet's primary CO_2 filter: trees. One million trees were planted in Los Angeles during the 1984 Olympics. They are currently involved with the American Forestry Association in developing the "Global Re-leaf" program to plant 100 million trees across the United States by 1992. Their program activities include citizen forestry training, working with school children in environmental education, and occasional disaster relief.

Union of Concerned Scientists
26 Church Street
Cambridge, MA 02238
(617) 547-5552

Conducts scientific and technical research concerning advanced technologies. This coalition of scientists, engineers and other professionals is concerned with health, safety, environmental and national security problems posed by the country's nuclear programs.

United Nations Environmental Programme
North American Regional Office
DC 2-803
#2 United Nations Plaza
New York, NY 10017
(212) 963-8093

UNEP has published studies on the ozone layer, global warming and the environmental impact of energy production methods, as well as on a wide range of other environmental issues. Call or write for information.

World Resources Institute
1709 New York Avenue, NW
7th Floor
Washington, DC 20006
(202) 638-6300

A research and policy institute helping governments, the private sector, environmental and development organizations meet human needs and nurture economic growth while preserving the environment. Major research, policy formation and public advocacy work on global warming.

Periodicals

Global Climate Change Digest
Elsevier Science Publishing Co.
655 Avenue of the Americas
New York, NY 10010

The best available news on technical and scientific publications, climate-related articles, legislation, conference reports, upcoming conference listings and other events. For the specialist. $175 per year.

In Context
P.O. Box 11470
Bainbridge Island, WA 98110

A quarterly review of humane sustainable culture. Its entire summer 1989 issue is devoted to the social and political aspects of climate change. Number 22. $5.

Books

Global Warming.   Dr. Stephen Schneider.
San Francisco: Sierra Club Books, 1989.

One of the preeminent scientists in the field explains the issues to the layperson, making atmospheric physics and chemistry understandable.

Arming the Heavens.   Jack Manno. New York: Dodd, Mead & Company, 1984.

Basic historical background of the military roots of the US space program in the attitudes of the Pentagon strategists and German scientists brought to the US to refine the weapons of world domination they had created under Hitler.

Beyond Spaceship Earth.   Eugene Hargrove, editor. San Francisco: Sierra Club Books, 1987.

A thorough and thoughtful exploration of the environmental impacts of space exploration. Confronts not only the environmental questions of pollution and weapons in space, but the ethical questions of how spacefaring humans should deal with alien lifeforms and ecologically-destabilizing planetary colonization.

Entropy: A New World View.   Jeremy Rifkin. New York: Bantam, 1989.

A reworking of the author's well-known book, with added material on the greenhouse crisis.

The Home Planet.   Kevin W. Kelley. Boston/Moscow: Addison-Wesley/Mir Publishing, 1988.

Jointly published in the US and the USSR, this handsome oversized book contains 150 beautiful color photographs of the Earth taken from space. The images are coupled with the actual words of astronauts and cosmonauts from 18 nations. The emotional impact of viewing our home planet from space has been brought back to Earth in this historic publication.

A Matter of Degrees: The Potential for Controlling the Greenhouse Effect.   Irving M. Mintzer. Washington, DC: World Resources Institute, 1987.

Research report that describes three likely scenarios for global warming under three different projections of economic and emission growth.

101 Ways to Save the Earth . . . and How You Fit into the Puzzle.   Washington, DC: Greenhouse Crisis Foundation, 1989.

The best current guide to individual lifestyle changes that can help mitigate global warming. Call (202) 466-2823 to order.

Out of the Cradle: Exploring the Frontiers Beyond Earth.   William K. Hartmann, Ron Miller and Pamela Lee. New York: Workman, 1984.

One of the most beautiful and informative books on the possibilities of space exploration. Crammed with page-filling paintings of scientifically accurate visual prophecies, the chapters cover the history of *space adventure, environmental pressures pushing us into space and plans to exploit the moons, asteroids and planets.*

Proceedings of the Second Annual North American Conference on Preparing for Climate Change. John Topper, editor. Washington, DC: Climate Institute, 1989.

Scientific and technical papers on climate change and a wide array of related issues.

Star Wars: A Defense Expert's Case Against the Strategic Defense Initiative. Dr. Robert M. Bowman. Los Angeles: J. P. Tarcher, 1986.

A rare insider's indictment of why Star Wars won't work. Lt. Col. Bowman, formerly head of the USAF's Advanced Space Program and an executive with General Dynamics, now heads the Institute for Space and Security Studies. The book's appendix includes copies of the ABM Treaty, President Reagan's "Star Wars" address and suggested wording for a treaty to ban weapons in space.

The State of the World 1989. Lester Brown, et al. New York: W.W. Norton, 1989.

Excellent overview of the greenhouse crisis in relationship to other major global issues. Includes a global action plan.

Turning Up the Heat: Our Perilous Future in the Global Greenhouse. Fred Pierce. London: The Bodley Head, 1989.

Some of the worst scenarios as described by the editor of Science News.

World Resources 1988-89. World Resources Institute, IIED and UNEP. New York: Basic Books, 1988.

An indispensible assessment of the resource base that supports the global economy, with an excellent section on the interactions among pollutants and atmospheric processes and the relationship among ozone depletion, acid rain and global warming.

PART TWO
BEYOND OPPRESSION

Embracing Diversity: Building Multicultural Alliances

MARGO ADAIR AND SHARON HOWELL

OUR CULTURE DEFINES success as material gain and progress as technological development. Whether or not we view our own lives with these values, living in industrial society has embedded destructive patterns deep in each of us. We are socialized with views that disdain nature and degrade those who do work that brings us closest to her—caring for the young, old and ill; picking and preparing food; cleaning homes and streets. This socialization maintains exploitation and oppression.

Relationships of domination and submission are re-created in the taken-for-granted assumptions of daily life. Industrialism divides us from one another and our own nature, alienates us from the Earth and creates a deep psychic fear of those "different" from ourselves. This view produces a hierarchical society in which some are valued and others not. In the name of efficiency we have created a monoculture in which

power is centralized. The complexity and interdependence that is intrinsic to life are replaced by sterile procedures.

Those of us who identify as environmentalists know that diversity is vital to nature's well-being. Yet we find ourselves reflecting only a narrow segment of society—the white middle class. We need to ask ourselves why. This is particularly perplexing when it is the least powerful among us who are most directly affected by the environmental crisis. Native Americans' land is desecrated for uranium and coal mining; farm workers are poisoned as they care for our food; neighborhoods in our inner cities are used for toxic dumps and giant incinerators; children are born into violence and poverty, inheriting a world devoid of meaning or social purpose. A legacy of struggle is being replaced with drug culture and the crime that comes with it. Human and spiritual devastation are made invisible by a view of "nature" devoid of people. We block out the

Margo Adair and **Sharon Howell** are both political activists, teachers, speakers and writers. They have been exploring how people duplicate relationships of domination and subservience while intending otherwise. Adair and Howell serve as consultants to labor, women, environmental, lesbian, gay and youth organizations. They have recently published a monograph, *The Subjective Side of Politics*, and have a forthcoming book, *Breaking the Power Taboo*.

What is NOT always addressed in the policy discourse of multiculturalism is the segregated division of labor in which, more often than not, white arts structures of intellectual institutions provide racism while control in which white Producers als theorise about materials ethnic Film and video testimony supply "experiential" or in which in the form of solicits token third wo and documentary, to theorise about the White intelligentsia that is, the problem of RLD intellectuals for the White inte the question these divisons contri the "other to the continuation Illig critical cultural apartheid white of the multicultural ve of reg ardless Given these problems it should neer. Come as no surprise that fear come Third world org anizations, that the current m exist within will ultimately hurt, not help them. multicultural impetus

"Border Axes" San Diego's Border Art Workshop/Taller de Arte Fronterizo suggests that "the border looks the same from both sides; that one crosses the border from one side to the same *side; that there is no border; that the border exists in the heart of society and within cultures as well as between them."* BORDER ART WORKSHOP/TALLER DE ARTE FRONTERIZO, 1987

pain of industrial society and with it the inspiration we could get from communities organizing to create dignified ways of living in the face of destruction. The environmental movement has come to mean those who "protect nature," not those struggling to make a home within her.

We need to ask ourselves why the defense of Big Mountain, the boycott of table grapes, the neighborhood organizing against toxins and the efforts of mothers to stop gang violence and killings of children are not considered ecological struggles. Why don't those carrying out these struggles identify as environmentalists? Why don't "environmentalists" consider these struggles worth their concentrated efforts?

What is it going to take for environmental activism to encompass the diversity of our country—a diversity made invisible within the political and social atmosphere we create? Until we become multicultural, the environmental movement will remain marginal, lacking the passion, creative energy and vision that is unleashed when people are struggling out of the immediate circumstances of daily life.

In those rare moments when we do work with "others," we soon find they are no longer showing up at meetings. We are baffled as to just what went wrong, given our intentions to be inclusive.

The very nature of the so-called melting pot makes invisible, at best, and degrades, at worst, all that is not considered "normal" by white, male, middle-class standards. In order to be taken seriously, most of us feel compelled to trivialize or hide those aspects of our being which don't fit this narrow norm. In order to be trusted and have our contributions welcomed, those of us from communities that are not of the white middle class find ourselves in the position of needing to dismiss entirely too much of who we are. People of European descent, in the effort to become "white," are cut off from any heritage they can respect. In this "wonderbreading" process, we all feel that we are continually having to prove ourselves under the scrutiny of one another's judgment. This creates an atmosphere in which competition rules, and our humanity is diminished. Out of all of this striving to fit in, we create a monoculture.

Breaking out of the patterns that make invisible the lives and perspectives of those from different circumstances is key to creating multi-cultural alliances. This entails coming to know the multitude of approaches we bring. Native Americans, African Americans, gays and lesbians, ethnic communities struggling to preserve language and traditions, people of conscience working to expand our understanding of our relationships with one another and the Earth, all offer rich wisdom.

We need to commit ourselves to learning about the historical legacy and present conditions of those who are different from ourselves. Just what is it, that a straight person can take for granted that a lesbian or gay cannot, that a wealthy person can take for granted that a poor person cannot, that an able-bodied person can take for granted that a disabled person cannot, that a Christian can take for granted that a Jewish person cannot? How is it that people maintain their humanity despite adversity? Learning about the ways oppressed groups have maintained integrity is indispensable not only for building trusting relationships, but for broadening perspectives to organize effectively.

The common solution is "outreach." This usually means getting people different from ourselves to work with us. We are oblivious to the fact that we have defined the problems and the resulting agenda without any awareness that the agenda itself would be altered if other perspectives were included from the beginning. Then, to create a comfortable atmosphere in which everyone feels included, we minimize all differences. We say, "We're all people." But this backfires. People justly feel their experiences are then invisible. There is no reason to believe these organizing efforts will change the painful and dehumanizing aspects of their own life and the lives of those with whom

they identify. Differences that would otherwise make us stronger are stifled. The cumulative effect of these patterns softens our minds, sharpens our hearts and depresses our spirits. Instead of our diversity making us strong and securing the future, we have only created one more arena in which we are alienated.

Sustaining work together across our differences will be uncomfortable because we are continually learning unfamiliar ways of being. There is no quick fix to this situation. Creating relationships of trust, in which everyone's contributions are honored, means breaking some of the most powerful taboos in our culture. It means consciously acknowledging the real power differences that exist among us.

Until everyone's reality is made visible, those of us with privilege cannot assume that our view is the only one operating. We have the responsibility of naming the price others have had to pay for the privileges we enjoy. For example, when we state as a simple fact that we are living on stolen land, Native American struggles are no longer invisible. The power of naming expands the parameter of the situation, and when done by those with privilege, it avoids the common dynamics of blame and guilt. Naming the realities with which we *all* have to grapple, creates an atmosphere that welcomes other cultural approaches. The death-courting monoculture breaks down and the life-sustaining customs from all our diverse groups weave the fabric of a resilient culture capable of protecting the sanctity of life.

ACTION*

Changing Patterns of Power

The monoculture is upheld by patterns that form the unspoken assumptions causing us to duplicate the very roles we are trying to transform. They permeate our every interaction from the intimate to the occasional. It is these patterns that keep us separate from each other, unable to appreciate what each of us has to contribute. Alliance building is close to impossible.

The behavior we aspire to, what is accepted as normal, is that of the dominators. They are our most visible role models. Even those of us who have lived with enforced submission find ourselves dominating others.

The following are common patterns that block our ability to work together. The hierarchical and competitive nature of our society gives everyone plenty of opportunities to experience both sides.

Altering either side of this dynamic forces changes on the other. Power exists as a relationship. Changing our own tendencies towards domination or submission cultivates a context of trust and cooperation that includes everyone's contribution.

To discover what behavior patterns we each need to change in our lives so as to be better able to build trusting relationships and work together, we need to ask:

Have I informed myself of the present conditions and history of the peoples with whom I work?

Are the humanity, intelligence, sensitivity and contribution of each person respected?

*Action section by Margo Adair and Sharon Howell

Am I taking up more or less time than others?

Do I interrupt?

Do I censor myself?

Are people dismissed for making mistakes or supported in changing?

Are differences minimized or is pride encouraged in each of our ethnicities and struggles?

Are decisions about the use of resources shared?

Is there an awareness of the differences in our access to resources?

Is there a generosity of spirit, or are guilt and blame operating?

Are distinctions drawn between where someone comes from and what s/he strives to defend and protect?

Are the activities of care for one another and the land at the center of what is valued?

Do we create ways of sharing and celebrating the sanctity of life?

Respect for the lives and work of her people is essential in healing the Earth. We are bound to one another as we are to nature. The protection of power and privilege has eroded all of our connections. They can only be restored as we engage in life-affirming processes that take joy in our diversity.

Behavioral Patterns that Perpetuate Relations of Domination

An individual from the . . .

Dominant Group	*Oppressed Group*
Defines parameters, judges what is appropriate, patronizes.	Feels inappropriate, awkward, doesn't trust own perception, looks to expert for definition.
Assumes responsibility for keeping system on course. Acts unilaterally.	Blames self for not having capacity to change situation.
Self-image of superiority, competence, in control, entitled, correct.	Self-image of inferiority, incompetent, being controlled, not entitled, low self esteem.
Views self as logical, rational. Sees others as too emotional, out of control.	Often thinks of own feelings as inappropriate and a sign of inadequacy.
Presumptuous, does not listen, interrupts, raises voice, bullies, threatens violence, becomes violent.	Finds it difficult to speak up, timid, tries to please. Holds back anger, resentment, rage.
Initiates, manages, plans, projects.	Lacks initiative, responds, deals, copes, survives.
Sees problems and situations in personal terms.	Sees problems in social context, results of system, "them."
Often needs to verbalize feelings.	Sees no point in talking about feelings.
Sees solutions to problems as promoting better feelings.	Sees solutions to problems in actions that change conditions.
Thinks own view of reality is the only one. Disagreements are result of lack of information, misunderstandings, personalities.	Always aware of at least two views of reality, their own and that of the dominant group.
Believes certain kinds of work below their dignity.	Believes certain kinds of work beyond their ability.
Does not acknowledge constraints in current situations.	Sees current situations in terms of past constraints.
Regards own culture as civilized, regards other's as underdeveloped, disadvantaged.	Feels own culture devalued, under assault.
Turns to others' culture to enrich humanity while invalidating it by calling it exotic.	Uses cultural forms to influence situation; uses humor, music, poetry, etc. to celebrate collective experience. Sees these forms as being stolen.

Human Rights

MEDEA BENJAMIN AND ANDREA FREEDMAN

"There were two very important aspects which influenced the government to order my release. First, the workers' refusal to permit the continuation of rights violations. Second, the massive response from the international solidarity movement. I want to personally thank all those who worked to achieve my freedom."

—HUBERTO CENTENO, EXECUTIVE COMMITTEE, NATIONAL UNITY OF SALVADORAN WORKERS (UNTS), MARCH 16, 1988

"HUMAN RIGHTS" is a relatively young concept. The Universal Declaration of Human Rights was adopted by the United Nations in 1948. It set forth rights evolving from the Western political tradition, such as equal protection under the law, protection against cruel or unusual punishment, freedom of expression and the right to participate in government through periodic elections. But it also established a series of economic rights, affirming that everyone has the right to a standard of living adequate for health and well-being, including housing, clothing, medical care and food.

These official declarations reflect the inextricable link between different categories of rights. Political rights are meaningless when the majority of citizens remain economically disenfranchised. Likewise, exercising one's economic rights becomes impossible against a backdrop of political repression, and under a government that remains unaccountable to the majority. People who speak out under these conditions risk their lives.

Medea Benjamin is Executive Director of the San Francisco-based Global Exchange, and author or co-author of several books, including *Don't Be Afraid, Gringo: A Honduran Woman Speaks From the Heart; No Free Lunch: Food and Revolution in Cuba Today;* and *Development That Works: Grassroots Solutions to Hunger and Poverty.* **Andrea Freedman,** a writer and researcher, works at the Center for US-USSR Initiatives. This article is excerpted from Andrea's and Medea's most recent book, *Bridging the Global Gap: A Handbook to Linking Citizens of the First and Third Worlds.*

The Universal Declaration of Human Rights signaled to all citizens that they not only hold certain basic political and economic rights as human beings, but also that individuals are responsible for defending human rights for themselves and for other people. While the Declaration is not legally binding on governments, it provides a certain "code of ethics," and has been followed up by numerous declarations and laws that give the Declaration increasingly more clout in determining international standards for basic needs and rights.

The Declaration has also become the cornerstone for a movement that has since grown to include human rights organizations in nearly every country of the world. Some, like Amnesty International, safeguard the rights of political prisoners. Amnesty works on behalf of over 6,000 political prisoners every year, from Central America to the Philippines, from Libya to the United States, from the Soviet Union to South Africa. Human rights groups like Survival International and the Food First Infor-mation and Action Network are working to ensure economic and cultural survival of indigenous groups and the poor who are struggling to organize and feed themselves. Groups like the Marin Interfaith Task Force on Central America and Peace Brigades International provide bodyguard services to threatened members of local human rights organizations.

Many of the US human rights organizations—Human Rights Advocates, the Lawyers Committee on Central America, Americas Watch—are professional and legal organizations. They use their knowledge of national and international law to press for wider recognition of human rights, as well as punishment for human rights violators. The Lawyers Committee for Human Rights, for example, sponsored a fact-finding mission in 1985 to study human rights abuses against black children in South Africa. Their findings, published in the book *The War Against Children: South Africa's Youngest Victims,* documents the repression and violence used by the state against young

Langa township, Cape Town. July 18, 1988. Youths with posters of Nelson Mandela sing and dance in the streets following a church service marking the jailed African National Congress leader's seventieth birthday. ERIC MILLER, IMPACT VISUALS

people, and calls for stronger US government sanctions against the apartheid regime.

One example of how human rights law works for the poor in our own country comes from Sandra Coliver, a founding member of Human Rights Advocates, an organization providing resources to lawyers defending human rights cases in the United States.

One dramatic illustration of the use of international human rights law came about in 1986. The question raised by a certain case in Merced, California, was, "Could a county cut back its welfare payments?" The court in Merced looked to international standards of what are considered basic needs, and ruled that Merced could not make the planned welfare cuts because it would reduce the standard of living for people to a level below these standards.

Dozens of cities and countries around the world have incorporated human rights laws into their constitutions. One reason why [former Philippines President] Marcos didn't want to stay in the United States is because we have precedents for being able to try him for his human rights violations in the Philippines.

But to believe that only lawyers can understand human rights—let alone defend them—would be a serious mistake. "What strengthens human rights is the mobilization of *public* pressure," says Sandra Coliver. "The grassroots campaigns on behalf of prisoners in the US and other countries will tip the scales in favor of human rights. Economic and political oppression are the common enemies of all of us, whether in the advanced industrialized countries or in the Third World. We must therefore all begin to speak the same language, educating others about human rights and actively working to make our voices heard.

ACTION*

1. **Defend individual victims.** Letter writing is one of the most common forms of human rights advocacy on behalf of individual victims. It is an easy course of action for individuals wanting to improve the human rights situation for a person who has been arbitrarily arrested. It works, it doesn't take much time, it's nonviolent, and the protest exemplifies the freedom of expression citizens of every country should possess.

2. **Support regional human rights organizations.** Perhaps equally as important as working on behalf of individuals in other countries is *strengthening a group's capacity to monitor human rights within its own country.* In 1975, representatives from 35 nations came together to sign the Helsinki Accords. The Accords gave human rights issues a prominence in international relations that was lacking previously, and provided human rights advocates with a standard by which to measure the performance of their own and other countries. The Accords also stated that citizens have the right to know about and act upon violations of their rights within their own countries. In the spirit of the Helsinki Accords, Helsinki Watch began in 1979 as a watchdog for

*Action section by Medea Benjamin and Andrea Freedman

human rights organizations in Eastern Europe, attempting to ensure that human rights monitors did not become victims of violence simply for their human rights activities. Subsequently, America's Watch and Asia Watch were formed.

One can directly protect human rights groups by the physical protection of local activists through one-on-one or group presence. Peace Brigades International (PBI) advocates and trains people for nonviolent conflict resolution throughout the world. One of PBI's tactics in the fight against human rights abuses is the personal escort. For three to 12 months each year, international volunteers form teams of unarmed escorts and accompany members of local human rights commissions in El Salvador and Guatemala. They hope that just the presence of international observers will deter the death squads and military assassins. It's risky, but volunteers know that their protection lies in the repercussions—dramatic turnarounds in US popular opinion—that can occur if they are injured or killed by another government's military.

3. **Tie labor rights to trade relations.** A new focus for international human rights work has been tying workers' rights to trade agreements. The purpose of this strategy is to give preferential treatment to those countries that respect labor rights, and to sanction those that do not. At the forefront of this movement is the International Labor Rights Education and Research Fund, which helps draft laws making US trade preferences conditional on nations' compliance with labor rights.

The American Bar Association recently passed a resolution urging US policymakers to consider the right to food in all foreign policy decisions, including trade, debt service payments, agricultural development and land distribution recommendations.

4. **Support the Sanctuary movement.** A very personal connection to human rights emerges within our own borders. Refugees fleeing political repression—from Haiti, Eritrea, El Salvador or Guatemala—bring human rights stories to life. Organizations in this country help refugees secure their status, support them in their struggle to survive here and work with them so that their stories are heard.

The Sanctuary movement is one of the best organized responses to the needs of political refugees in the United States. It began in a formal way on March 24, 1982, on the second anniversary of the assassination of Salvadoran Bishop Oscar Romero. Almost simultaneously, churches in Tucson, San Francisco, Seattle, Los Angeles and Chicago declared the legal process of seeking refugee status unjust, and declared themselves Sanctuary churches. By 1986 the number of public sanctuary sites had grown to 300. For every congregation that publicly declared sanctuary, there may be ten others working underground. Some 27 cities in the United States have declared themselves cities of refuge. The cities of New York and Chicago have urged non-cooperation with the Immigration and Naturalization Service by asking city workers not to turn over undocumented workers from Central America.

Indigenous Rights

JOHN MOHAWK

I N 1406, SPANISH and French soldiers landed on Lanzarotte Island in the Canary Islands and commenced what would prove to be a 90-year war with the indigenous population of the islands. Those peoples, known as Gaunches, were finally defeated in 1496, the survivors taken as slaves to plantations in the Azores and throughout the Canaries. The Gaunches were probably the first distinct people of the modern world that ceased to exist as such, but they were far from the last.

Should distinct peoples—usually but not always indigenous to the lands or at least to the continents they inhabit—have rights to a continued existence as distinct peoples? The question has been the subject of papal pronouncements, an interesting 16th-century debate at Validolid, and international treaty law for centuries. Since World War II the question has become a matter of international human rights law.

The history of indigenous peoples has centered on their struggle to survive the rapid expansion of modern nation-states. During the late 15th and early 16th centuries whole peoples were decimated, whole islands depopulated of indigenous peoples. Major civilizations disappeared in Central and South America, and indigenous peoples were relegated to conditions of slavery and serfdom. The mistreatment of natives and the genocide systematically waged against them caused exterminations of populations of peoples in places such as Tasmania, Newfoundland, Southern California, Texas and Puerto Rico. This process of pressure and extermination or near-extermination has continued into the 20th century and is currently most dramatically seen in El Salvador, Brazil, Guatemala, Alaska, East Timor, and many other places where the right of peoples to survive is in distinct contradiction to the plans of the nation-state to conscript their lands and people into the national economy.

Indigenous peoples have suffered outrageously at the hand of nation-states during recent decades. Some peoples of the South Pacific were removed from their

John Mohawk teaches American Studies at the State University of New York at Buffalo. He writes for numerous periodicals and is currently the editor of *Daybreak* magazine.

Sarawak tribal elders in Borneo defy rainforest developers. Multinational corporations have been destroying the rainforest of Southeast Asia, including Borneo, where some of the last indigenous people continue their traditional hunting and gathering lifestyle. FRIENDS OF THE EARTH, UK

homelands after World War II so their islands could be used to test atomic bombs. Their waters are invaded by huge fishing fleets that deplete their fisheries, and by intercontinental ballistic missiles; and sometimes their homelands have simply been opened up for settlement by nation-states seeking room for excess populations.

Indian peoples in Canada have been forced to relocate because the government wanted to use their lands as a gunnery range. In many areas of the world, but dramatically in the United States, Canada and the Philippines, huge hydroelectric projects have displaced entire indigenous nations and continue to threaten to do so in the fu-

ture. In the rainforest areas of the world, development, usually part of a national strategy, threatens the rainforest and the rainforest people. There has been little international agreement about rights indigenous people may have against the assertions of nation-states, which define practically every plan in terms of "national security" or "national welfare." These national needs, the argument goes, outweigh the rights and needs of indigenous peoples, most of whom do not have paper recognition of their ownership of land, though they may have occupied it since time immemorial.

Most of the rights distinct peoples would need to continue to exist as distinct peoples are, today, theoretical rights. Few nation-states recognize the principle that indigenous peoples have a right to lands, and those who do, recognize very limited rights. This has resulted in a situation in which nations such as Brazil have failed to delineate and protect lands needed by the Yanomani for their future survival. In some countries such as the United States, national laws recognize treaties made with Indian nations as the highest law of the land. But treaties are subject to the Plenary Power Doctrine, under which the courts recognize the right of the United States to do anything it pleases to Indian nations—including the right to destroy Indian peoples as peoples.

The Plenary Power Doctrine was used during the 1950's to justify the Termination Policy. Under that policy, Indian nations were simply declared "terminated." They no longer existed in the eyes of the United States. In recent times, this has been the most dramatic way of ending the existence of distinct peoples in North America.

President Nixon declared the termination policy at an end in the 1970's, but the United States enacted the Alaska Native Claims Settlement Act in 1974. Under that act most of the Alaska Natives will soon experience something very similar to Termination when their land rights are dissolved and their homelands will become, essentially, open to the market.

Struggles for a continued existence sometimes cross continental boundaries and ideological lines. For example, during the 1970's and continuing to the present, Australia's indigenous peoples, the Aborigines, have waged a vigorous campaign for recognition of their rights. Aborigines were hunted for sport well into this century. Their peoples have been driven from their lands, their children taken from their communities, and their members subjected to second-class status in every way, including recognition of land rights. They have found allies in labor unions and human rights advocates, and today are moving toward re-establishing their societies throughout Australia.

One of the most dramatic indigenous struggles involved the Indian peoples of the East Coast of the Central American country of Nicaragua. Following the Nicaraguan Revolution, some of the Miskito moved to press land claims that had been outstanding for about a century. The Managua government saw the land claim as a reactionary attempt to dismember Nicaragua, a position Indian leaders asserted was an over-reaction. When Indian leaders who were asserting the land claim issue were arrested, there were demonstrations on the East Coast. People were killed during these demonstrations and the unrest escalated until Indian guerrilla units were attacking Sandinista army units.

This conflict was presented in the North American press generally, and some of the liberal press specifically, as part of the East/West phenomenon of surrogate warfare.

The Sandinistas were proposed to represent the socialist world, and the Indians were accused of being manipulated by the CIA. The initial history of the conflict and the real issues were largely obscured and the rights of the Miskito and other Indian peoples of the Atlantic Coast have been generally ignored. Recently the Managua government has been proposing that the Indians function with a degree of autonomy, but the details of that proposal have also proven controversial and very tentative.

Many of these conditions of oppression under which Indian people struggle to survive can be influenced by public opinion. In the winter of 1988-89 Brazil was accused of inaction in cases in which Indians were being abused by woodcutters who had invaded the Indian country. Publicity about these cases has embarrassed the Brazilian government. Public outrage would cause Brazil to pay more attention to the issue.

Concerned people need to be informed about indigenous issues and support the development of principles of indigenous rights. Most of the abuses to indigenous peoples occur far from the capitals and population centers of the world and are slow to enter into the mainstream press, so people should read the publications which speak to these issues. People should also act on their consciences in these matters. Write letters to Congress, to the offending governments, to local newspapers to help publicize the issues. Unless we act, indigenous peoples will never be accorded rights by governments that covet their land, their water, their labor and that often deny that any indigenous people even exist within their borders. Informed people can make a difference, which would save lives throughout the world.

————————— *ACTION**—————————

1. Education is Action:

- Encourage your university, high school, or community center to hold seminars led by Indian people involved in current issues. Do independent studies, research papers in classes, and media projects on contemporary Indian affairs. Find out what conflicts exist for Indians in your community. Trace the history of Indian people in your region. See list of organizations to contact for events.

- Write letters to the editor of your paper, and put pressure on the media to cover current issues affecting Indian people. Often issues are covered, but the perspective of Indian people affected is neglected or distorted. (The threat to Athabascan subsistence posed by drilling in the Alaska National Wildlife Refuge is but one of many cases where the media act as if there are no Indian people affected in unique ways.)

2. General Popular Support:

- Establish grassroots solidarity groups in your community or school. (Contact the International Indian Treaty Council for information concerning resources for such a group.)

- Maintain contact with native rights groups, and organize media campaigns, community education projects and letter-writing campaigns based on the priorities of these groups.

3. Political Support:

- Research threats to Indian self-determination in your area, such as racist

backlash legislation seeking to abrogate treaty rights (Wisconsin, 1988); the desecration of sacred sites; and violations of religious freedom (Big Mountain relocation in Arizona, Gaskett-Orleans Road in California, geothermal development in Hawaii, mineral extraction in the Black Hills of South Dakota, and interference with prisoners' religious practices). Contact your Congressional representative, expressing the need to uphold the rights of indigenous people.

- The attack on Alaska Native Sovereignty: 1991 will be a crucial year for the future of Alaska. In 1991 the provisions of the Alaska Native Claims Settlement Act (ANCSA) will come to fruition. The sovereignty of the Alaska Native people and the future of Alaska Native children are greatly threatened by this Act. There are various opposing views, depending on who gets to benefit by the opening up of Alaska lands to non-natives, as provided by ANCSA. Contact the Alaska Native Sovereignty Network or the International Indian Treaty Council. Much public support will be needed for the traditional people fighting to retain their lands, and rights to subsistence.

4. Confront divide and conquer strategies:

Historically, Indian people have been manipulated by occupying powers to fight their own people. Current examples include the public relations media campaign describing a Hopi/Navaho "range war" in need of a government land dispute settlement. This strategy

*Action section by Karl Erb

fragmented communities in both tribes covering up the historical and current interests of uranium and coal development which is a central cause of the "land dispute". Traditional people, who feel that they are not represented by tribal councils, face an overwhelming task in fighting the misinformation about their struggle for unity and land. (Read *The Second Long Walk* by Jerry Krammer.)

Another current example of divide and conquer is the manipulation by the CIA and other US foreign policy organs of the historical tension in Nicaragua between Atlantic Coast Indians and pre- and post-revolutionary governments in Nicaragua. The Sandinista government's literacy campaign of 1980 insensitively imposed a Spanish language program on the mostly English-speaking Atlantic Coast. The Sandinistas subsequently acknowledged their mistake and initiated dialogue with the Atlantic coast peoples including Miskito, Rama, Sumu, Garifono and Creole. As a result of the dialogue, the Nicaraguan constitution is the only one in the Americas that contains a statute granting rights of autonomous government to the indigenous peoples within its boundaries. The International Indian Treaty Council and other organizations see this historic step as an example that serves to embarrass nation states throughout the Americas, like the US which espouses democracy but continually falls short of awarding these rights to indigenous people.

Women: Still the Second Sex

BELLA ABZUG AND MIM KELBER

F ROM THE RICHEST TO the poorest nation, in not one country of the world
have women yet achieved equal social, economic or political status with men.

This has been a century of revolutionary changes, and in many instances, progress for women, with the concept of liberation and equal rights for our numerically
superior sex stirring them into action in virtually every part of the globe.

But enormous and widening gaps exist
between the quality of lives of women in the
industrialized West and those in the foreign-
debt-plagued, underdeveloped countries of
Africa, Latin America, Asia and the Middle
East. Even within the United States and
Western Europe, where women have made
the most notable advances, extreme poverty, poor education and health care, and denial of basic human rights still afflict millions of women, many of them heads of
fatherless families.

In a 1988 Population Crisis committee
study of 99 countries, representing 2.3 billion women (92 percent of the world's female population), women's well-being was
measured in five sectors; health, marriage
and children, education, employment, and
social equality. Scores were ranked from
Excellent (100) to Extremely Poor. No nation scored excellent. Only seven countries
had total scores of 80 or above, giving them
a rank of Very Good. Sweden, with 87,
scored highest. Among the highest scoring
nations, the United States ranked first in
achievements in education; 16th in health;
18th in marriage and children; 12th in employment; and 20th in social equality. Bangladesh, with a score of 21.5, ranked lowest.
In all, some 51 out of 99 countries fell into
the study's three bottom categories: Poor,
Very Poor and Extremely Poor. The study
found that over 60 percent of all women and
girls in the world live under conditions that

Bella Abzug is co-chair of the Women's Foreign Policy Council, former Democratic member of Congress
(1971-76), co-founder of Women's Strike for Peace, and has taken a leading role in various international
women's conferences over the last two decades. She recently published *Gender Gap: Bella Abzug's Guide to
Political Power for Women*. **Mim Kelber** is co-chair and Editorial Director of the Women's Foreign Policy
Council, former Policy Consultant for President Carter's National Advisory Committee for Women, a researcher, writer and peace activist.

threaten their health, deprive them of choice about childbearing, limit educational opportunities, restrict economic participation, and deny them equal civil and political rights with men.

United Nations data released in 1985, at the conclusion of the UN Decade for Women, revealed that women do two-thirds of the world's work but earn only 10 percent of its income and own only one percent of property. Worldwide, one-third of all households are headed by women, and they are disproportionately poor. (In the US, more than three-fourths of all people living in poverty are women and children.) Among the world's fast-growing refugee population—people fleeing from wars, political persecution, economic dislocation, famines and droughts—80 percent are women and their dependent children.

Each year an estimated 500,000 women die from causes related to pregnancy and childbirth; 99 percent of these deaths take place in underdeveloped countries. They die of hemorrhages, infections, toxemia, accentuated by malnutrition and anemia. Fifteen million children under age five die each year, most of whom could be saved through simple medical interventions and preventive health care, including nutritional monitoring, immunization, better hygiene, safe drinking water and better birth spacing.

Although women produce more than half the world's food, in many nations tradition decrees that men and boys are served first. In the best of times, women and girls get less food than males; in times of famine and drought, they are the most vulnerable. UNIFEM, a UN agency that works with Third World women, estimates that in Africa women spend as much as 2,000 to 5,000 hours a year in unpaid labor transporting water, fuel and goods to and from their households. The alarming shrinkage of the world's forests, the dependency of women on wood for fuel, the pressures created on

these finite resources by uncontrolled population increases and "austerity" economic measures, the resulting soil erosion and transformation of once-fertile lands into deserts are among the many factors further imperiling the already miserable lives of millions of Third World women.

Women are not only a majority of the oppressed, but because of their sex, they are also victimized in distinctive ways. Domestic violence is a worldwide epidemic, affecting women in the US as well as in those countries where women still have few legal rights. In a continuing horror story, an estimated 84 million women and little girls, primarily in Africa and the Middle East, have been sexually mutilated by genital circumcision.

Women are turned into sexual commodities, sold as products in the international sexual slavery trade, exploited for profit in the sex tourism rackets of the Far East, shipped abroad to work as maids and to send their money back home, and drafted as prostitutes to service the thousands of American GIs in US military bases, in the Philippines and elsewhere, where many are impregnated, abandoned and infected with disease.

For a majority of women throughout the world, human rights, as defined in the West, in the press and by traditional human rights organizations, is the icing on a cake they have never tasted. They still seek plain, ordinary bread and water. Desperate as their situation is, women everywhere are organizing to fight for their rights, for economic justice and equality. Their struggles are focused around their local needs as well as the basic rights guaranteed them by the UN Universal Declaration of Human Rights, approved in 1948, and two subsequent UN documents: the Convention on the Elimination of Discrimination Against Women (signed by President Carter in 1979, but not yet ratified by the US Senate) and the

COMADRES *march in San Salvador. This movement in El Salvador was inspired by Las Madres de la Plaza de Mayo, the Argentinian women's group whose protests over disappeared relatives continued for years under a dictatorship that succeeded in silencing most dissident voices. "Disappearances" are also a major human-rights issue in El Salvador.* JIM TYNAN, 1987, IMPACT VISUALS

"Forward-Looking Strategies" statement that emerged from the UN-sponsored international women's conference in Nairobi in July 1985. Nairobi was the place where global feminism came of age—a symbol of sisterhood, of internationalist feminist networks, of women's determination to win economic, social and political equality, not only for their own betterment but to infuse more balanced, humanist values into our society.

As the Women's Foreign Policy Council says in a Women's Declaration of Interdependence that is being circulated within the US and internationally: "Women's views on economic justice, human rights, reproduction and the achievement of peace must be heard at local, national, and international forums, wherever policies are made that could affect the future of life on Earth. Partnership among all peoples is essential for the survival of the planet."

ACTION*

1. **Organize against threats to women's rights.** Currently, a woman's right to an abortion is under attack both legislatively and in the realm of community action. A national group called Operation Rescue is physically attempting to block entrances to abortion clinics. Organize to defend women's legal right to abortion and to counter-demonstrate, disrupt and discredit Operation Rescue's infringement of women's rights. Contact National Abortion Rights Action League.

2. **Fight rape**—and learn to defend yourself. Contact your local rape prevention center, rape crisis center or university women's center for information.

3. **Campaign for equal pay for equal work,** and compensation for housework. Currently women in the US earn approximately 60 cents on every dollar that's earned by a male wage earner.

4. **Investigate equal access to services and resources in your city.** Do women have equal opportunities in your workplace? In your local government? Is there a local government commission for women's rights in your city? Quality childcare and healthcare are critical services that must be provided in order to allow women to have full participation in today's society.

5. **Start a women's support center** in your town or region.

6. **Join a local chapter** of one of the many women's organizations; start a local chapter if there isn't one.

7. **Read and share women's history,** largely ignored and untold in our country.

8. **Develop your own consciousness** regarding gender balance in organizations that you are a part of. Take a look at the number of women in leadership positions. Are women's issues represented in your discussions? How can you help support women to achieve more experience and leadership?

9. **Examine your own sexism.** Both women and men need to look at what

*Action section by Florence Gardner and Brad Erickson

they expect from women as compared to what they expect from men.

10. **Campaign to elect women to political office.** Only 26 out of 535 Senators and Congressmembers are women, yet women make up more than 50 percent of the country. No wonder women's issues are under-represented in policymaking.

RESOURCES

Organizations

American Civil Liberties Union, Political Asylum Project
122 Maryland Avenue, NE
Washington, DC 20002
(202) 543-4651
Provides information on policies toward El Salvador by the United States. Provides documentation for lawyers working on political asylum cases for El Salvadoreans.

Alaska Native Sovereignty Network
P.O. Box 1105
Chickaloon, AK 99674
A coalition of traditional peoples fighting for recognition of their right to sovereignty and self-governance. Working to protect those threatened by the Alaska Native Claims Settlement Act. Write for information.

American Indian Support Group of New York
P.O. Box 1587, Cooper Station
New York, NY 10276
(212) 505-9323
AISGNY is a local support group for national Indian issues. Works for human rights and Indian sovereignty over their lands.

Amnesty International
322 8th Avenue
New York, NY 10001
(212) 633-4200

International human rights action group that focuses on the release of prisoners of conscience, and the abolition of torture and the death penalty. Their bimonthly periodical, Amnesty Action, costs $25/year.

Anti-Racist Action (ARA) Chicago
P.O. Box 11211
Chicago, IL 60611
One of a growing number of anti-racist skinhead and punk groups around the country. While the white supremacist movement recruits skinheads to their agenda, skinhead groups like ARA are resisting the racists.

Big Mountain Support Group
316 W. 95th Street, #731
New York, NY 10025
(212) 226-2675
AND
2150 47th Avenue
San Francisco, CA 94116
(415) 665-1743, 664-1847
The BMSG is an activist membership organization dedicated to stopping the unlawful relocation campaign launched by the United States federal government in its effort to exploit the mining of uranium-rich, ancestral lands of the Dineh (Navahos) of Big Mountain Arizona. Opportunities to get involved range from legal work to front-line confrontation with the federal government to community support. The San Francisco BMSG publishes the national Big Mountain Newsletter.

Center for Third World Organizing
3861 Martin Luther King Jr. Way
Oakland, CA 94604
(415) 654-9601

CTWO works with activists and community organizations to promote the interests of Asian, African-American, Latino and Native American peoples. Projects include the Minority Activist Apprenticeship Program, the Campaign for Accessible Health Care, media training sessions, seminars on women's issues and leadership training. Their periodical, The Minority Trendsetter, *is available for $20 per year.*

Church Coalition for Human Rights in the Philippines
Box 70
110 Maryland Ave NE
Washington, DC 20002
(202) 543-1094

Promotes education in the Ecumenical Church regarding US policy and human rights. Their bi-monthly newsletter, Philippine Witness, *costs $10/year.*

Clergy and Laity Concerned (CALC)
198 Broadway
New York, NY 10038
(212) 964-6730

Interfaith peace and justice organization that disseminates information and advocates citizen action on issues of militarism, economic justice, human rights and social justice.

Columbia River Defense Project
P.O. Box 6564
Portland, OR 97228
(503) 289-4585

The CRDP has been working with the Indian people of the Pacific Northwest for many years. The primary threat to the sovereignty and subsistence of the Columbia River people has been the continued assault on their traditional fishing rights by the US government and commercial interests on the Columbia River. The CRDP is currently trying to fight the eviction of families along the river, including those of elder David Sohappy, Johnny Jackson and other "Salmon-Scam" defendants. CRDP issues press releases, circulates petitions and can help coordinate speakers.

Global Exchange
2940 16th Street, Room 307
San Francisco, CA 94103
(415) 255-7296

Global Exchange is a research, education and action center aimed at fostering direct people-to-people ties between US and Third World citizens. Projects include "reality tours" to the Third World, sister city and sister schools programs, human rights networks and ethical trade. They work to improve US foreign and corporate policies.

Gray Panthers
311 S Juniper Street
Suite 601
Philadelphia, PA 19107
(215) 545-6555

The Gray Panthers challenge ageism and advocate fundamental change to eliminate injustice, discrimination and oppression. They act independently and in coalition with other groups to build a new power base to achieve short-term social change and ultimately a society that will put the needs of people above profits. Their newsletter, Gray Panther Network, *is $12 per year.*

Guatemalan Human Rights Commission
1359 Monroe Street NE
Washington, DC 20017
(202) 529-6599

The GHRC works to provide information on specific violations of human rights, and to provide a forum in the United States and elsewhere for the people of Guatemala. Their aim is to develop a core of concerned individuals in the United States who speak out in support of persons and groups in Guatemala whose rights have been violated or seriously threatened. Their bi-monthly newsletter, Information Bulletin, reports quarterly with human rights alerts.

Highlander Research and Education Center
Route 3, Box 370
New Market, TN 37820
(606) 248-8213

The Highlander Research and Education Center is dedicated to adult education, empowering people at the grassroots to become more effective in organizing their own communities. Highlander provided key support for the labor movement in the 30's and 40's, for the civil rights movement in the 50's and 60's and now works with the grassroots anti-toxics movement. Their STP Schools (Stop the Poisoning, Save the Planet) are free weekend training sessions held monthly. Call for schedule.

Huichol Center for Cultural Survival and Traditional Arts
414 41st Street
Oakland, CA 94609
(415) 655-0111

The Huichol Center was established to help the Huichols of Central Mexico preserve their cultural, spiritual and artistic heritage while adapting to the demands of the twentieth century. The Center provides shelter and nutritious food, and medical, economic and legal aid for migrant Huichols working on the tobacco plantations near the small urban center of Santiago Ixcuintla, Nayarit. The Center also helps the Huichols use their artistic talents, providing art supplies at a reduced price and purchasing finished artwork for marketing.

Human Rights Advocates
P.O. Box 5675
Berkeley, CA 94705
(415) 841-2928

A fully accredited Non-Governmental Organization, HRA participates in the activities of the United Nations and the Organization of American States, testifying on human rights aspects of issues such as mass exoduses, religious persecution, independence of the judiciary, prisoners of war, armed conflicts, genocide, the right to food, and refugees' rights. HRA also assists lawyers in international human rights-related law suits. $15 membership ($10 for students) includes newsletter and announcements of events.

Human Rights Watch
36 West 44th Street, #911
New York, NY 10036
(212) 840-9460

HRW is a collection of existing watch committees that monitor governments' human rights practices. The committees pressure violators by publishing reports of the violations and launching international protests. They publicize discrepancies between governmental practices and claims, relying on public embarrassment to secure change. HRW provides updated lists of their extensive publications from 41 countries.

International Indian Treaty Council
710 Clayton Street #1
San Francisco, CA 94117
(415) 566-0251

As the international arm of the American Indian Movement (AIM), IITC became the first indigenous support organization to be recognized by the United Nations as a credentialed non-governmental organization in the Economic and Social Council in 1977. The IITC represents and credentials delegates from many regions of the world at the United Nations Human Rights Commission, the UN Working Group on Indigenous Populations and other forums. Write for information on letter writing campaigns, speaking tours and other political strategies.

The IITC can also refer you to local organizations working in their communities in the Pacific Northwest, Hawaii, the American Southwest, Alaska, the Pacific Rim, South America and other parts of the world. A donation of $10 or more brings Treaty Council News, *a quarterly.*

International Women's Rights Action Watch

Humphrey Institute of Public Affairs
University of Minnesota
301 19th Ave. South
Minneapolis, MN 55455

Monitors implementation of the Convention on the Elimination of All Forms of Discrimination Against Women.

John Brown Anti-Klan Committee (JBAKC)

220 Ninth Street, No. 443
San Francisco, CA 94103

Named for the 19th-century white abolitionist, JBAKC is a national organization that fights the racist violence of the KKK and Nazis, and the system of white supremacy. The group builds solidarity with the black liberation movement and supports struggles for human rights and self-determination. Subscriptions to their newspaper, No KKK! No Fascist USA!, *are $6 for 8 issues.*

Leonard Peltier Defense Committee— International Office

P.O. Box 583
Lawrence, KS 66044
(913) 842-5774

Works to free Leonard Peltier, an American Indian given two life sentences for alleged involvement in the killing of two FBI agents in Pine Ridge in 1975. The LPDC has information on resources, including videos of TV newscasts, interviews, articles, speakers, news of the struggle and communication from Leonard.

MONITOR—Center for Democratic Renewal

P.O. Box 50469
Atlanta, GA 30303
(404) 221-0025

A national clearinghouse that monitors hate groups. Their bi-monthly periodical, Monitor, *covers the Ku Klux Klan, Aryan Nation, and issues surrounding the New Right.*

Mozambique Support Network

343 South Dearborn, Suite 601
Chicago, IL 60604
(312) 922-3286

A solidarity movement for anti-apartheid support that has sponsored US speaking tours for Lina Magaia, Graca Machel and Samora Machel, the widow of Mozambique's first president. MSN publishes a bimonthly newsletter.

The Multicultural Project, Inc.

186 Lincoln Street, 8th Floor
Boston, MA 02111

Committed to promoting social justice and fostering respect for cultural diversity, MPI provides training on issues of race, culture and the relationships among different forms of oppression.

National Abortion Rights Action League (NARAL)

1101 14th Street NW, Suite 500
Washington, DC 20005
(202) 371-0779

A 290,000-member organization divided into four divisions: The Political Action Committee, the NARAL Foundation for Educational Campaigns, the NARAL Lobbying (responsible for media campaigns), and the Nationwide Petition Campaign (with 34 affiliates). Publishes a periodical, Naral News.

National Commission Against Repressive Legislation

236 Massachusetts Avenue NE, #406
Washington, DC 20002
(202) 543-7659

Maintains that without our constitutional liberties, all other freedoms are endangered. Provides information about constitutional freedom and First Amendment rights. Their bi-monthly periodical, The Right to Know and the Freedom to Act, *monitors developments related to First Amendment rights and is available for a $15 donation. Also available are pamphlets on rights issues, such as "Black Voting Rights: A Case Study in Racial Harassment."*

National Committee to Defend New Afrikan Freedom Fighters

P.O. Box 1184
Manhattanville Station
New York, NY 10027

Provides legal support for black nationalist political prisoners in the US.

National Gay Rights Advocates

540 Castro Street
San Francisco, CA 94114
(415) 863-3624

A public interest law firm that does litigation on behalf of lesbians, gay men and people infected with the HIV virus. Challenges laws and policies that discriminate on the basis of sexual orientation and HIV-positive status. Publishes a national newsletter, the NGRA Quarterly, *available for a donation.*

Native American Rights Fund

1712 N Street NW
Washington, DC 20036
(202) 785-4166

A legal firm that defends Native Americans' land and water claims. Issues a newsletter, Indian Law Support Center, *as well as an annual report.*

New Afrikan People's Organization

P.O. Box 2348
New York, NY 10027

A revolutionary nationalist black organization that fights for land, independence and socialism for the black nation inside the US. Also has offices in Los Angeles, Chicago and Jackson, Mississippi.

New Bridges/Unlearning Racism

3708 Mt. Diablo Boulevard
Lafayette, CA 94549

Each year New Bridges brings together young people and adult staff in a one-week intensive summer camp to develop a diverse community of mutual trust and respect.

Pacific Concerns Resource Center

General Coordinating Office
P.O. Box 9295
Newmarket, Auckland
Aotearoa (New Zealand)
Ph. 64-9-375-862

PCRC is the Secretariat of the Nuclear Free and Independent Pacific Movement, working in concert with a number of organizations. Provides information on the struggles of Pacific peoples, and contacts in Palau, other South Pacific Islands, Maori, and Australia. PCRC also has offices in Sydney, Australia.

Peace Brigades International

4722 Baltimore Avenue
Philadelphia, PA 19143
(215) 727-0989

Advocates and trains people for nonviolent conflict resolution throughout the world. Peace Brigades sends teams to countries at war, establishes contacts with all parties involved and works to improve communications and reconcile conflict.

People for the American Way
2000 M Street NW, Suite 400
Washington, DC 20036
(202) 467-4999

A non-partisan Constitutional liberties organization whose members work together to lobby local, state and national officials. Created a legal defense fund to protect education from censorship, and helped to override Reagan's veto of the Civil Rights Restoration Act. They issue a quarterly periodical entitled Forum. Their publications include: Government Secrecy: Decisions Without Democracy ($8.95), Values, Pluralism and Public Education ($6.95) and 1987 Censorship Report ($5.95).

Peoples Institute for Survival and Beyond/ Undoing Racism
1444 No. Johnson Street
New Orleans, LA 70116

Provides workshops on community organizing/undoing racism.

Rural Advancement Fund
2124 Commonwealth Avenue
Charlotte, NC 28205

A non-profit farm advocacy group working toward a just and sustainable system of agriculture based on family farms and environmentally sound methods.

The Southwest Organizing Project
1114 7th Street NW
Albuquerque, NM 87102

Includes a community environmental program organizing in low-income Hispanic communities to protect their neighborhoods.

The Seventh Generation Fund
P.O. Box 3245
Flagstaff, AZ 86003
(602) 774-7222

Supports appropriate development projects on Indian lands. Their quarterly, Native Self-Sufficiency, available for a do-

nation, contains information on other publications on development and indigenous rights issues.

Sisterhood is Global Alert
c/o Ms. Foundation, Suite 62
141 Fifth Avenue
New York, NY 10010
(212) 689-3475

Organizes campaigns of support for women who are victims of human rights violations.

Sojourners
P.O. Box 29272
Washington, DC 20017
(202) 636-3637

A ministry of Sojourners Community that educates and organizes in US churches for faith-inspired action against nuclear weapons. Publishes the monthly Sojourner's Magazine ($15/year).

South and Meso-American Indian Information Center (SAIIC)
P.O. Box 7550
Berkeley, CA 94707
(415) 834-4263

A peace and justice organization dedicated to the education of the general public in the US and human rights organizations abroad, about the struggles for survival and self-determination of the Indian peoples of South and Meso-America. Publishes a quarterly newsletter.

Tenantzin Land Institute
1446 Bridge Boulevard
Albuquerque, NM 87105

Advocates traditional land rights for native and Chicano people.

Tools for Change
P.O. Box 14141
San Francisco, CA 94114

An institute for adult education, mediation and consultation for organizational and individual empowerment. Offers workshops on patterns of power, racism, classism and multi-cultural alliance building. Publications include "The Subjective Side of Power" ($5), a pamphlet by Margo Adair and Shea Howell that is useful for those wanting to build alliances across race and class differences.

United Nations High Commission on Refugees
UN Secretariat, Room S931
New York, NY 10017
(212) 963-0032

The UNHCR has two offices in the United States—one in New York and one in Washington, DC. The Commission works on political asylum and relocation issues, and assists people seeking refugee status—those escaping persecution because of race, religion or political beliefs. Publishes the monthly Refugee magazine, and offers an extensive list of publications, including the United Nations Universal Declaration of Human Rights.

Weaving Project
P.O. Box 865
Kykotsmoui, AZ 86039
(602) 527-2757

An indigenous rights group providing support for the Dineh people at Big Mountain.

Women Against Imperialism (WAI)
3543 18th Street, Box 14
San Francisco, CA 94110
(415) 995-4735

An activist organization of lesbians and straight women whose work touches on issues of reproductive rights, lesbian liberation, Central America, the Philippines, political prisoners, anti-racism, women's oppression, imperialism, patriarchy, and the conditions of women and lesbians.

WomanEarth Institute
P.O. Box 2374
Stanford, CA 94309

A network of ecofeminists dedicated to creating a context for political work that maintains parity between women of color and white women.

Women's Foreign Policy Council
1133 Broadway
New York, NY 10010
(212) 691-7316

Current projects include a women and environment program to ensure women's presence and participation in US government and United Nations meetings on environment.

Periodicals

Against Racism
Anti-Racism Literature Project
P.O. Box 2902
Brooklyn, NY 11202

For anti-racist organizers; published five times a year.

Akwesasne Notes
Mohawk Nation
P.O. Box 196
Rooseveltown, NY 13683-0196

Focuses primarily on issues in Northeastern America; also covers national and international native news; includes features and poetry. Six issues a year.

Cultural Survival Quarterly
11 Divinity Avenue
Cambridge, MA 02138

Informs the general public and policy makers in the US and abroad to stimulate action on behalf of tribal peoples and ethnic minorities. $20 per year.

Green Letter
P.O. Box 9242
Berkeley, CA 94709

A quarterly newspaper that covers grassroots organizing efforts of people to protect and reclaim their communities.

Books

A Documentary History of the Mexican Americans. Wayne Moquin and Charles Van Doren, eds. New York: Bantam Books, 1972.

Arranged chronologically, 65 documents reveal the Mexican-American experience in "Anglo" America from 1536 through the 1960's.

America's Original Sin: A Study Guide on White Racism. Washington, DC: Sojourners Magazine, 1988.

Moving stories and sharp analyses with vision and a challenge for a just future.

A People's History of the United States. Howard Zinn. New York: Harper Colophon Books, 1980.

A history of the American people from the point of view of those who have been exploited politically and economically and whose story has been largely omitted from most histories. The stories of blacks, women, Native Americans, poor laborers and union organizers are told with extensive quotations from them. Events usually ignored are covered here, from the railroad strike of 1877 to the brutal suppression of the Philippine independence movement at the turn of the century, to the secret bombings, massacres and cover-ups of Vietnam.

Basic Call to Consciousness. Mohawk Nation, via Rooseveltown, New York: Akwesasne Notes, 1978.

Challenges many basic assumptions in Western philosophy and includes a history of the self-governance of the Iroquois, which influenced the writers of the US Constitution.

Black and White Styles in Conflict. Thomas Kochman. Chicago: University of Chicago Press, 1981.

Captures the differing assumptions about conflict, and suggests that understanding them will help us avoid unnecessary conflict.

Bridging the Global Gap: A Handbook to Linking First and Third World Citizens. Medea Benjamin and Andrea Freedman. Cabin John, MD: Seven Locks Press, 1989.

Discusses the myriad ways US citizens can hook up with poor people struggling for peace, justice and sustainable development in the Third World. $11.95 from Global Exchange.

The Desperate People and **The People of the Deer.** Farley Mowat. Boston: Little, Brown, 1959.

A detailed account of the forced relocations of the Eskimos and the attempts to destroy their religion and culture. Sad books that show how companies and governments abuse and disregard native peoples.

Feminist Theory from Margin to Center. Bell Hooks. Boston: South End Press, 1984.

Clearly argued critiques of white feminist theory, stressing the need for feminist thinking to begin with the experience of women at the bottom.

Healing The Wounds: The Promise of Ecofeminism. Judith Plant, ed. Philadelphia: New Society, 1989.

Essays that probe questions of feminism and ecology, organizing and strategies.

Indians of the Americas: Self Determination and International Human Rights. Roxanne Dunbar Ortiz. New York: Praeger Publishers, 1984.

A survey of the international nature of indigenous resistance, and the standards that have been developed in the last 20 years defining the rights of indigenous peoples. Contains case studies, and discusses the basis for indigenous nationhood.

Killers of the Dream. Lillian Smith. New York: Norton & Company, 1978.

A sensitive account of race and class dynamics in the South before the civil rights movement. Strange Fruit, also by Lillian Smith, is a novel brilliantly depicting relations between the races in the South.

Nations Within: The Past and Future of American Indian Sovereignty. Vine Deloria and Clifford Lytle. New York: Pantheon Books, 1984.

Explains the position of American Indians in relation to the United States government. Contains a history of the Indian Reorganization Act of 1934, the debate surrounding it, and discusses its political implications today. (Deloria's other books, which encompass the legal, political, cultural and religious issues affecting and involving American Indians, are likewise recommended.)

Nobody Knows My Name. James Baldwin. New York: Dell, 1963.

Passionate reflections on the American character, the role of African Americans and the relationships between blacks and whites. Captures flavors of the early 60's and raises essential questions for today.

Racism and the Class Struggle: Further Pages from a Black Worker's Notebook. James Boggs. New York: Monthly Review, 1970.

Essays dealing with the fundamental relationship of race and class to the development of the US.

Sister Outsider. Audre Lorde. Trumansburg, New York: Crossing Press, 1984.

Essays that reveal many of the dynamics that maintain relations of domination.

The First Freedom. Nat Hentoff. New York: Delacorte Press, 1980.

A chronicle of battles for freedom of speech in the US, from 18th-century newspaper editor Peter Zenger, whose case won the press the right to criticize government officials, to Mary Beth Tinker, the junior high school student who got expelled for wearing a black armband to protest the Vietnam War.

The Hidden Wound. Wendell Berry. Boston: Houghton, Mifflin, 1970. Out of print. Portions reprinted in Berry's Recollected Essays, 1965-1980. Berkeley: North Point Press, 1981.

Berry, who comes from many generations of white small farmers in the South, explores the impact of racism on the psyche of whites.

There is a River: The Black Struggle for Freedom in America. Vincent Harding. New York: Vintage, 1981.

History from the slave trade to the Civil War; a poetic account describing the African American experience building the foundation of the United States, and emphasizing their intellectual contributions to the Abolitionist movement.

The Second Long Walk: The Navajo-Hopi Land Dispute. Jerry Kammer. New Mexico: University of New Mexico Press, 1980.

An overview of the forced relocation of the Navajo and Hopi peoples mandated by the Land Settlement Act. Kammer was a *journalist in the Southwest, and the book is well researched and documented.*

The Woman Warrior. Maxine Hong Kingston. New York: Vintage, 1975.
Novel about a Chinese American woman growing up in California.

This Bridge Called My Back: Writings by Radical Women of Color. Cherríe Moraga and Gloria Anzaldúa, eds. New York: Kitchen Table/Women of Color Press, 1981.
Prose, poetry, personal narrative and analysis by African American, Asian American, Latina, and Native American women. An uncompromised definition of feminism by women of color in the US. Includes an extensive bibliography.

Thousand Pieces of Gold. Ruthanne Lum McCunn. New York: Dell, 1981.
The story of Lalu Nathoy, a Chinese immigrant who made a life for herself in California in the late 19th century despite racist laws that limited Chinese people's citizenship rights.

Tribal Peoples and Development Issues: A Global Overview. John H. Bodley. Mountain View, CA: Mayfield Publishing Company, 1988.
A survey of past and current literature on the term tribal, *the uniqueness of tribal people in relation to development models, and the debate on acculturation versus maintenance of traditional practices. Contains many useful case studies.*

Village Journey: The Report of the Alaska Native Review Commission. Thomas R. Berger. New York: Inuit Circumpolar Conference/Hill and Wang, 1985.
Testimony documenting the effects of the Alaska Native Claims Settlement Act (ANCSA), useful in understanding how the traditional people will be affected by the Act in 1991.

Wasi'chu: The Continuing Indian Wars. Bruce Johansen and Roberto Maestas. New York: Monthly Review Press, 1979.
A history of American Indian activism in the 1970's, the rise of the American Indian Movement (AIM), Wounded Knee, and domestic counterinsurgency. Also discusses the broader international implications of the domestic political situation.

Voices from Wounded Knee. Mohawk Nation via Rooseveltown, New York: Akwesasne Notes, 1974.
Personal accounts of the struggle at Wounded Knee, giving insight into native people's effort to protect their land.

When and Where I Enter . . . The Impact of Black Women on Race and Sex in America. Paula Giddings. New York: William Morrow, 1984.
A comprehensive portrayal of the largely untold history of African American women from after the Civil War to the 1980's.

"The question is not whether we will be extremists, but what kind of extremists we will be. . . . The nation and the world are in dire need of creative extremists."
—MARTIN LUTHER KING, JR.

PART THREE

CONFRONTING THE COLONIAL LEGACY

Global Resource Distribution

VANDANA SHIVA

Before independence, Gandhi was asked by a British official,"Once India gains her independence, how long will it take her to reach Britain's standard of living?" Gandhi answered, "It took Britain half the globe's resources to reach its current standard of living, how many globes will it take India to reach Britain's standard of living?"

T HE RECENT PERIOD in human history contrasts with all the earlier ones in its strikingly high rate of resource utilization. Ever-expanding and intensifying industrial and agricultural production has generated increasing demands on the world's total stock and flow of resources. These demands are mostly generated from the industrially advanced countries in the North and the industrial enclaves of the underdeveloped countries in the South.

Paradoxically, the increasing dependence of the industrialized societies on the resources of nature, has been accompanied by the spread of the myth that increased dependence on modern technologies means a *decreased* dependence on nature and natural resources. This myth is reinforced by the introduction of long and indirect chains of resource utilization, obscuring the real material resource demands of the industrial processes. Through this combination of resource intensity at the material level and resource indifference at the conceptual and policy levels, the conflicts over natural resources generated by the new pattern of resource utilization are generally shrouded and ignored. The conflicts become open and visible when the resource- and energy-intensive industrial technologies threaten

Vandana Shiva is Executive Director of the Research Foundation for Science and Ecology in Dehra Dun, India. A founder of the World Rainforest Movement and India's Chipko Movement, and an active member of the Asia Pacific Peoples' Environment Network, she is also the author of a recent book on women and ecology.

the resource base of communities whose survival depends on the conservation of those resources.

Ecology movements emerging from the conflicts over natural resources and rooted in the people's right to survival are spreading in regions of the Third World where most natural resources are already being utilized to satisfy the basic needs for the survival of the large population. The introduction of resource- and energy-intensive production technologies as the main tool for economic development has, thus, the consequence of creating economic growth for a small minority in the formal sector while, at the same time, undermining the material basis for the survival of the larger majority.

Economic Growth Against Survival

Peruvians packing crates of melons for shipment to Europe (in boxes marked El Colono). The global economic scheme forces many third-world countries to export food while their own citizens go hungry or malnourished. RAY WITLIN, WORLD BANK

For centuries, vital natural resources like land, water and forests had been controlled and used collectively by tribal and peasant village communities, thus ensuring sustainable use of these renewable resources. The first drastic change in resource management was associated with colonial domination of this part of the world. This led to the introduction of major conflicts over natural resources induced by non-local factors. Colonial domination systematically transformed the vital common resources into commodities for generating profits and growth of revenues. During the first industrial revolution, Western Europe's demand for resources was to a large extent supported by this transformation of commons to commodities. Vast tropical resources became available to the European industries, and the biologically rich tropics were turned into the under-developed Third World. Britain's take-off at the end of the 18th century

was made possible by the underdevelopment of three continents. The destruction of the Indian textile industry and Indian agriculture, the slave trade from Africa and the genocide of the indigenous North American people were the preconditions for growth in the centers of modern industry in Britain.

With the collapse of the international colonial structure and the establishment of sovereign countries in the region, this international conflict over natural resources was expected to be reduced and replaced by resource policies guided by comprehensive national interests. However, development, as defined and financed by institutions like the World Bank and the International Monetary Fund, became another name for colonialism. Resource policies continued along the colonial pattern, leading to a second drastic change in resource use. The most seriously threatened interest group in this conflict is the large but politically weak

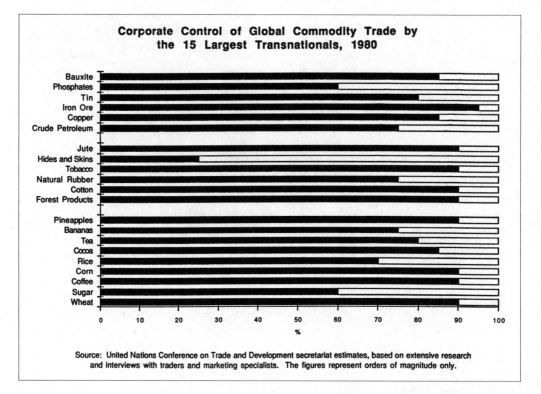

Corporate Control of Global Commodity Trade by the 15 Largest Transnationals, 1980

Source: United Nations Conference on Trade and Development secretariat estimates, based on extensive research and interviews with traders and marketing specialists. The figures represent orders of magnitude only.

UNITED STATES STUDENT ASSOCIATION

and socially disorganized group of poor people whose resource requirements are the lowest and whose lives are supported directly by the products of common natural resources outside the market system. Current changes in resource utilization have almost wholly bypassed the survival needs of this group. The changes are primarily guided by the requirements of the countries of the North and of the elites of the South. And as the countries of the North move to conserve their own natural resources, many resource-intensive and pollution-intensive industries—like those producing chemicals, pulp and paper, steel and aluminum—are being relocated to countries of the South. While the environmental burden shifts to tribal peoples, to peasants and women of the South, the political control of global resources shifts increasingly away from people into the hands of national governments, multinational corporations and multilateral development agencies and banks.

ACTION*

1. **Support popular movements, land reform and liberation struggles in the Third World.** Contact CISPES, Global Exchange, EPOCA, Nicaragua Network, Mozambique Support Network and other solidarity groups to learn about these movements.

2. **Challenge the activities of institutions of international lending and international trade.** Require them to adhere to the principles of the United Nations Universal Declaration of Human Rights and to ecological imperatives. Require the World Bank and USAID to share in the costs and responsibility of making reparations for the decades of exploitation. Perhaps it is better to close the World Bank, take over the IMF and establish institutions specifically designed to *serve* humanity and the Earth. Challenge power relationships, political systems and cultural institutions that support and legitimize depredations in the Third World. Besides the US government and US-controlled financial institutions, the activities of the Japanese government, the West German government and the European Economic Community also need to be watched, challenged and fundamentally changed to support and embody equitable international exchange.

3. **Support indigenous struggles, women's movements, environmental groups, and restoration projects in the Third World.**

4. **Support progressive non-governmental organizations (NGOs) in the Third World.** Contact Oxfam, International Development Exchange (IDEX) or Food First for more information on what they're doing and how you can help.

5. **Find out what the US government can be forced to do unilaterally to relieve pressure on the Third World.** For example, what "resources" does the government import for military uses? for space programs? for destructive and polluting technologies?

*Action section by Brad Erickson

World Hunger

FRANCES MOORE LAPPÉ

"Today, therefore, the question on the agenda must read, why should there be hunger and privation in any land, in any city, at any table, when man has the resources and scientific know-how to provide all mankind with the basic necessities of life . . . . There is no deficit in human resources; the deficit is in human will."

—DR. MARTIN LUTHER KING, JR.,
NOBEL LECTURE, DECEMBER 11, 1964

HUNGER IS NEEDLESS. Everywhere. Sufficient food is produced globally to make us all overweight. Yet worldwide at least 700 million people suffer from hunger, and here in our own food-rich country 20 million people go without adequate food.

But the cause of hunger is no mystery: Where a minority wield economic and political control over resources, people are deprived of the land, food and income they need for self-support. Today we see such concentration from the family, to the village, through the national level, to the level of international commerce and finance.

Hunger is thus the most horrific symptom of people's economic and political powerlessness. The challenging question is not "Why hunger?" but "Why do human beings allow decision-making power to concentrate in so few hands that hunger spreads, even amid plenty?"

To work effectively to end hunger means first understanding why people are unable, or feel they are unable, to address its obvious roots. And then changing that reality.

This means strengthening democracy, and deepening and extending democratic institutions and culture. Democracy? You

Frances Moore Lappé is co-founder and Senior Researcher at the Institute for Food and Development Policy. She is the author or co-author of a number of books on hunger and related issues, including *Food First: Beyond the Myth of Scarcity*, *Betraying the National Interest* and *Rediscovering America's Values*.

might ask: What has democracy to do with hunger?

If hunger reflects undue concentration of power, then its only antidote is democracy. And democracy must be understood not just as particular structures of government but as certain principles in action: the *accountability of leadership* to all those touched by its decisions and the *sharing of power* so that all can participate in community life—so that no one is left powerless. Realizing these principles in economic as well as political life is the only means of eliminating hunger.

This framework suggests that we can all be part of ending hunger, since its roots are so deep that they touch every aspect of our lives.

ACTION*

1. **First, educate! Only as we develop a solid understanding of the roots of hunger can we work effectively to change public policies. Since we all influence others every day, we can work to uproot the pervasive myths that disempower us:**

   Rapid population growth causes hunger because people are pressing against nature's limits.

   No. We must demonstrate a different cause and effect: It's people's powerlessness that leads to high birth rates and economic desperation, adding to environmental degradation.

   Absolute laws govern economic life, particularly the "free market." If the market prices some poor people out of food, this is too bad; but we can't correct the problem without destroying the market, hurting everybody.

   No. We must show that there are no god-given economic rules. The market is just a *device*. It can further human development only as citizens make rules governing economic life to ensure that everyone has purchasing power.

   Increasing agricultural production in the Third World to avert famine requires the introduction of the efficient, modern farm methods we use here.

   No. Farm technologies dependent on fossil fuels are not more efficient, when you calculate the cost of poisoning farmworkers and ground water as well as the erosion of topsoil. Besides, most Third World farmers can't afford them anyway! Traditional farming methods can be highly productive. The real problem is that most Third World people have no land on which to develop their more ecologically-sound agriculture.

   The sad truth is that most Americans would never allow Third World people truly to advance, for they would see it as a threat to their standard of living.

   No. We must show that the well-being of most Americans depends on the advancement of the majori-

* Action section by Frances Moore Lappé

Market worker in Mombasa, Kenya. Distribution, not scarcity, is the real cause of world hunger. KAY CHERNUSH, 1978, WORLD BANK

ties in the Third World. As long as they remain blocked from protecting their own rights to live and work in dignity, we here will be forced to sacrifice our own well-being in competition for jobs.

The powerlessness of the poor so conditions them to passivity that they cannot overcome their oppression, much less create democratic societies.

No. We must show that wherever people are hungry they are working for change.

Increasing US foreign aid is the best way to help relieve Third World poverty.

No. We must show that our responsibility is to remove the obstacles in the way of Third World people who are already seeking fair access to resources for self-support. These obstacles include not only specific US military and economic intervention but the narrow, materialistic economic dogma that the United States promotes, and in some cases imposes, abroad.

2. **Foster relationships of mutuality, not *noblesse oblige,* directly with Third World people and their organizations.** Avenues include personal tours and exchanges across national borders, alternative trade networks, "sister cities" links, citizen diplomacy, collaborative strategies for protecting human rights and workers' rights, and common programs for solving trade/debt/environmental problems. We can also offer material aid, but only in such a way that it abets local, democratic initiatives already underway.

3. **Work to democratize our own political and economic life.** Ending hunger means realizing democracy in America both for ourselves and to inspire others. We can work within citizen organizations to:

- Strengthen all avenues for citizen participation in discourse and decision-making in public life, from the neighborhood school board to the national media. Central to this work is electoral reform to remove wealth from its dominance in the political process.

- Work to extend the concept and practice of citizenship—with its rights and responsibilities—into economic life. The right to opportunity for gainful employment, for example, must become as essential to our concept of citizenship as the right to vote. And large corporate bureaucracies must be made democratically accountable, since their actions often have greater impact on our lives than do elected bodies of government.

Of course, we do not have to start the train moving. Much good work is underway. But to get on board, good will is not enough. We must be eager to learn.

Rethinking Population

BETSY HARTMANN

O N THE SURFACE, fears of a population explosion are borne out by basic demographic statistics. In the 20th century the world has experienced an unprecedented increase in population. In 1900 the global population was 1.7 billion, in 1950 it reached 2.5 billion, and today 5 billion people inhabit the Earth. Three-quarters of them live in the Third World. The United Nations predicts that world population will reach 6 billion by the end of the century and will eventually stabilize at about 10.5 billion by the year 2110, though such long-term projections are notoriously imprecise.

Initially, this rapid increase in population was due in part to some positive factors: advances in medicine, public health measures and better nutrition meant that more people lived longer. In most industrialized countries, the decline in mortality rates was eventually offset by declines in birth rates, so that population growth began to stabilize in what is called the "demographic transition." Many countries have now reached the "replacement level" of fertility and in some the population is actually declining.

Today birth rates are also falling in most areas of the Third World, with the exception of sub-Saharan Africa. In fact, the *rate* of world population growth has been slowing since the mid-1960's, and this decline is likely to accelerate in the years ahead. While world population is still growing in absolute terms, the "explosion" is gradually fizzling out.

Nevertheless, there is still a considerable discrepancy between birth rates in the industrialized world and birth rates in the Third World. Conventional wisdom has it that Third World people continue to have so many children because they are ignorant and irrational—they exercise no control over their sexuality, "breeding like rabbits." This "superiority complex" of many West-

Betsy Hartmann lived in Bangladesh and India for several years and has written for numerous journals on development issues in Asia, including *Le Monde Diplomatique, The Christian Science Monitor, The Nation* and *The New Internationalist.* Betsy is also the co-author with James Boyce of *Needless Hunger* and *A Quiet Violence,* and the author of *Reproductive Rights and Wrongs.*

erners is one of the main obstacles in the way of meaningful discussion of the population problem. It assumes that everyone lives in the same basic social environment and faces the same set of reproductive choices. Nothing could be further from the truth.

In many Third World societies, having a large family is an eminently rational strategy of survival. Children's labor is a vital part of the family economy in many peasant communities in Asia, Africa and Latin America. Children help in the fields, tend animals, fetch water and wood, and care for their younger brothers and sisters, freeing their parents for other tasks. Quite early in life, children's labor makes them an asset rather than a drain on family income. In Bangladesh, for example, boys produce more than they consume by the age of 10 to 13, and by the age of 15 their total production has exceeded their cumulative lifetime consumption. Girls likewise perform a number of valuable economic tasks, which include helping their mothers with cooking and the post-harvest processing of crops.

The other crucial reason for having children is security. In most Third World societies, the vast majority of the population has no access to insurance schemes, pension plans or government social security. It is children who care for their parents in old age—without them one's future is endangered. The help of grown children can also be crucial in surviving the periodic crises—illness, drought, floods, food shortages, land disputes, political upheavals—that unfortunately punctuate village life in most parts of the world.

High infant and child mortality rates are one of the most important causes of high birth rates. Each year in the Third World more than 10 million children die before reaching their first birthday. The average infant mortality rate is more than 90 deaths

per 1,000 live births, compared to 20 in the industrialized countries. The situation is especially severe in Africa, where 16 countries have infant mortality rates in excess of 150 per 1,000.

High infant mortality means that parents cannot be sure their children will survive to contribute to the family economy and to take care of them in their old age. The poor are thus caught in a death trap: they have to keep producing children in order that some will survive.

At first glance, it might appear that reductions in infant mortality would actually *increase* the rate of population growth, since there would be more surviving children to grow up into fertile adults. The Third World population surge of the 1950's and 1960's came about through such a reduction in mortality rates without a corresponding reduction in birth rates. Experience has shown, however, that once mortality rates fall to around 15 per 1,000 people per year, the average for the Third World today, each further decline in the mortality rate is generally accompanied by an even greater decline in the birth rate, as people adjust their fertility to improved survival possibilities. This has led UNICEF director James Grant to conclude:

> Paradoxically, therefore, a "survival revolution" which halved the infant and child mortality rate of the developing world and prevented the deaths of six or seven million infants each year by the end of the century would also be likely to prevent between 12 and 20 million births each year.

To date no country has achieved a low birth rate as long as it has had a high infant mortality rate.

The last (but not least) cause of high birth rates is the subordination of women. Male dominance in the family, patriarchal social mores, the systematic exclusion of women from the development process, and the absence of decent birth control services combine to force many women into having more children than they want. The social environment, in effect, leaves them little or no reproductive choice.

Behind the demographic statistics, then, lies a reality unfamiliar to many in the West, who do not have to worry from day to day about who will help in the fields, who will take care of them when they are old and sick, how many children they need to ensure that a few survive until adulthood. High birth rates are often a distress signal that people's survival is endangered. Yet the proponents of population control put the argument the other way around, insisting that people are endangering their own survival—and the survival of future generations—by having so many children. This is the basis of the Malthusian philosophy which for so long has defined the debate on the population problem.

In the 1960's and 1970's it was fashionable to attribute hunger to overpopulation. "The battle to feed all humanity is over," claimed Paul Ehrlich's 1968 book, *The Population Bomb.* "In the 1970's the world will undergo famines—hundreds of millions of people will starve to death." Computer projections, such as the Club of Rome's famous *Limits to Growth,* gave these dire predictions a pseudo-respectability, which the hard facts could not. The galloping horse of population had met its match in the steady march of the tractor: we were about to enter the era of food surplus.

Tremendous advances in agricultural productivity mean that today the world produces enough grain alone to provide every man, woman and child on Earth with 3,000 calories a day, well above the 2,200–2,500 calorie average considered a minimal-

ly acceptable dietary level. At least on the global scale, there is no shortage of food.

In the past three decades, world food production has grown *faster* than world population. World food production doubled between 1959 and 1980, and according to a recent United Nations Food and Agriculture Organization study, it could double again by the year 2000. The increase has been larger in the Third World than in the industrialized nations. With the exception of sub-Saharan Africa, most Third World countries have experienced rising per capita food output in the past two decades. Today most countries have enough food to meet the needs of their growing populations. Yet even when food is plentiful, millions of people go hungry.

They go hungry because individual families do not have land on which to grow food, or the money with which to buy it. The main problem is not that there are too many people and too few resources, but rather that too few people monopolize too many resources. *The main problem is not one of absolute scarcity but one of distribution.*

Like deforestation, desertification, which threatens almost 20 percent of the Earth's surface, is frequently attributed to overpopulation. "Excessive population pressure on limited land resources means desertification," claimed a United Nations news feature. "That is the bottom line."

But for many peasants there is another bottom line: the monopolization of land resources by the rich. El Salvador is a case in point. Just as the war ravaging this small Central American nation is often blamed on rapid population growth, so is its deteriorating environment. Today El Salvador faces accelerated erosion of an estimated 77 percent of its land. The country is steep and mountainous, with fertile lands located in the middle of volcanic slopes, river basins, and coastal plains. These few productive areas belong to large estates growing cotton, sugar, coffee and cattle for export.

El Salvador's land ownership pattern is highly skewed: fewer than one in a hundred farms is more than 250 acres, yet these large farms occupy half the total cultivable land in the country. Meanwhile, the peasants have been pushed onto the higher slopes, where in order to survive, they cut down vegetation and grow subsistence crops on land unsuitable for cultivation. Erosion is the inevitable result. El Salvador's peasants are putting pressure on marginal lands not because of their numbers alone but because they themselves have been made marginal by an agricultural system controlled by the rich.

Perhaps the most common economic woe laid at the door of rapid population growth is unemployment. Open unemployment is rare in the Third World for the simple reason that most people cannot afford to be idle; in the absence of unemployment benefits or social insurance, they must somehow try to earn enough to survive. The real problem is *underemployment* in low-paying, low-productivity occupations such as street vending, domestic service, and handicraft production, which constitute the bottom end of the so-called informal sector in Third World economies.

The problem of surplus labor in Third World countries dates from the colonial period, when European powers appropriated land and other productive resources in Asia, Africa and Latin America, while destroying any local industries that might compete with their own manufactured goods. Thrown off the land and thrown out of enterprises, thousands joined the ranks of underemployed labor. Political independence did not automatically break this pattern, as

industrial development largely continued to be dominated by multinational corporations and international financial institutions, who promoted capital-intensive rather than labor-intensive industries.

Despite the popular Western image of the Third World as a bottomless begging bowl, today it gives more to the industrialized world than it takes. Inflows of official "aid" and private loans and investments are exceeded by outflows in the form of repatriated profits, interest payments and private capital sent abroad by Third World elites.

This is not to say that rapid population growth poses no problem at all in the Third World. When agriculture and industry fail to provide employment to the underemployed, then population growth can have negative effects. Indeed, if the number of jobs stays fixed and more and more people vie for them, wages and living standards will tend to fall even for those jobs. If the numerator remains the same and the denominator swells, then the trend will be for each individual share of the economic pie to get even smaller—though the rich could well cut themselves an even bigger slice.

This "matter of simple arithmetic," however, is not an immutable mathematical law. The question is: *Why do all things remain equal?* Why are the majority condemned to a life of chronic poverty and low productivity—and consequently, to high fertility?

The Malthusians do not have the answer to this question because they do not bother to ask it. They do not bother to ask who owns the land, who fells the forests, who draws up the government budget, who steals the international bank loans, who were the colonists and who were the colonized. By a wave of some magic wand, they deny the role of the rich and powerful in creating and perpetuating the poverty of the powerless. Their ideological fervor masks a profound fatalism: the poor are born to their lot, and the only way out for them is to stop being born.

And what happens when the poor start demanding their rights? The Malthusians call that "political instability," and blame it too on overpopulation. Thus recent writers on US foreign policy, such as General Maxwell Taylor and Robert McNamara, believe the civil war in El Salvador results in part, if not in full, from population pressure, ignoring the extreme disparities of wealth in that country and the violent suppression of any peaceful attempts at social reform. Central America's problem in general is portrayed as too many underemployed young males, who, according to Leon Bouvier of the Population Reference Bureau, increase "the availability of people for revolutionary activity." In this way Malthusianism directly serves to legitimize the status quo: if poor people are rising up, it is only because their numbers are rising too fast.

The Malthusians are fundamentally wrong. The solution to the population problem lies not in the diminution of individual rights through population control, but in their *expansion*. This is because the population problem is not really about a surplus of human numbers, but a lack of basic human rights. Too many people have too little access to resources. Too many women have too little control over their own reproduction. Rapid population growth is not the cause of underdevelopment; it is a symptom of the slow pace of social reform.

Once people's physical survival is ensured and children are no longer their only source of security, history shows that population growth rates fall voluntarily. Higher living standards across the board were the motor force behind the demographic transition in the industrialized world. Similarly,

those Third World countries, whether capitalist, socialist or mixed economy, which have made broad-based development a priority have also experienced significant reductions in population growth, often at relatively low levels of per capita income. These include Cuba, Sri Lanka, Korea, Taiwan and China. Meanwhile, a country like India, where the benefits of substantial economic growth have flowed disproportionately to a small elite, still has high rates of population growth despite the massive resources the government has devoted to population control.

The right to a decent standard of living is necessary but not sufficient. The other critical right is the fundamental right of women to control their own reproduction. The expansion of reproductive choice, not population control, should be the goal of family planning programs and contraceptive research.

What exactly is reproductive choice? Narrowly conceived, it means offering women a broad range of birth control methods, including legal abortion, from which they can freely choose. But the choice is really less in the specific product than in the ongoing relationship between the provider and recipient of family planning services. Good screening, counseling, follow-up and genuine informed consent depend on respect for the needs and the experience of the individual woman (or man). She must be the ultimate arbiter in the decision of whether or not to use contraception and which method to choose. Her womb belongs to her.

The question of reproductive choice ultimately goes far beyond the bounds of family planning programs, involving women's role in the family and in society at large. Control over reproduction is predicated on women having greater control over their economic and social lives and sharing power equally with men.

While reducing poverty rates reduces births, so does reducing patriarchy. The sheer physical burden of many pregnancies in close succession means that women who are free to control their reproduction seldom opt for having all the children it is biologically possible for them to have. And when women have access to education and meaningful employment, they tend to want fewer children for the obvious reason that they have other options.

To say that guaranteeing these two basic sets of rights will help to reduce population growth is not to say that these rights should be pursued for this purpose. On the contrary, once social reforms, women's projects, and family planning programs are organized for the explicit goal of reducing population growth, they are subverted and ultimately fail. Instead, these basic rights are worthy of pursuit in and of themselves; they have far more relevance to the general improvement of human welfare than reducing population growth alone ever will.

ACTION*

1. **Work to improve the status of women in society** and to insure that all women have access to adequate health care, contraceptive choice and the right to a legal abortion.

2. **Work to secure food security for all peoples.** Land reform and participatory democracy are prerequisites for the broad-based development necessary to insure people's physical survival and security. Contact the Institute for Food and Development Policy (Food First).

3. **Help support literacy programs** and make sure that women's literacy is emphasized.

4. **Support grassroots-based development and restoration projects** that serve the needs of Third World poor people, empowering them and their communities. The massive prestige projects usually funded by multinational banks rarely help the economically disenfranchised. What is needed is clean water, local health service, small-scale agriculture and cooperative enterprises adapted to local conditions and based on principles of environmental sustainability.

* Action section by Brad Erickson

Third World Debt Crisis

SUSAN GEORGE

"Conquered states . . . can be held by the conqueror in three different ways.
The first is to ruin them, the second for the conqueror to go and reside
there in person and the third is to allow them to continue to live under
their own laws, subject to a regular tribute, and to create in them a government of a few who will keep the country friendly to the conqueror."

—NICOLO MACHIAVELLI, *THE PRINCE*, 1513

"Without being radical or over-bold, I will tell you that the Third World
War has already started—a silent war, not for that reason any less sinister.
This war is tearing down Brazil, Latin America and practically all the Third
World. Instead of soldiers dying there are millions of unemployed; instead
of destruction of bridges there is the tearing down of factories, schools, hos-
pitals and entire economies . . . . It is a war by the United States against the
Latin American continent and the Third World. It is a war over the foreign
debt."

—BRAZILIAN LABOR LEADER LUIS IGNACIO SILVA,
HAVANA DEBT CONFERENCE, AUGUST 1985

U UNDERSTANDING WHY Third World debt concerns all the inhabitants of the planet, no matter where they live, means first understanding the actions and the motives of the major actors in the crisis.

It is perhaps useful to recall that the debt and default crisis of the 1870's led directly to foreign, colonial occupation of several debtor countries. Today's debt crisis is leading to something similar. We already have an accelerated transfer of wealth from

Susan George is a fellow and Associate Director of the Transnational Institute in Amsterdam, the international wing of the Institute for Policy Studies. TNI's work "addresses the fundamental disparities between rich and poor peoples and nations of the world, investigates their causes and develops alternatives for their remedy." She is the author of several books, including *How the Other Half Dies—The Real Reasons for World Hunger* and *A Fate Worse than Debt*, from which the above is excerpted.

the poor countries to the rich, exactly as in "the good old days." Over $130 billion net—repayments minus loans—has left Latin America and landed in Northern banks in the past five years alone. Banks are also beginning to take over national industries and other assets in the Third World in lieu of interest payments.

The US learned from its failure in Vietnam. Highly visible, debilitating and exhaustively reported interventions have given way to low intensity conflict. LIC has become the officially sanctioned and widely practiced strategy against movements popular in the Third World and governments unpopular in Washington. It costs little in money and in manpower; above all, it costs little in political opposition and turmoil at home, because it is so hard to focus on. Real, overt wars have to be based on consensus, or they eventually come to grief, as the Pentagon has learned to its cost. LIC allows the intervenor to bypass this need for approval, or at least acquiescence, at home. Branding "the enemy" part of the "global communist conspiracy" usually suffices for successful manipulation of Congress and public opinion. For the victim, on the other hand, LIC is high-cost conflict. Defense spending, for example, requires nearly 60 percent of Nicaragua's national budget.

Now let me take the LIC concept one step further. I'll call it FLIC, or financial low intensity conflict. Third World debt is now, perhaps, less a "crisis"—though I have followed convention and called it that—than an ongoing, dialectical FLIC waged against the South; a permanent global struggle exactly like LIC but played out on another terrain. As with LIC, FLIC does not seek to "win," because total victory—complete payback—would also mean total bankruptcy for the debtors. The war would be over, and everyone would have lost.

For waging modern warfare, debt is an efficient tool, allowing one to accomplish

the major goals of classical war except, of course, territorial expansion. It insures access to other peoples' raw materials and infrastructure on the cheapest possible terms. Dozens of countries must compete for shrinking export markets and can export only a limited range of products because of Northern protectionism and their lack of cash to invest in diversification. Market saturation ensues, reducing exporters' incomes to a bare minimum while the North enjoys huge savings. Likewise, debt-for-equity swaps and massive privatization facilitate foreign takeovers—sometimes in partnership with local businessmen—of indebted countries' national manufacturing and service capacity. Whatever looks like it will be profitable is fair game; the debtors are welcome to the rest.

In traditional warfare, a clever strategist will also make the adversary pay for his own oppression. Since the beginning of the debt "crisis," the poor have financed the rich on an unprecedented scale. In 1982, commonly accepted as the first year of the debt crisis, resources transferred from the poor countries to the rich ones for the first time exceeded the resources received. Ever since then, the gap has continued to grow. Total transfers since the beginning of the decade show over $200 billion in the North's favor. But if we eliminate the pre-debt crisis years of 1980 and 1981, the contrast is even more stark: $552 billion inflow, $838 billion outflow; net gain to the industrialized countries, $286 billion.

A further goal of classical warfare is to prevent the adversary from challenging the dominant system, in this case the one organized by the North. Debt effectively discourages such challenges. For example, when Oscar Arias announced his peace plan for Central America, the United States immediately placed unusually strict bans and restrictions on Costa Rican imports; it further refused, for the first time, to intervene with US commercial banks on Costa Rica's behalf. With $4.5 billion in debt to service—a huge sum for such a small country—Costa Rica found itself ineligible for further bank loans; the US move also held up agreements with public sources of credit. Other leaders will doubtless think twice before taking political initiatives unwelcome to a major creditor.

Debt also leads to direct and unmistakable violence when people riot against sudden and unsustainable increases in the cost of survival. Peruvian economist Denis Sulmont provides a valuable résumé of the major anti-austerity uprisings in 22 countries. His figures (probably low since he takes them from Western press tallies) add up to some 3,000 dead, 7,000 wounded and 15,000 arrested. These casualty figures do not include the more recent Venezuelan riots.

Peru tried to limit debt service to 10 percent of export revenues and has been effectively isolated by the "international community"; by late 1988 its economy was in shreds. Peruvian defiance of the banks received no support from anyone, but creditors' harsh reactions show that the strategy was feared and could have been successful had it been adopted by several debtors at once. Brazil declared a moratorium on payments for 19 months in 1987-88, then backed down under internal and external pressures, promising its creditors "Never again" in order to qualify for fresh money. Without solidarity and the safety of numbers, defying the banks has worsened the economic and social situation of countries that have tried it, and this fact has not been lost on those who haven't.

Joint repudiation by the South seems an unlikely prospect because Southern elites and governments have so little to gain from it. They rarely suffer and sometimes profit from the debt crisis. When public services

deteriorate, they can afford private ones. They go on eating however much hunger and malnutrition grow around them. They have larger, more miserably paid labor forces to draw upon as a result of IMF measures. They want to be first-string players in the international financial system, and have more in common with their counterparts in New York or London than with their fellow citizens. Most of their money is abroad anyway, safe and sound.

Assume that private banks and public creditors pretend to accept demands for cancellation; that they forgive, say, 50 percent or less of the debt, but insist that debtors then remit with no further discussion both interest and principal on the remainder. Either the situation for Latin America would become worse, or would be unchanged, since the continent is now servicing only 50 percent of its loan charges.

UNCTAD has called for 30 percent cancellation. Either this UN agency has not grasped the financial realities of Third World debt or it is on the side of the creditors. Other advocates of cancellation may retort that they want not 30 percent or 50 percent, but 100 percent. No doubt. Alas, one rarely obtains 100 percent of any political demand. In the present case, getting half a loaf or less would be a disaster.

Substantial, meaningful cancellation is in any event unlikely. Creditors may well be tempted to create an illusion of largesse while actually reducing their overall aid contribution. But even if they don't, the relevant questions remain "Aid to whom?" and "Cancellation for whom?" Unconditional cancellation means writing a blank check for debtor governments. If one trusts Third World governments and elites to share the benefits of cancellation with their peoples, fair enough. My own confidence in them is admittedly limited.

Even if it were to occur, I fear that can-

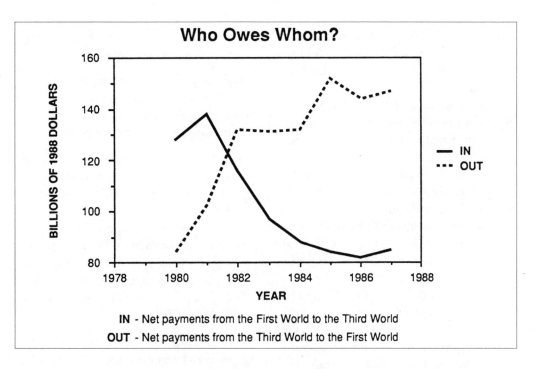

Who Owes Whom?

IN - Net payments from the First World to the Third World
OUT - Net payments from the Third World to the First World

cellation would not enhance popular control over the elites who would be the chief beneficiaries of debt relief and who would, in the absence of other changes, remain in power. Even if we assume the most unlikely scenario: 100 percent cancellation *and* fresh money in the form of aid or new loans, this could simply provide governments with a license to go right back to the disastrous and discredited development models that got them into trouble to begin with. Those practicing these models are not generally noted for their sensitivity to the needs of poor people.

People who believe cancellation would automatically work to the benefit of Third World majorities must have faith in the "trickle down" process. Precious little has trickled down for the past 30 years: why should it begin to do so today? A single example: eight Sahelian states received $14 billion in aid during the decade ending in 1984. This comes to about $44 per person per year. Only 4.5 percent of the total aid received went to rain-fed, as opposed to ir-

rigated, agriculture—even though rain-fed agriculture accounts for 95 percent of Sahelian cereals production. Less than 5 percent went to the livestock sector. These eight governments thus invested less than 10 percent of all aid money in the activities upon which over 90 percent of their populations depend.

As I see it, the Third World has three options. The first, still accepted at the end of 1988, is acquiescence to FLIC. Under the FLIC scenario, the South remains divided, accepts the dominant, export-oriented, outward-looking model, goes on playing the game on the North's terms, and sees its lifeblood gradually drained—though never quite emptied—through reimbursement.

The second option is total or partial repudiation, but this only works when undertaken jointly, as shown by the cases of Brazil and Peru.

The third option is a negotiated settlement recognizing that debt is not an economic but a political problem, and that it can be in everyone's interest to resolve it. My own basis for such a settlement is called "creative reimbursement" or the "3-D solution," standing for debt, development and democracy.

The basic idea of the 3-D solution is that countries are allowed to pay back interest and principal over a long period of time in local currency, calculated so as not to create inflation. Their payments are credited to national development funds whose uses are determined by authentic representatives of the people working with those of the state. For the creditors, 3-D would come to mean the same thing as cancellation since the local currency would be used internally.

The second component of the creative reimbursement formula is reimbursement in kind. Even so-called "poor" Africa is home to natural, material and cultural treasures that are part of humankind's heritage. Under pressure from present development strategies, these treasures are being squandered, eroded or irrevocably destroyed.

Mobilization of local people's energies for "reimbursement in kind" projects would accomplish a great deal more useful work, and more cheaply, than could international aid and outside experts. Foreign assistance should fulfill only a pump-priming function.

Examples of possible payments in kind:

- soil conservation/anti-erosion measures;

- reforestation with local varieties of trees and shrubs, or, if imported, tested by and for the peasantry and pastoralists;

- development and improvement of wells and small-scale irrigation techniques;

- collection, recording and, where appropriate, improvement of building techniques, particularly for traditional earthen architecture, and new con-struction, particularly public buildings, employing these techniques;

- development of new biomass sources for energy purposes as an alternative to wood and charcoal and as an alternative source of income for poor people;

- collection and recording of traditional agriculture, medical, nutritional and pharmaceutical knowledge; establishment of scientific institutes to examine (and in some cases upgrade) this knowledge in light of Western science and technology, generally and often erroneously assumed to be more "modern"; a particular effort to collect female knowledge should be made;

- improvement of local and village level food and water storage facilities;

- establishment of mobile services for pastoralists, particularly for health and education;

- compilation of dictionaries and grammars of local languages;

- revalorization and dissemination of these alternative stocks of knowledge through the schools; new texts, teacher training, literacy campaigns for men *and* women based on rural, life-enhancing themes.

One could easily add to this list; the main thing, however, is the recognition and remuneration for past and future contributions to our common heritage. People who participate in reimbursement-in-kind projects should be paid a democratically-determined minimum wage out of the development fund. Ecological renewal simply will not happen unless people are paid to do it, because they cannot take time from vital short-term survival activities to plant trees, dig irrigation ditches, and so on.

The goal of repayment in kind and in local cash is to strengthen the peasantry, the pastoralists and the agricultural sector. Thus the 3-D program would work toward the elimination of hunger and poverty, help rehabilitate the environment and provide income-generating activities for the people who live in it. In short, 3-D seeks greater equality and social justice.

Because governments contracting for a 3-D solution would have to accept greater popular control over the development process, a kind of conditionality would still apply; but the conditions, unlike those of the IMF, would promote real development and encourage real democracy. Politically speaking, the chief advantage of 3-D—and, to be honest, a huge obstacle to its acceptance—is that it would get money, and the power that goes with money, down to the grassroots majorities that have never enjoyed either before.

Utopia? Maybe. Still, like past political ideals such as ridding the world of slavery or the divine right of kings, creative reimbursement is plausible. Because virtually everyone, in both North and South, is losing from present debt management strategies, exceptional opportunities exist for coalition-building to push for the use of debt as an instrument of development and democracy. In the North, environmentalists, peace activists, women's movements, trade unions, farmers and export-oriented industries, as well as Third World support groups and non-governmental organizations, all have an interest in the changes 3-D would encourage. Together, they might oblige Western governments to put their money where their mouths are in defending democratic values.

Is 3-D affordable to the creditors? Absolutely. The international financial system would not collapse even if the Third World debt went entirely unpaid. Since 1982, the banks have drastically reduced their risk; by 1988 Third World loans accounted for only 6 percent of their total loan portfolios. The debt crisis is now only a crisis for at most two or three large US banks. Their minority interests should not be allowed to prevent a viable political solution.

My proposals have been criticized on grounds that they violate the principle of national sovereignty. What, then, have the IMF and the World Bank been doing all these years? Another objection is that Western governments are not exactly shining examples of democracy themselves and have no business preaching to others or imposing any conditionality at all. Democratic conditionality does not necessarily imply Western-style parliamentary institutions; it does concern citizen access to, and accountability of, the institutions making decisions that now harm untold numbers of people. The Universal Declaration of Human Rights, whose fortieth anniversary is observed as I write, is the best basis for determining the guiding principles of creative reimbursement.

Some governments opting for a 3-D plan would try to get around the conditions. I don't propose we try to start with, say, Zaire! Other governments, however, have already recognized that the state can't do everything; they admit the need for decentralization and for sharing development tasks with popular organizations. As the UN has said in innumerable documents, it's a question of political will; the will of Northern and Southern institutions to set up adequate machinery for the 3-D process. This is not the place to draw up blueprints for the machinery, which could be readily assembled if the political will were present. The task is for activists to push for this political will.

ACTION*

1. **Consumers can put pressure on banks** and corporations using moral persuasion. Corporations don't want the embarrassment of a bad record. Shareholders have a direct effect on private corporations and commercial banks. Taxpayers have a clear right and responsibility to be involved in decisions regarding international loans, especially loans from the World Bank, the IMF, Export/Import Banks, USAID, and other Multilateral Development Banks.

2. **Push Congress to legislate debt relief.** Join campaigns to put pressure on banks. Relief should not be conditional upon austerity plans dictated by the lenders. To find out about current campaigns, contact one of the organizations in the resource list at the end of this section.

*Action section by Brad Erickson

3. **Insist that debt forgiveness be conditional on democratic principles** and the protection of human rights, the environment and indigenous peoples' rights.

4. **Insist that recipient governments respect land rights and the environment,** solicit the participation of indigenous peoples and that proposed projects meet the following principles: proper public notification, the right to be informed, and the right to go to court. Put the onus on recipient governments to provide evidence of meeting these principles before each loan is approved. Future loans should be made with the clear condition that the people affected are given due process and the right to participate in the decision to approve projects and the right to challenge any project.

Intervention and History

BILL HALL

War is a racket. . . . It may seem odd for me, a military man, to adopt such a comparison. Truthfulness compels me to. I spent 33 years and 4 months in active service as a member of our country's most agile military force—the Marine Corps . . . And during the period I spent most of my time being a high-class muscle man for Big Business, for Wall Street and the bankers. In short, I was a racketeer for capitalism . . . .

Thus I helped make Mexico and especially Tampico safe for American oil interests in 1914. I helped make Haiti and Cuba a decent place for the National City Bank boys to collect revenues in. I helped in the raping of half a dozen Central American republics for the benefit of Wall Street. . . . I helped purify Nicaragua for the international banking house of Brown Brothers in 1909-1912. I brought light to the Dominican Republic for American sugar interests in 1916. I helped make Honduras "right" for American fruit companies in 1903 . . . .

Looking back on it, I feel I might have given Al Capone a few hints. The best *he* could do was to operate his racket in three city districts. We Marines operated on three *continents*.

—MAJOR GENERAL SMEDLEY D. BUTLER,
TWO-TIME WINNER OF THE CONGRESSIONAL MEDAL OF HONOR

Bill Hall's experience as a community activist spans the anti-apartheid, Central America, anti-nuclear, and Green movements. As assistant to the Director of Project Abraco, he worked in solidarity with the grassroots movements of Brazil and organized popular education on the Third World debt crisis and US intervention. He is currently an Associate of the Environmental Project on Central America (EPOCA) in San Francisco, and an editor of the journal *Capitalism, Nature, Socialism*. Bill dedicates this essay to Linda Evans and all North American political prisoners jailed for their beliefs and associations.

IN THE NOVEL *1984,* author George Orwell portrays the daily pain and humiliation of life in a totalitarian nation of the future. Although the main character Winston Smith is a lowly bureaucrat, he nonetheless performs an administrative function vital to his society's dictatorial order. Each day at his desk Smith methodically searches through past newspapers and magazines to change names, dates and events. He removes information deemed politically objectionable by his superiors and destroys all record of it. Orwell's protagonist literally rewrites the past to suit the ideology of the present. History is lost into a bureaucratic "memory hole."

In part a response to *1984, Brave New World* presented a dictatorial society based not on the coercion applied to and administered by Orwell's Winston Smith, but instead on what author Aldous Huxley considered a far more insidious tool of control: consent. In *Brave New World,* totalitarianism has become so effective that repression is unnecessary. The oppressed submit to their masters willingly; they love their servitude. Censorship is unneeded, because there is no interest in hearing nonconformist views. The citizens of *Brave New World,* engrossed in the distractions of drugs or endless day-to-day entertainment, themselves allow history to slip down the memory hole.

The message of both novels is clear. Whether it is because of repression and censorship, or because of indifference and omission, a society that forgets its history loses its freedom. To allow our past to be written by others, and the truth to be lost to the memory hole, is to surrender our future to totalitarianism.

It is now more than 36 years since the US began its sponsorship of South Vietnamese dictator Ngo Dinh Diem, propping up a corrupt and violent regime dependent on growing infusions of US money, training—and eventually troops—to stay in power. Fifteen years later support for Diem had ended in US defeat and withdrawal from Vietnam, with more than four million deaths. "The Vietnam War" is now considered part of our past. The war's lessons about our government, lessons that seemed so clear during the war, are fast being forgotten, lost down the memory hole of a society seemingly committed to repeating its own tragic history.

Today nearly half a million US troops occupy 40 foreign countries. The majority of US "defense" spending is devoted to overseas commitments. US training and weapons nurture war and repression in the Philippines, in El Salvador, Guatemala, Peru, Indonesia, Thailand, Chile, Zaire, Lebanon and dozens of other countries. The same policy-making elite that invoked "national security" in order to violate the 1954 Geneva peace accords (which called for free elections in a unified Vietnam instead of stepped up US intervention and a divided country) now invokes "national security" to continue waging war in the poverty-stricken islands of the Philippines. The same Pentagon that dumped more than 18 million gallons of dioxin-laden defoliants on Vietnamese land —land that still cannot produce food—now claims that "national security" demands we ship more bombs to the Salvadoran Air Force to reduce the countryside of El Salvador to desert. Today the same State Department that funded mercenary armies of Montagnard tribesmen with profits from heroin trafficking in Laos claims the moral high ground in an increasingly militarized war on drugs—and "subversives"—in Peru, Bolivia and Colombia. The same CIA Director, William Colby, who, as head of the CORDS (war-related US relief and "development aid") agency, directed the systematic assassination of tens of thousands of "Vietcong suspects" in Operation Phoenix,

In the US Capitol, Witness for Peace demonstrators protest the Reagan-Bush administration's Nicaragua policy of Contra aid, which the World Court and the Organization of American States also condemned. Names on the crosses are those of victims of the Contras.
RICH REINHARD, 1986, IMPACT VISUALS

now informs us that "international terrorism" necessitates political investigations and police-state tactics at home.

Only by recovering the history of US intervention in Vietnam from the memory hole can we begin to understand how the war continues in the form of US intervention today. And only by recovering that history can we learn our power to stop intervention.

The US government assaulted the Vietnamese resistance movement—a movement President Eisenhower said would have surely won free elections—with more firepower than it used in all of World War II. Yet the world's most powerful country was defeated at the hands of an army of illiterate—but committed—farmers. The White House considered using nuclear weapons to exterminate this enemy that it could not conquer. But that option was made impossible by

policy-makers' fear of opposition at home, as hundreds of thousands of people confronted Vietnam not with fear or denial, but with courage and rage. They rose up in a militant mass protest movement and threatened to shake the very foundation of order in our country. And they helped stop the war in Vietnam, and return some of the destiny of Southeast Asia to the people who live there.

The history of the Vietnam War and what it took to stop it shows that US intervention in the Third World is not just the result of "failed policies" or imprudent decisions. Intervention against efforts at greater democracy in the Third World—whether in Southeast Asia, Grenada, or Chile—arises from the lack of genuine democratic control in the US. From General Smedley Butler to more modern day "racketeers for capitalism," the interests of cheap labor, abundant resources and military dominion guide the decision-makers behind US foreign policy.

The history of the Vietnam War is also the history of how policy makers respond when their wars are challenged at home. As the opposition movement swelled into the millions, the government began to consider the US a kind of "second front" in the war in Vietnam, and unleashed a repressive campaign of domestic counterinsurgency to battle its enemies at home: the peace movement and all protest groups. COINTELPRO, the FBI Counterintelligence Program, sought explicitly to sow paranoia, cause division, destroy reputations with rumor and lies and "neutralize" activists and groups. It was a clandestine campaign to destroy opposition at home, and it went far outside the limits of law. Chief among the program's aims was suppressing activism at its early stages, as well as preventing coalitions from developing between anti-war activists and people challenging elite control of the society from other positions—the Black Power movement, Native Americans, Chicanos, farm workers and others. Not just a few, but dozens of activists were assassinated by the police, FBI and FBI-backed right-wing vigilantes as part of COINTELPRO. Repression set back—but did not eliminate—a powerful movement that had begun to unearth the roots of intervention.

When the Vietnam War protest movement did succeed in narrowing their latitude for action, the Nixons, Kissingers and Oliver Norths took it as a lesson. They concluded that US politics was suffering from "too much democracy"; a passive, pliant public was much preferable to the active and critical one the war had generated. If the nominal checks and balances of democracy were limiting the freedom of the Pentagon and CIA in any way, these men saw only one solution: circumvent the checks and balances of democracy.

Covert actions, mercenary armies, self financing, "off-the-shelf" operations, the "privatization" of foreign and domestic policy—all serve to remove more and more repressive activity from potential scrutiny by Congress and accountability to the electorate. The "covert actions" abroad (such as the Iran-Contra scandal) and "anti-terrorism" at home (such as the infiltration and break-ins of Central America peace groups) are pursued in secret not because their visibility would cause a "national security risk." Rather, the US ruling elite knows that if people were aware of these actions, there would be strong opposition from domestic "enemies" on the "second front."

Escalation of war in Vietnam failed to defeat independence fighters. Escalation of repression at home has likewise not rendered protest movements powerless. In Nicaragua, a country with only one (highly unreliable) working elevator and a population mostly under the age of 16, a revolution is surviving a US military and economic war, and remains committed to comprehensive social programs and environmental protection not only because of its own courage, but also because of the US peace movement's efforts. Clergy, students and human rights activists across the US were able to force the Reagan Administration to adopt the toughest anti-South Africa sanctions ever as the anti-apartheid movement surged in power in the US and around the world.

Ending military aid to "allies" and keeping the Marines in their barracks and not on the beaches can be achieved, but it takes an outspoken and militant anti-intervention movement. It takes a movement that understands that a more humane government in Nicaragua or South Africa may or may not choose to call itself "socialist"; the point is that if steps are being taken to defend justice and human rights, then we should support whoever is taking those steps. It takes a movement that can condemn US intervention without ignoring Soviet intervention, a movement that rejects the history written for us and instead reclaims its own. It takes a movement unafraid to speak the truth, unhesitant to seek listeners in all corners of society and unashamed to reach out to the compassion and love that lies dormant deep within so many people in this country.

To see its task clearly, the anti-intervention movement must relearn its history and again attack the roots of exploitation and power that anchor intervention in our economy and political system. To gather the strength needed to win, the movement must forge alliances with all of those working against the same system of power. The banner of this movement is *solidarity*, the solidarity of the poor against the rich, of the powerless against the powerful, solidarity that knows no borders, no division by race or nation.

Whether our country's will to struggle has for the time being been ripped from us, or whether it is merely abandoned for more entertaining pursuits, we must seek out ways to live without Orwell's memory hole, ways to recover human identity and compassion in an age of denial and barbarity. In the words of Eduardo Galeano, an Uruguayan writer and activist once forced into exile by a US-backed dictatorship: "I think that fighting to change the world, to restore it, gives sense to the human adventure. In this fight I recognize myself in others. In this fight I become a compatriot and contemporary of those who are moved to action by the will for justice and the will for beauty. I am their compatriot though they were born in another country. I am their contemporary though they lived in another age. And thus I feel and know that I am a breeze of a wind that will continue when I am no longer. . . ."

ACTION*

- Monitor the alternative press for news behind the headlines of US foreign policy. Respond among friends and acquaintances to such mass media propaganda as the "War on Drugs," "overpopulation," "terrorism," and "national security." Look to the root causes and political uses behind such misinformation.

- Recover the history of US intervention and movements in opposition to it, by consulting books, films, radio shows, and other sources, as well as seeking out the stories of people involved. Begin a small resource library of books and tapes with your friends. Gather a small group of friends to read or go to lectures together and then discuss the implications.

- Investigate the economic motives that underpin US foreign policy, in order to understand how lack of democracy and justice at home relates to militarism abroad.

- Write letters to the Editor.

*Action section by Bill Hall

- Get on as many mailing lists of peace and solidarity groups as possible; get to know what the movement looks like in your area.

- Participate in discussion about strategies, outreach, methods and priorities.

- Promote coalition building and linking of issues around broad demands for greater democracy and justice.

- Phone radio talk shows to inform other listeners.

- Write your representative and Senators.

- Get in touch with and volunteer with peace and solidarity groups in your area. If you can't donate your time, donate money. If you can't donate money, then let your support be known in other ways.

- Train yourself in civil disobedience protest and participate in blockades, sit-ins and occupations for a change in policy.

- Let everyone you know hear about your commitment to social change, and address people's fears and ignorance about it. Try to keep others informed, and challenge their misunderstandings. Such small efforts can have tremendous reverberations where people have not considered these issues before.

- Encourage others to get involved.

- Zero in on hesitations you might have about liberation struggles in the Third World. Are your concerns based on informed advocacy of democracy and justice? Or are you failing to critically examine assumptions given to you by television and our government?

- Write to activists in the US who are imprisoned for their political beliefs and efforts.

- Send material aid to liberation movements.

- Travel to the Third World.

- Support refugees in your community.

RESOURCES

Organizations

Action in Support of the Mexican Garment Workers
c/o AFSC
1501 Cherry Street
Philadelphia, PA 19102
Supports Mexican women who formed a dynamic union after the 1985 earthquake with tours, material aid and letter-writing.

American Committee on Africa
198 Broadway
New York, NY 10038
(212) 962-1210

Supports African people in their struggle for freedom and independence. Initiates projects to inform and mobilize Americans to support African freedom through changes in US foreign policy. Publishes the free ACOA Action News, twice annually.

Amnesty International
322 8th Avenue
New York, NY 10001
(212) 633-4200
International human rights group that focuses on the release of prisoners of conscience and the abolition of torture and the death penalty. Their bi-monthly periodical, Amnesty Action, costs $25/year.

Bread for the World
802 Rhode Island Avenue NE
Washington, DC 20018
(202) 269-0200

A Christian citizens advocacy organization, which trains their 40,000 members to become activists—using letter-writing campaigns, phone trees, etc. Local groups lobby their Congresspersons on international and domestic debt and hunger issues. Their quarterly, Bread, *is $25/year.*

CANNICOR
P.O. Box 6819
San Francisco, CA 94101
(415) 885-5102

A church-supported agency that examines the social responsibility of mostly private banks, both nationally and internationally. Their quarterly, Of Prophets and Profits *($15 to $25, sliding scale), reports on activities of the group and on the situation in Latin America and South Africa.*

Center for Constitutional Rights
853 Broadway
New York, NY 10003

A law office that defends persons facing political repression and monitors harassment and surveillance of protest organizations. Has worked on the FBI infiltration of peace groups and the murder of Benjamin Linder by US-funded Contras in Nicaragua.

Central American Historical Institute
Intercultural Center, Georgetown
  University
Washington, DC 20057

A research and analysis organization that publishes Update *and* Envio—*resources on Central American issues ranging from Guatemala's constitution to women's rights in Nicaragua.*

Chile Humanitarian Aid
347 Dolores Street, #109
San Francisco, CA 94110
(415) 863-0681

Raises money for grassroots projects in Chile: helps political prisoners and supports indigenous peoples.

The Christic Institute
1324 North Capitol Street NW
Washington, DC 20002
(202) 797-8106

An interfaith center for law and national policy in the public interest that commits its resources to legal investigations selected for their potential to advance human rights, social justice and personal freedom at home and abroad. Their investigation of the Contragate conspiracy uncovered and tracked an international criminal network involved in drug trafficking, political assassinations and covert warfare directly to the White House and the CIA. A $20 donation brings Christic Institute publications for one year.

**CISPES (Committee in Solidarity with the
  People of El Salvador)**
P.O. Box 122056
Washington, DC 20005
(202) 265-0890

Works to stop intervention and to direct the support of people in civil disobedience, demonstrations, rallies, marches, human rights campaigns, fund raising and directory services. Publishes a yearly newsletter, Alert: Focus on Central America.

Clergy and Laity Concerned
198 Broadway
New York, NY 10038

Once known as Clergy and Laity Concerned About the War in Vietnam, this religious affiliation has for decades been a leader in the US peace movement.

**Committee for US-Central American
  Relations**
731 8th Street SE
Washington, DC 20003-2866
(202) 547-3800

Provides the media, government and public with an analysis of the development policy and its relation to military intervention.

Development Group for Alternative Policies

1400 I Street NW, Suite 520
Washington, DC 20005
(202) 898-1566

The Development GAP is a non-profit organization that seeks to strengthen grassroots development in the Third World, advocating changes in aid and other social development policies that affect the poor. Development GAP is studying and acting on issues related to the World Bank and developing mechanisms for building initiative policies by and for the poor, including symposia with the US Foreign Affairs Committee and with foreign NGOs.

Energy Probe and Probe International

225 Brunswick Avenue
Toronto, Ontario M5S 2M6
Canada

Provides literature on the debt crisis, including model letters. An organizing and networking force in Canada, providing information on local, regional, national and international issues.

Environmental Project on Central America (EPOCA)

Earth Island Institute
300 Broadway, Suite 28
San Francisco, CA 94133
(415) 788-3666

Organizes against the devastating environmental impact of US military and economic intervention in Central America. Through its publications, speakers bureau, and award-winning video, EPOCA is showing the link between social justice and environmental protection. EPOCA's environmental reforestation brigades to Nicaragua (co-sponsored with the Nicaragua Network), assistance to Central American conservation projects and protest campaigns to

change US foreign policy all work to forge alliances between the Central America solidarity and environmental movements in the US and around the world. A $25 donation (less for low-income people) brings EPOCA's Green Paper series and other publications. Local organizers, volunteers and interns are welcome.

Eritrean Relief Committee

475 Riverside Drive #251
New York, NY 10015
(212) 870-2727

Supports refugees under attack by the Ethiopian government and promotes self-determination.

Free Puerto Rico Committee

c/o Breakthrough
P.O. Box 14422
San Francisco, CA 94114

The country's leading network of groups working in solidarity with the movement to end US colonialism in Puerto Rico. Also networks with Puerto Rican immigrants living in the US.

Food First/Institute for Food and Development Policy

145 9th Street
San Francisco, CA 94103
(415) 864-8555

Food First was established 14 years ago by Frances Moore Lappé and Joseph Collins, whose extensive research demonstrated that the scarcity of food in the world is due to politics, and not natural shortages. Food First acts to correct this crisis through research and education, and offers a large publication list.

Friends Committee on National Legislation

245 2nd Street NE
Washington, DC 20002
(202) 547-6000

A Quaker organization that attempts to bring spiritual values to bear on public policy decisions. Priorities include strengthening participation of all people in the decisions that affect their lives; reducing threats to the environment; redefining national and global security; US compliance with agreed upon standards of international law and justice, and efforts to improve those standards. The FCNL Washington Newsletter *chronicles Congressional voting records on the above priorities, and costs $20/year. FCNL encourages people to write letters to their Congresspersons, to newspapers, and to become involved in action networks.*

Gabriela
National Women's Coalition
2017 Francisco Street
Berkeley, CA 94709
(415) 841-1439

Provides assistance to the national network of Filipino women's groups struggling for democracy, human rights and an end to US intervention.

GATT-Fly
11 Madison Avenue
Toronto, Ontario M5R 2S2
Canada
(416) 921-4615

By far the best source for information on the debt crisis. GATT-Fly's position is, "The debt has already been paid." Write for their publication catalog or their superb book, Debt Bondage or Self Reliance, *a popular perspective on the debt crisis (US $6; Canadian $7.95).*

Global Exchange
2940 16th Street
Room 307
San Francisco, CA 94103
(415) 255-7296

Promotes direct, constructive ties, through trade and mutual aid, between North Americans and communities and organizations in the Third World. They have a speakers bureau and three solidar-ity groups people can get involved with: Africa, Central America and Caribbean Exchanges. Global Exchange recently published Bridging the Global Gap: A Handbook to Linking First and Third World Citizens, *an excellent and practical guide ($11.95). Membership (includes their newsletter) is $25.*

Grassroots International
P.O. Box 312
Cambridge, MA 02139
(617) 497-9180

A non-profit organization working to promote grassroots development initiated by the poor. Supports small-scale programs in all areas of the Third World.

Honduras Information Center
P.O. Box 1750
Jamaica Plain, MA 02130
(617) 522-6240

Independent information and research center focusing on political, social and economic issues within Honduras, the effects of US foreign policy and particularly human rights. They provide information to journalists and publish the monthly Honduras Update, *featuring original analysis by research staff, scholars and eyewitnesses, and translations of documents issued by Hondurans. Subscriptions are $14/year.*

Institute for Policy Studies Debt Crisis Network
1601 Connecticut Avenue NW
Washington, DC 20009
(202) 234-9382

Liberal-left think tank in Washington committed to sweeping reforms in the political and economic order. Their Debt Crisis Network documents the hidden impact of the debt crisis and unites groups across the US to promote international economic policy based on social justice. Write for a publication catalog of hundreds of books, such as Winning America: Ideas and Leadership for the 1990's.

International Alliance for Sustainable Agriculture
The Newman Center
University of Minnesota
1701 University Avenue SE, Room 202
Minneapolis, MN 55414

Promotes sustainable agriculture through an international educational network, and offers practical alternatives to high-input agriculture.

International Development Exchange (IDEX)
777 Valencia Street
San Francisco, CA 94110
(415) 621-1494

Supports small-scale community development projects in Asia, Africa and Latin America and works to educate and involve Americans in Third World community development. Currently IDEX is supporting over 60 projects, linking them with sponsoring individuals and organizations. Among the projects IDEX supports are a Philippine youth training center, community gardens in Botswana, a Nepalese drinking water system and a Mexican artisans center.

International Monetary Fund
700 19th Street NW
Washington, DC 20431
(202) 623-7000

If you want to find out what the bankers say about what they do, contact the IMF. The IMF acts as a forum for 151 countries who have joined to maintain a system of buying and selling their currencies. They issue a weekly topical report of the Fund's activities, IMF Survey, which gives an insider's view of countries' large-scale investment patterns.

Lasting Links
6231 Leesburg Pike #612
Falls Church, VA 22044

Promotes partnerships between people in the US and grassroots development projects in the Third World.

Mozambique Support Network
343 South Dearborn, Suite 601
Chicago, IL 60604
(312) 922-3286

An anti-apartheid solidarity group. Sponsored US tours for speakers Lina Magaia, Graca Machel, and the widow of Mozambique's first president, Samora Machel. They issue a bi-monthly newsletter.

National Labor Committee in Support of Democracy and Human Rights in El Salvador
15 Union Square
New York, NY 10003

Organizes to promote solidarity in the US labor movement toward Central American workers.

Network in Solidarity with the People of Guatemala
1314 14th Street
Washington, DC 20005
(202) 483-0050

NISGUA sends material and human aid and provides grassroots Central America committees with programs and activities on Guatemala. Their magazine, Report on Guatemala (five issues per year for $10), covers current events, political trends, government insurgency, popular movements and political activity in the US. NISGUA also offers internships and organizes activist tours to Guatemala.

New El Salvador Today (NEST)
P.O. Box 411436
San Francisco, CA 94141
(415) 864-7755

Provides direct financial support to organizations and communities working to build a democratic alternative and laying the foundation for a new society in El Salvador. Seeks to raise public awareness about the role of US government in El Salvador. NEST raises $1 million in aid per year.

Nicaragua Network
2025 I Street NW, #1117
Washington, DC 20006
(202) 223-2328

A network of 300 local committees working to stop contra aid and provide humanitarian assistance, such as the "Oats for Peace" Fund. Co-sponsors environmental, housing and harvest brigades. Their newsletter, Nicaragua Network News ($10/year), and quarterly magazine, Nicaragua Perspectives ($12/year), provide in-depth analysis and thoughtful reporting of issues affecting Nicaragua and the US peace movement.

North American Congress on Latin America (NACLA)
151 West 19th Street
New York, NY 10011

The country's leading progressive research organization on Latin America and the Caribbean. Readily makes referrals on a wide number of issues. Publishes the award-winning bi-monthly magazine Report on the Americas.

Oxfam America
115 Broadway
Boston, MA 02116
(617) 482-1211

An international agency that funds self-help development projects and disaster relief in poor countries in Africa, Asia and Latin America. Also prepares and distributes educational materials for Americans on the issues of development and hunger. Oxfam America is a non-sectarian and non-profit organization which neither seeks nor accepts US government contributions. All contributions are tax-deductible to the extent provided by law.

Palestine Solidarity Committee
P.O. Box 27462
San Francisco, CA 94127
(415) 861-1552

A North American organization working for Palestinian rights in the US, with 30 chapters that educate the public through forums, publications, speaking tours and telegram and postcard campaigns. A membership of $30 brings their bi-monthly Palestine Focus and monthly newsletters, leaflets and other information bulletins.

Peace Brigades International
4722 Baltimore Avenue
Philadelphia, PA 19143
(215) 724-1464

PBI seeks to establish international and non-partisan approaches to peacemaking and to the support of basic human rights. Upon invitation, PBI sends unarmed peace teams into areas of violent repression. These teams work to reduce the violence and support local social justice initiatives. A donation brings Peace Brigades newsletter.

Planned Parenthood
810 7th Avenue
New York, NY 10019
(212) 541-7800

Seeks to alleviate overpopulation through international campaigns to facilitate family planning, with medical, educational and counseling services. Planned Parenthood advocates sex education and the availability of birth control devices around the world.

Population Resource Center
622 Third Avenue
New York, NY 10017
(212) 888-2820

A non-advocacy organization providing demographic analysis of social issues for policy-makers. PRC is funded by major US foundations and corporations, and their service is sought largely by established conservative agencies. But PRC's demographic analysis appears unbiased and in-depth, and may be of use to progressive environmental/population activist organizations.

Prairie Fire Organizing Committee
P.O. Box 14422
San Francisco, CA 94114

Works to build the anti-imperialist struggle in the United States. Their quarterly journal, Breakthrough ($10/year), covers the experiences and strategies of national liberation movements, political prisoners and anti-sexism and anti-racism organizers, providing resources, analysis and interviews.

Project Abraço
515 Broadway
Santa Cruz, CA 95060
(408) 423-1626

Project Abraço (which means "embrace" in Portuguese) is the US's only organization working in solidarity with the popular organizations of Brazil. The newsletter Terra Nossa ("our land") covers developments in Brazilian politics, economics and the struggle for social change. Abraço has done widely acclaimed educational work on the human and ecological impacts of the Third World debt crisis, has sponsored "reality tours" for North Americans who want to learn about Brazil, has brought Brazilian leaders of the nonviolence movement to the US, leads human rights protest campaigns, and is now working to build alliances between environmental and social justice organizations to protect the Amazon.

Third World Coalition
1501 Cherry Street
Philadelphia, PA 19102
(215) 241-7178

Part of the American Friends Service Committee, networks Third World organizations and community people, often working on the local level. The Third World Coalition offers support and helps with the networking process.

Trans-Africa
545 Eighth Street SE
Washington, DC 20003

(202) 547-2550

Lobbies on Capitol Hill for a progressive foreign policy toward Africa and the Caribbean, and also coordinates a number of citizen chapters. Their newsletter, TransAfrica News, is $12.50 a year.

United Methodist Church
777 United Nations Plaza
New York, NY 10017
(212) 682-3633

Promotes research, education and action on peace and development issues, UN affairs, militarism, economic justice and US foreign policy.

United Nations High Commission on Refugees
UN Secretariat, Room S931
New York, NY 10017
(212) 963-0032

With two offices in the United States— one in New York and one in Washington, DC—the UNHCR works on political asylum and relocation issues, and assists people seeking refugee status—those escaping persecution because of race, religion or political beliefs. They publish the monthly Refugee magazine, and an extensive list of publications, notably the United Nations Universal Declaration of Human Rights.

United Nations Non-Governmental Liaison Service
DC2-1103 2 UN Plaza
New York, NY 10017
(212) 963-7234

Provides information services, speakers, and helps other agencies to find the networking systems (both personnel and electronic) that work best for them. NGLS publishes and disseminates materials on development, including newsletters, calendars, NGO directories, information kits, pamphlets and annotated bibliographies. Six times a year they issue NGLS News.

Washington Office on Latin America

110 Maryland NE
Washington, DC 20002
(202) 544-8045

WOLA has two central purposes: to monitor human rights practices, political developments and US policies in Latin America and the Caribbean, and to provide US policy-makers and the public with information and analysis about the region. Its goal is to help shape a foreign policy that advances human rights, democracy and peace in the hemisphere. WOLA provides objective documentation and analysis to foreign policy decision-makers and promotes informed debate through public seminars, meetings, reports and investigative missions. They publish Latin America Update ($18/year).

World Hunger Year
201 West 35th Street, Room 1402
New York, NY 10001
(212) 629-8850

Founded in 1975 by singer Harry Chapin and Bill Ayres, it works to inform the public, the media, and policy-makers about hunger in the Third World and in the US, and to initiate programs to relieve hunger and homelessness.

Periodicals

Across Frontiers
P.O. Box 2382
Berkeley, CA 94702

An informative source of news and analysis on Eastern Europe's popular movements against militarism and for greater democracy. Avoids the establishment anticommunist perspective on these movements and offers concrete ways to act in solidarity. $10/year.

Contra Watch
P.O. Box 40601
San Francisco, CA 94140

Exposes the activity of counter-revolutionaries and terrorists backed by the US government, from the UNITA army fighting against Angola to the contras fighting Nicaragua from bases in Honduras.

Development
Society for International Development
Pallazzo della Civilta del Lavoro
Rome 0144, Italy

Offers a critical perspective on prevailing development models and effective debate about emerging alternatives. $25/year.

Food Monitor
201 West 35th Street, Room 1402
New York, NY 10001

Focuses on hunger and poverty in the US, as well as the international development crisis. $18/year.

Guardian
33 West 17th Street
New York, NY 10011

The country's leading weekly of the grassroots protest movement. Extensive coverage of efforts in solidarity with the Third World. Samples free; $27.50/year.

MERIP Reports
P.O. Box 3122
Washington, DC 20010

An excellent magazine on Middle East affairs from a social justice and peace perspective. MERIP—the Middle East Research and Information Project—is also a resource for information and research on Palestine, the Occupied Territories, Islamic nationalism and other issues.

New Internationalist
P.O. Box 1143
Lewiston, NY 14092

Best overall introduction to these issues. Highly readable. Great for classroom use. $25/year.

Seeds
22 East Lake Drive

Decatur, GA 30030

Focuses on hunger in the United States and our ties to the hungry abroad, from a Christian perspective. $12/year.

Third World Resources
464 19th Street
Oakland, CA 94612
(415) 536-1876

A quarterly review of resources from and about the Third World, including organizations, books, periodicals, pamphlets and articles, and audiovisual items. TWR collects, catalogs, annotates and publicizes resources from around the world on Third World regions and issues. Fantastic for the activist/organizer. $25/2 years (individuals); $25/year (organizations).

Books

Aid as Obstacle: Twenty Questions About Our Foreign Aid and the Hungry. Frances Moore Lappé, Joseph Collins and David Kinley. San Francisco: Food First Books, 1980.

Betraying the National Interest. Frances Moore Lappé, Rachel Schurman and Kevin Danaher. San Francisco: Food First Books/Grove Press, 1987.

Shows why US foreign assistance backfires, failing to address the needs of the hungry or to serve the interests of the American people.

COINTELPRO: The FBI's Secret War on Political Freedom. Nelson Blachstock. New York: Anchor Foundation, 1988.

A comprehensive overview of how the US government countered the power of the anti-war and other popular movements in the 1960's and 1970's. An introduction by Noam Chomsky provides historical background and analytical context.

Don't Be Afraid, Gringo: A Honduran

Woman Speaks from the Heart. Medea Benjamin. San Francisco: Food First Books, 1987.

A courageous peasant labor leader makes vivid the devastating impact of US policies on the hungry in Central America— and the strength of the movement to resist those policies.

A Fate Worse Than Debt. Susan George. San Francisco: Food First Books/Grove Press, 1987.

Dramatizes how the Third World debt burden is carried by the world's poorest people, and offers an innovative solution.

Fire in the Lake: The Vietnamese and the Americans in Vietnam. Frances Fitz-Gerald. New York: Vintage Books, 1989.

A vivid introduction to the hidden history of the US war in Southeast Asia and what it meant to the people affected by it. An important antidote to historical amnesia.

Food First: Beyond the Myth of Scarcity. Frances Moore Lappé and Joseph Collins. New York: Ballantine Books, 1979.

Fifty questions and answers probing the links between hunger and rapid population growth, environmental devastation and foreign aid.

I . . . Rigoberta Menchu: An Indian Woman in Guatemala. Elisabeth Burgos-Debray, editor. New York: Verso, 1983.

Testimony of a Guatemalan Indian whose siblings were poisoned by pesticides while working the fields and whose father was burned to death by the Guatemalan military during a land protest. This compelling oral history of Quiche Indian life weaves together the story of the land and the people of Guatemala.

Open Veins of Latin America: Five Centuries of the Pillage of a Continent. Eduardo Galeano. New York: Monthly Review Press, 1973.

Galeano's masterpiece, burned in the plazas of Santiago, Chile, after the 1973 military coup, journeys through the continent's history of agony and resistance. Galeano has the passion of a novelist and the precision of a historian; his sensitivity to the pillage of natural resources gives the book an underlying ecological perspective.

The Philippines: Fire on the Rim. Joseph Collins. San Francisco: Food First Books, 1989.

Filipinos—from the poorest sugar worker to the wealthiest landowner—tell their stories, taking the reader behind the headlines of the new Philippine "democracy."

The Price of Power: Kissinger in the Nixon White House. Seymour M. Hersh. New York: Summit Books, 1983.

A frightening account of power politics at the height of the Nixon machine during the years of saturation bombing in Vietnam, the invasion of Cambodia, Watergate and the corruption of the 1972 presidential elections, and the engineered coup against democratically elected Chilean socialist Salvador Allende and the massacres that followed. Hersh, a New York Times journalist, won the Pulitzer Prize for a book that exposed Nixon's drinking problems, the cavalier attitude to war and the profoundly undemocratic nature of state foreign policy planning.

Rediscovering America's Values. Frances Moore Lappé. New York: Ballantine Books, 1989.

A dialogue exploring the meaning of America's core values—freedom, democracy and fairness. Lappé invites readers to rethink our own and our nation's values as guides to address hunger and environmental destruction.

Reproductive Rights and Wrongs: The Global Politics of Population Control and

Contraceptive Choice. Betsy Hartmann. New York: Harper and Row, 1987.

A critical reexamination of population issues that places third world and women's perspectives in the center of the population debate.

Turning the Tide: US Intervention in Central America and the Struggle for Peace. Noam Chomsky. Boston: South End Press, 1985.

The Real Terror Network. Edward S. Herman. Boston: South End Press, 1982.

The Washington Connection and Third World Fascism. Noam Chomsky and Edward S. Herman. Boston: South End Press, 1979.

These three books dispel myths perpetuated by the mass media and offer powerful, meticulously documented proof of the US empire's activities, including training foreign police in torture techniques, assassinating domestic and foreign political opponents, and recruiting Nazis for work with the CIA. Herman's book reveals a shocking correlation between US aid and human rights violations in the Third World. Bibliographies offer further resources.

Women in the Global Factory. Annette Fuentes and Barbara Ehrenreich. Boston: South End Press, 1983.

An accessible, 60-page analysis of the exploitation of Third World women factory workers by multinational corporations and the kinds of organizing needed to combat it. Shocking, enraging and empowering—an essential feminist perspective on global imperialism.

World Hunger: Twelve Myths. Frances Moore Lappé and Joseph Collins. San Francisco: Food First Books/Grove Press, 1986.

A pithy, hard-hitting introduction to the interrelated causes of hunger and what we can do to end it. Also available is an illustrated fold-out fact sheet, Hunger Myths and Facts.

PART FOUR

ECONOMIC JUSTICE

Share the Wealth

SUSAN DEMARCO AND JIM HIGHTOWER

"If a free society cannot help the many who are poor, it cannot save the few who are rich."

—JOHN F. KENNEDY

THE US ECONOMY cannot long withstand the level of damage done to it during the Reagan/Bush years. We've suffered the economic loss—and ethical bankruptcy—that results from busting unions, ruining farmers, squeezing out small business, stifling minority enterprise, shrinking people's paychecks and shutting the escape hatch on the poor.

We might as well say out loud, then, what a growing number of people already know: America is headed straight for a new depression. The economic agenda of the Reagan/Bush years produced one of the quickest and most regressive redistributions of wealth in US history. For all its impassioned rhetoric about removing government as a force in our financial affairs, the Reagan/Bush government injected itself more

enthusiastically into the economy than any administration since Lyndon Johnson's Great Society. Indeed, the Reagan/Bush administration took so much money from the pockets of middle- and lower-income Americans and shoved it up to the wealthiest 10 percent in our society that a top-heavy structure now threatens to come crashing down on us.

The nation is in a deeper hole than most realize. It is not merely that a few hapless souls are having hard times or that a few badly managed firms are succumbing to "free market realities." American families are being pulled down in the swirl of this economic decline:

- Since 1981, more than 620,000 productive farm families (20 percent

Susan Demarco, a public policy analyst who lives in Austin, established and directed the economic development programs of the Texas Department of Agriculture. **Jim Hightower** is the elected Texas Commissioner of Agriculture and founder of the Texas Populist Alliance.

of the total) have been put out of business.

- The rate of small business failures has jumped dramatically in the 1980's, with 56,000 going under in 1986 alone.

- From the end of World War II until 1981, only 170 banks failed in the United States, but 621 banks failed from 1981 to 1988, with the number of failures increasing sharply every year.

- An estimated 12 million Americans lost jobs since 1981 as a result of plant closings and layoffs. For those laid off, there is only a 62 percent chance of finding another job within a year.

- More than 44 percent of the new jobs created in our economy during the eighties pay less than $7,400 a year— 35 percent less than a poverty-level income for a family of four.

- The number of Americans having to work in jobs paying the $3.35-an-hour minimum wage ($6,968 a year) grew from 5.1 million in 1981 to 7.8 million in 1987.

- Since 1979, there has been an increase of 35 percent in the number of families with children living in poverty.

To understand how this mess developed and to find our way out, we must come to grips politically with a vital subject that slipped from the center of our political discourse after about 1940: the undemocratic spread of America's wealth.

In 1976, the wealthiest 1 percent of America's families owned 19.2 percent of the nation's total wealth. By 1983, those at this 1 percent tip of our economy owned 34.3 percent of our wealth. Since each 1 per-

cent of this wealth represents more than $100 billion, even fractional shifts up or down the scale make significant differences.

It had taken more than 50 years of historic struggle by citizens' groups—pushing the New Deal, Fair Deal, New Frontier and Great Society—to reduce the total wealth owned by the top families from the estimated 36 percent share they clutched before the Depression to the "more democratic" share inherited by Mr. Reagan. But, in a historic blink, Washington wiped out the struggles of half a century, altering the rules governing taxes, spending and interest rates to move an unprecedented share of America's money up the economic ladder. Today, the top 1 percent of Americans possesses more net wealth than the bottom 90 percent.

Like Willie Sutton, who explained that he robbed banks because that's where the money is kept, the Reagan/Bush team's first move was on the public treasury. The 1981 and 1986 tax bills turned the US tax code into a front-end loader for the truly rich, cutting their ostensible tax rate from 70 percent in 1981 to 28 percent in 1988, which is the same rate now assessed to most of the middle class. These two bills have effectively eliminated America's 60-year commitment to progressive taxation.

The skewing of the tax code was done, as such things usually are, under the rubric of doing something for everyone. Most of us, however, actually received much less of a reduction in our income taxes than we imagined, thanks to the fact that our social security taxes, which are extremely regressive, were quietly hiked even before the presidential signature dried on the loudly touted tax-cut bill. It was the wealthiest who made the real gains.

The greatest contortions of the tax code were engineered for the benefit of the country's largest corporations. The 1981 tax bill so skewed fairness that some hugely profit-

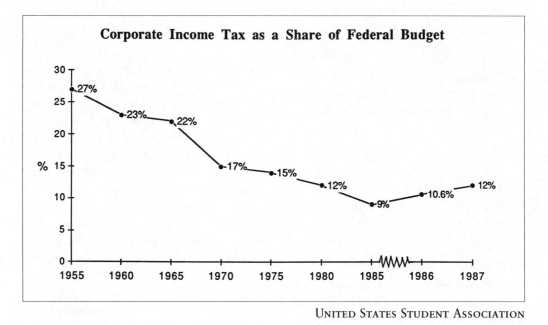

Corporate Income Tax as a Share of Federal Budget

UNITED STATES STUDENT ASSOCIATION

able conglomerates were paying a lower effective tax rate than a typical $16,000-a-year worker on one of their production lines. Tax gimmicks were stuck into the code like private beer taps in a huge keg, draining hundreds of millions of dollars in tax benefits that flowed mainly to the largest one-tenth of a single percent of America's corporations. Among the biggest beneficiaries were Dow Chemical, General Electric, PepsiCo, ITT, Boeing, Tenneco and Texaco, corporate citizens that used these gimmicks so successfully between 1981 and 1984 that they avoided federal income taxes altogether—even though the average profit of these firms was $2.9 billion.

In 1960, corporations shouldered 23 percent of the federal tax burden. Their share dwindled to 12.5 percent by 1980, and the Reagan/Bush program shrank it to 6.9 percent by 1986, saving the corporate sector—and costing the individual taxpayers—$120 billion in that year alone. Once again federal policy moved money from the bottom and middle of our economic ladder toward the top.

In the Mexican-American communities of South Texas, there is a saying that richly expresses the responsibility facing us today: "El dinero es como el abono; de nada sirve si no se desparrama," which translates roughly as "Money is like manure; it does no good unless it is spread."

Just as Reagan and Bush did for the wealthiest of Americans, we must now get our hands dirty in the mechanics of wealth distribution on behalf of the rest of Americans. Three rudimentary levers of governmental power are used to direct the flow of wealth: tax policy, spending policy and credit policy. To achieve any real and lasting progress toward economic growth and economic democracy, we must be willing to yank these policy levers into position so that (1) the wealthy finally begin to pay their fair share of taxes; (2) rational new public spending is initiated to restore the country's economic infrastructure; and (3) the central banking system is brought under democratic control. Progressive taxation, productive spending and democratization of credit—those are the three keys to economic justice and grassroots prosperity.

Often when activist groups or politicians propose programs to cure obvious ailments in the economy, they are dismissed with this deadly question: "Oh yeah, where you gonna get the money from?" The answer is: "Get it from where it went!" Having squandered their opportunity to foster real economic growth, the wealthy now must surrender their tax breaks so that those with the desire to invest talent and labor in our economy will have the opportunity to do so. A tax system with genuinely progressive rates, requiring the major corporations and the wealthiest families to meet their obligations, is central to America's ability to rebuild its productive capacity.

The fiscal tools of government, taxing and spending are always the subject of much political debate. But an equally powerful tool of wealth distribution—the secretive world of monetary policy—is rarely the subject of national debate and has been wrongly set above public control.

The formal structure for administering this power is the Federal Reserve System, which operates through a Washington-based seven-member board, 12 regional Reserve banks, and 6,000 commercial banks around the country. The Fed is the nation's central bank, a hybrid of a private, central banking system that has full governmental authority. The Fed described itself in 1939, oddly but accurately, as an "independent department" of government.

The attitude that "money matters" are best left to these specialists and kept above the hurly-burly of political debate must be challenged, because few decisions have as broad an effect on the public as do these money decisions. On a national level, the availability and cost of credit determines whether a strategy for industrial redevelopment can succeed. On a personal level, a decision to keep credit tight and interest rates high redistributes money up the economic ladder from borrowers to those who have the money to lend.

Participants in the Texas WIC (Women, Infants, Children) program using food stamps at the San Antonio Farmers Market.
KAREN DICKEY, TEXAS DEPT. OF AGRICULTURE

To democratize the creation and distribution of wealth, and fuel a grassroots surge of economic growth, we must loosen the Fed's oligarchic grip on the public's money supply. At the very least, the Fed must be opened to direct representation by much broader public interests than those of bankers, and its policies must be brought within the purview of the President and the Congress. Ways to widen participation include citizen membership (farmers, small business and labor) on the boards of all banks in the central system and popular election of these boards.

There should be Congressional oversight of the Fed's budget and policies as well. A more significant reform would be to make the Fed an integral part of the government's economic machinery, as most other nations do, by establishing it as a subdivision of the Treasury Department. Another path is to create an alternative credit system, using the money-creating power of the US government (which the Fed now monopolizes) to buy the bonds of farmer-owned, employee-owned, cooperative-owned or community-owned trusts in order to finance new capital ventures and spread ownership of wealth-creating enterprises.

Even the mildest of these reforms will elicit howls of protest, of course, and initiate a struggle of historic proportions. The control of our money supply is the greatest power that the wealthy have, and they are not about to relinquish it voluntarily so

Americans can have a more productive, more democratic economy. It would be a difficult fight, but the stakes are so high that the battle is worth waging.

We need to confront head-on this core issue of the control of wealth, unfurling the old banners and giving new spirit to the populist theme "Share the Wealth!" We must seek the widest possible sharing of America's wealth because it is the only true means of achieving full, productive participation in our economy, because it is the best way to restore prosperity to the whole country, and because it is the right thing to do.

ACTION*

1. **Urge your Congressional representatives to support progressive taxation,** forcing the wealthy to pay their share of the tax burden. Insist that they fight against industry protectionism and corporate tax exemptions.

2. **Actively participate in your union and/ or support the unionizing efforts of other workers.** The historical and continued effort of the labor movement is the reason that we now have a five-day, 40-hour work week, health benefits and workers' compensation for injuries on the job. Yet many employees still do not have even these minimal rights. We need to address the democratization of unions, and advocate solidarity between communities and unions in order to gain control over our own lives. Communities should decide what will be produced and how.

3. **Demand popular election of the boards of all banks in the central system** and the representation of labor, farmers and small business.

4. **Insist on a minimum wage that keeps all workers above the poverty level.** Some activists suggest a *maximum wage* of $100,000 per year as a way of approaching economic equity. Those who think this outrageous should reflect on the absurdity of an economic system that allows a talk show host to earn a million dollars a year while other full-time workers live below the poverty level.

5. **Require that rents be determined by community control** and that they reflect a percentage of individual income. No one should pay more than 25 percent of their monthly income for rent.

*Action section by Brad Erickson

Co-ops: Democratic Alternatives to Business as Usual

BOB SCHILDGEN

"Capitalism is the extraordinary belief that the nastiest of men for the nastiest of reasons will somehow work for the benefit of us all."

—JOHN MAYNARD KEYNES

COOPERATIVES PROVIDE ALTERNATIVES for creating more equitable income distribution and bringing democratic control to any field in which the cooperative method is applied. They are economic democracy in action because they provide democratic ownership and control of assets, something that is glaringly absent from the US economy.

One-half of one percent of the families in the US own over 25 percent of the wealth. The top 10 percent possess over 65 percent of the wealth. The *control* of assets is completely out of the hands of most shareholders. For example, workers holding the billions of dollars worth of stock owned and held by pension funds, have no voice in the policies of companies in which they own shares. In cooperatives, the people who own them also govern them on a one-person, one-vote democratic basis.

Co-ops can exist in virtually any form of endeavor in which people wish to use them: retail stores, food supply, housing, wholesale, medicine, electric power, financial service, marketing, manufacturing, nursery schools, the arts—even cable television co-ops and cooperative funeral societies. Co-ops range in size from tiny natural food stores or worker co-ops of a half dozen members to nationally-known marketing giants, such as Sunkist, Sun Maid and Blue Diamond. Credit unions, which have over 50 million members nationwide, are financial cooperatives. Ten million people in the rural US are served by electrical co-

Co-op authority **Bob Schildgen** is author of *Toyohiko Kagawa: Apostle of Love and Social Justice,* a biography of Japan's famed co-op organizer. In 1987-88, he was Co-op Scholar-in-Residence at Oberlin College. He has also served as editor of *Co-op News,* the weekly publication of the Consumers Cooperative of Berkeley.

operatives, which were formed by farmers themselves when private companies refused to serve rural areas, claiming it wasn't profitable.

Regardless of the type, size or ideology of individual cooperatives, what they all have in common is that they give members economic and social power that they would never have if they acted merely as individuals.

Underlying the specific economic activities of a cooperative is a philosophy of human solidarity, with an emphasis on working together for the common good rather than accumulating excessive wealth for private gain. Because of this philosophy, it is not surprising that some cooperatives have taken leadership roles in consumer and environmental protection, and other reforms. In Japan, for example, which has some of the world's largest and strongest co-ops, the cooperative movement is also a leader in the peace movement. In the Scandinavian countries, where cooperatives do about 20 percent of the retail trade, these businesses have led the way in providing pure food and more environmentally sound methods of distribution and packaging.

Cooperatives are owned and controlled by the people who use them, rather than by outside shareholders as in a conventional capitalist enterprise. The co-op has a dual nature as both a business and a membership organization, founded and capitalized by the members it serves. For example, in a cooperative such as REI, a major outdoor goods supplier, the members provide the funds to set up and maintain the business by purchasing shares, as in any other business. (Generally, there is a limit on the number of shares any individual may own—this is to keep any individual from "taking over" the co-op, which would run counter to the democratic purpose of cooperatives.) If there are net earnings at the end of the fiscal year, the co-op may return this money to the members in the form of a "patronage refund"—a rebate based on the percentage of the total amount of patronage the individual member has done with the cooperative. Or the co-op may invest in new co-op or other activities selected by the members. Or it may use revenue to offer products or services unavailable elsewhere. Therefore, instead of going to outside shareholders, these earnings are recycled to the members.

The other most important feature of the co-op is democratic control. Boards are elected on a one-person, one-vote basis. This means that the poorest individual has as much voice in the cooperative as the most wealthy, the person with five shares has as much voice as the person with five thousand. In a conventional business, votes are based on the number of shares owned. The more shares owned, the more votes. In a cooperative, governance is based not on the amount of assets you own, but on what you as a person want and need from the co-op.

Because of these features, the co-op is oriented toward giving service to members rather than profiting from customers. Members expect the co-op to satisfy their economic and social needs rather than the needs of investors. Co-ops are, as Ralph Nader has said, "buyer sovereign" rather than "seller sovereign."

What follows are just a few examples of some of the many types of cooperatives in the US alone. (There are more than 500 million co-op members worldwide.)

Food Co-ops. Anyone interested in changing our wasteful, environmentally unsound and anti-farmer food distribution system should look to food cooperatives. The ruling idea in food co-ops is "Food for People, Not for Profit."

In Oberlin, Ohio, the Good Foods Co-op is run from the basement of a student housing cooperative. Unlike a giant supermarket, with its huge overhead, Muzak and

Zimbabwe co-op members work their fields. Since independence in 1980, the government of Zimbabwe has implemented reforms including paying higher prices for crops, assistance to small farmers and providing fertilizer—resulting in a massive increase in food output, self-sufficiency in basic food crops—and has redistributed land to tens of thousands of peasant families. Anna Zieminski, 1987, Impact Visuals

10,000 products, Good Foods carries a simple inventory of basic foods and is open a few hours a week, staffed by members, who get healthful food at slightly over wholesale prices. They save money by avoiding the "supermarket trap," where the store design and marketing techniques are set up to tempt people to spend the maximum amount (notice, for example, the massive array of junk food at the checkout counter). Small co-ops literally created the natural foods movement by their refusal to carry overprocessed, overpackaged, and over-priced items.

But food co-ops can also come in the form of larger, supermarket-sized stores, such as the North Coast Co-op, a four-store chain in northern California. This co-op puts out a newspaper full of consumer information and ideas on how to eat better for less.

Food co-ops like North Coast influence public policy by educating members on a host of issues, from sound nutrition to workers' rights. Because so many of the products sold may be environmentally hazardous or produced by exploited workers, the co-op is in a perfect position to call attention to such abuses. The Consumers Cooperative of Berkeley—often called "the store with a conscience"—was a significant factor in shaping Berkeley's famed activism, simply because of the information it presented at the point of sale and through publications, guest speakers, forums, etc. Members became more aware than any other group of consumers in the United States about questions such as farm workers' attempts to organize, the threat to dolphins from tuna netting and the dangers of pesticides.

Credit Unions. Financial co-ops with boards of directors elected on a one-person, one-vote basis, credit unions often give more favorable terms of interest on loans, deposits and checking accounts than do banks. They also recycle money in the community of members, rather than allowing it to be siphoned away. The credit union's "profits" are redistributed among the members rather than sent to shareholders, as in a conventional bank. Credit unions avoid questionable banking practices, such as inserting hidden charges on checking accounts or making loans to irresponsible leaders in debt-stricken nations. Credit unions emphasize keeping capital within a community or group, to help improve the quality of life of ordinary people.

Housing Cooperatives. Cooperatively owned apartments can give low- and middle-income people control over housing which ordinary tenants seldom enjoy. The member of a cooperative housing project is not subjected to constant increases in rent: the monthly payment remains stable, like a mortgage. With ownership comes a sense of empowerment, rather than the alienation tenants feel when they are victimized by a landlord. The most promising type of housing cooperative, the "limited equity" co-op, puts an upper limit on the price someone moving out can charge for their stake. This helps prevent speculation, a major factor in driving up the cost of housing. (Millions of people are forced to spend over half their income merely for shelter.)

Related to the housing cooperative is the concept of "co-housing," where people share common kitchens, laundry facilities, gardens and so forth. This approach is far more efficient than the typical single-family housing, which underutilizes both space and equipment.

Student housing cooperatives have been shown to save students a thousand dollars a year or more in their rental and food costs, compared to dormitories or private housing. They can also provide students with a sense of community and valuable experience participating in a democratic organization.

Worker Cooperatives. In a worker-owned cooperative, the individual employees are also the owners: they hold the controlling interest in the company and hire the management. There is considerably more equity in pay in a worker cooperative than in a hierarchical corporation, and job satisfaction and morale are heightened because workers have far more control over their work. As owners of the enterprise, workers take a direct interest in its efficient operation; there is often less of the middle management that burdens a typical corporation.

Few people realize that 10 percent of the plywood produced in the US comes from worker cooperatives in the Pacific Northwest. Studies show that these co-ops are generally more profitable and efficient than the competition. In Philadelphia, stores from the A&P chain were bought out by the employees and converted into a successful chain, O&O—standing for Owned and Operated (by the workers).

Perhaps the most outstanding worker cooperatives in the world today are those of the Mondragon group in the Basque region of Spain. Organized in the 1950's, the organization has grown to a democratically owned and -controlled group of factories manufacturing heating units, appliances and electronic equipment with 20,000 member-owners and sales of over a billion dollars a year. These cooperatives outperform similar industries in the area. One of the reasons for its rapid development is a mechanism that puts earnings from the co-ops into a bank also owned by the members. The worker-controlled funds in this bank are used to capitalize new cooperative enterprises.

These are merely a few of the ways in which cooperatives can be applied by those who seek solutions to economic and social problems caused by business as usual.

ACTION*

1. **Find and support co-ops.** Think of co-ops first when you do business. Wherever you live, seek out the local cooperatives, join and patronize them. Remember, although co-ops are alternative businesses, they still need strong, loyal patronage to be successful.

   If possible, become active in the co-ops you are part of. Co-ops benefit from an involved membership.

   - The smaller co-ops, such as local food co-ops, child care co-ops, buying clubs, and worker co-ops sometimes require a bit of research to find. But locating them can be exciting and will link you up with other activists. Once you make some contacts in the co-op world, you will begin to learn about all the co-ops in your area.

   - See if there is a credit union you are eligible to join. These are often sponsored by a specific union, employee group or other organization.

   - Consider starting your own co-op on a small scale, such as a buying club for food.

   - Investigate the possibilities of cooperative housing or co-housing as lower-cost, more sociable alternatives to renting or buying single-family units.

   - Support worker-owned businesses. Determine whether your workplace or business would benefit from being worker-owned and -controlled.

   - Encourage solidarity among cooperatives.

2. **Challenge exploitive business practices and business as usual.** Question the corporate right to surplus profit. Monopolized economic control by a wealthy minority violates the right of the economically disenfranchised to adequate food, housing, education and medical care.

   - Push for the democratization of economic power and control. Who decides what our economy produces? Who determines whether it is investment or production based? Who decides who can make profits and how much?

   - Support unions as workers struggle for control over their working conditions and terms.

   - Support women's efforts for wage parity and equality in society.

   - Support people's challenges to corporate poisoning and destruction of the Earth, and the waste of our limited common natural resources.

   - Resist the military/industrial complex. Join INFACT's boycott of General Electric.

   - Explore the idea of transforming giant multinationals into co-ops.

*Action section by Bob Schildgen and Brad Erickson

Homelessness

DAVID LYLE LIGHT SHIELDS

"Poverty is the parent of revolution and crime."
—ARISTOTLE

HOMELESS AMERICANS, whose very existence reveals the inhumanity of the current economic policy, are everywhere—sleeping on steam vents in big cities, living in old cars in the suburbs, walking the dusty roads of rural America. Their numbers are officially (under)estimated at about 300,000. The actual number is closer to 3 million. The numbers would be higher still if homeless children did not die at an alarming rate.

During the 1980's, the homeless population increased at an average of almost 30 percent a year, as measured by demand for emergency housing. Such a rate of inflation would galvanize the public and rivet the attention of policy-makers if the numbers referred to dollars and not people. Who are these homeless citizens? Consider the following facts:

- About half the homeless are single men; 15-20 percent are single women. About a third are families.

- In most areas, young children are the fastest growing segment of the homeless population.

- Almost a third of the homeless are veterans.

- One third are mentally ill. Some hit the streets with a history of mental problems, others developed symptoms from life on the streets.

- Homelessness is probably our nation's most successful affirmative-action recruiter: the homeless are a rainbow of minority and white women and men, girls and boys.

David Shields is the Director of the Hunger Action Center at Unitas, a Christian campus ministry at the University of California at Berkeley and a lecturer in the Peace and Conflict Studies Program there.

■ One in five homeless persons holds a job, half have high school diplomas and more than one in four have attended college.

In addition to the indisputably homeless, there are the marginally housed, those living part of each month in welfare hotels and low-rent apartments, those shifting from the couch of one relative to the cot of another. There are the elderly on fixed incomes who live with the constant fear of eviction as neighborhoods gentrify.

The effects of homelessness are debilitating. Health care for everyday problems such as headaches, diarrhea and sore throats is nonexistent. Dental care is rare. More serious health problems, such as circulatory diseases and malnutrition, are common, yet largely unattended.

Homeless toddlers lag behind their peers in such developmental milestones as learning to walk and talk; many children attend school only sporadically. Homelessness is devastating to self-esteem, and most of the homeless struggle with depression and anxiety.

In addition, the civil rights of the homeless are often violated, many having suffered from illegal evictions, sexual harassment and crime. Homeless shelters are frequently run like prison camps.

The homeless face myriad obstacles to re-entering housed society. They must find a job, but they have nowhere to clean up and no phone number and address to leave a prospective employer. They must search for housing, for which they need first and last months' rent plus cleaning deposit. Often they must spend hours walking from one meal program to another just to eat. On top of these tasks, there are the daily strains of a disrupted family life, the frustrations of trying to work with the bureaucracy of the welfare system from which they receive precious little assistance, and the swelling feelings of guilt and shame, reinforced by the cold shoulder received from the general public.

Causes of Homelessness

The situation of the homeless may be likened to an image created in an amusement park mirror with Uncle Sam standing in front of it. They reflect in distorted and exaggerated ways the economic and social realities of our nation. All the homeless share two realities: poverty and a convergent lack of support from family, friends and government.

Poverty is a relative term. The ability of poor people to purchase a house or make rent payments is relative to the cost of those commodities, which, in turn, is influenced by the purchasing power of those with greater financial resources.

The trend since 1980 has been an increasing gap between the rich and poor. The wealthiest 0.5 percent of the population controls more than a third of the nation's net wealth; the bottom 90 percent controls only 28 percent. The gap between rich and poor is wider now than at any point since 1947, when the Census Bureau first began collecting these data. Furthermore, the income of the typical poor family is further below the poverty line than ever before.

In addition, financial assistance to the poor has declined. In constant dollars, benefits declined 33 percent between 1970 and 1986.

While the poor have been getting poorer, the real costs of owning a home have skyrocketed. Housing costs soared above the rate of general inflation by 65 percent between 1973 and 1982. The total cost burden for first-time home buyers, measured as a percent of the income of young renters,

Haight Street, 1988. PAUL WHITEHEAD

rose from 14.3 percent in 1973 to 37.4 percent in 1982. Currently, the rate of home ownership is at its lowest level in 15 years.

Costs of rental housing also have climbed substantially. Adjusting for inflation, average rents in 1987 were 12 percent higher than they were in 1973. More importantly, the ratio of rent to income has increased substantially. In 1974 heads of households aged 25 to 34 paid about 19 percent of their income for rent; in 1987 the same group paid 26 percent of their income for rent. In the latter part of the 1980's nearly half of all poor renter households paid at least 70 percent of their income for housing.

Ironically, federal backing for low-income housing decreased as housing costs increased. Since 1981, federal support for activities to help replenish the shrinking stock of low-rent housing has been cut by more than two-thirds. In a recent study, the US Conference of Mayors found that the average waiting period for assisted housing is 18 months; over two-thirds of the 23 cities surveyed had closed the waiting lists.

Not all poor people, of course, are homeless. Some are able to afford the housing that is available. Many others, at least for a time, are able to avoid the streets by doubling or tripling up with relatives. In New York City, for example, there are an estimated 100,000 "couch people" camped in the living rooms of family members or friends.

The poor who end up on the street either have no family or community to turn to for support or they have exhausted these resources. Disaffiliation is a distinguishing mark of the homeless.

Some of the homeless are former patients in mental institutions. In 1955, about 560,000 people lived in public mental hospitals. By 1980, that number had dropped to about 120,000 as part of the effort to de-institutionalize the mentally ill in favor of treatment in community settings. But the money never followed the former patients out into the community as intended. Furthermore, community health centers were ill-prepared to deal with issues of housing and jobs, or to train people to adapt to independent living.

Of course, there are less tangible but perhaps even more important causes of homelessness. The policy choices that have led to rampant housing speculation, escalat-ing incomes for the rich and declining support for the poor are rooted in value perspectives that blame the victims for their troubles. People are homeless because in our rich nation we have placed the rights and privileges of the wealthy above the basic needs of the most vulnerable. People are homeless because those with homes have developed a callousness to those on the streets, viewing them as a different class or breed of human being from themselves. Attitudes and values are as important in defining the causes of homelessness as policies and economics.

ACTION*

The multiple problems of homelessness need to be dealt with concurrently. Emergency shelter is needed, but shelters must not be allowed to become permanent institutions. A united effort by the government, the private sector and the public must focus on affordable housing, economic support for the poor, job training with related support services such as childcare and adult literacy programs, and adequately funded community-based mental health systems.

Here are some ideas of how you can get involved:

1. **Volunteer time at a local homeless shelter.** Many non-profit and religious organizations operate shelters or soup kitchens and need volunteer assistance. Through your work, you may get to know homeless people personally, relationships you will find enriching and valuable.

2. **Find out what is being done about homelessness in your community.**

Check with your city and county governments, church and synagogue leaders, private service organizations, and emergency meal providers. Ask each person what is currently being done to assist the homeless and what needs are going unmet. Share these findings with the groups and organizations to which you belong. Ask how they can get involved.

- **Find out what is being done in your community about low-income housing.** Are special tax advantages given to first-time home buyers? Does your community have rent control?

- **Organize a business/homeless cooperative program** where business people hire homeless people to clean up the streets, do odd jobs and skill-building jobs.

3. **Write to your Congressional representative** and Senators, urging support

*Action section by David Shields

for legislation that benefits the homeless. Contact the National Coalition for the Homeless (202/659-3310) for current information on federal legislative efforts.

4. **Generate popular support.**

   ■ Arrange to have homeless persons, or those who work with the homeless, talk to organizations to which you belong.

   ■ Check with local school principals and school boards to see if homeless issues are dealt with in school curricula. If not, encourage them to sponsor speakers in the schools.

   ■ Contact local television and radio stations. Ask them to air a program on the homeless. Ask if you might make a public service announcement.

   ■ Write a letter to the editor of your local newspaper inviting others to join you in working on the homeless issue.

The Impact of AIDS

PATRICIA CASE

"In *societal* terms, compassion must be seen as the collective will and political acts that bring about resources, structures, institutions, behaviors, and norms directed at the care of the sick, the prevention of illness, and the promotion of health."

—GERALD FRIEDLAND, M.D.

I T IS THE ACTS of compassion that are so compelling in the midst of the AIDS epidemic. In the face of the most hateful combinations of contempt, deliberate neglect, and outright denial, there have been individual and collective actions that have forced public health policy somewhat in the direction of a compassionate approach to treatment and prevention of AIDS. However, in the face of an epidemic of this magnitude, much more will be required in the years to come, to reverse the criminal neglect of this medical emergency and social disaster.

The virus knows no borders. Acquired Immune Deficiency Syndrome (AIDS), a consequence of viral infection by Human Immunodeficiency Virus (HIV), is an emerging global pandemic. The numbers worldwide are chilling. As of March, 1989, 146,569 actual AIDS cases were reported to the World Health Organization (WHO), with as many as 10 to 50 percent of AIDS cases going unreported, for a variety of reasons. Recent data from researchers in San Francisco suggest that the median time from infection with the virus to onset of AIDS is eight to ten years. Thus, even if all new infection were to stop today, the cumulative AIDS cases would increase each day for perhaps another twenty years.

There are as many as 10 million people infected with HIV worldwide and WHO estimates that 1 million people will develop AIDS by 1991. The United States has over half of the AIDS cases reported, but a num-

Patricia Case is a member of Prevention Point, an unsanctioned needle exchange program in San Francisco that is concerned with preventing transmission of HIV between intravenous drug users.

Visitors to the Names Project quilt, which commemorates victims of AIDS, on display at Capitol Mall in Washington, DC. MARCEL MIRANDA III, 1988

ber of African and Caribbean countries have serious epidemics. The Bahamas, for example, reports 1,345 cases per million population, and the Congo reports 595 cases per million. Unless current rates of infection can be slowed, the future of this epidemic in some African countries holds a toll large enough among the 20-49 year-old age group that economic, social and political destabilization will result.

Here in the United States, AIDS has primarily affected gay men but threatens many communities with deadly efficiency. In New York City, particularly hard hit by the epidemic, AIDS is the now leading cause of death for women of childbearing age. One out of every 61 babies born there is HIV infected. In the United States, over 80 per cent of heterosexual intravenous drug users (IVDUs) with AIDS are people of color and 70 percent of the women with AIDS are Black or Latina. It is the vicious combina-

tion of racism and classism that has worked to make services, education, health care, and drug treatment less available or accessible to people of color, placing those communities at far greater risk.

As the dimensions of the epidemic emerged, it became clear that a massive, internationally organized public health effort would be necessary to stem the rising tide of the epidemic.

Yet precisely the opposite occurred. In industrialized nations, political and ideological agendas have taken priority over the public health effort. In the United States, the current and previous administrations have been so preoccupied with a moralistic approach to gay men and IV drug users that the development of vitally needed AIDS prevention programs that have been demonstrated to reduce the behaviors that transmit the lethal virus has been slowed or thwarted. It is bitter hypocrisy that in a climate of "just say no" to drugs, treatment programs are so underfunded that those seeking treatment must wait from six weeks to two years for a publicly funded treatment slot.

There are endless examples of the government's inability to act with compassion, one of the most notable being the Food and Drug Administration's heartless approach to possible new treatments, requiring lengthy experimental trials before licensing drugs for use. Thousands of people may have died because of the withholding of new treatments. In addition, the prohibitive profits being reaped by the pharmaceutical companies for those few drugs that may slow the course of the disease has kept needed treatment from countless others.

Solutions, both effective and ineffective, are being attempted in countries all over the world. Mandatory testing and quarantine is often proposed as a solution. Cuba, for example, quarantines indefinitely every person infected with the virus as soon as detected, in conjunction with mandatory testing of all adults. By June 1988, 268 persons were being held in a hospital in Havana. In South Korea, where selective quarantine is lawful, 23 people have been forcibly interned. Other countries that can impose selective quarantine on certain HIV-infected individuals are South Africa, the Soviet Union, Iceland, Sweden, and the West German state of Bavaria. In the United States, 13 states require forced testing of anyone charged with or convicted of prostitution and many prisons require testing of prisoners and separation of those who test positive. In addition, many state legislatures are considering laws that will impose some form of quarantine. Since a person with AIDS does not present a risk to the community through contagion or casual contact, the only effect of quarantine policy is to create a coercive legal situation that keeps people from being tested or treated for the consequences of the disease.

In contrast to programs of mandatory testing and quarantine, other countries have launched AIDS education programs. Culturally appropriate prevention messages are being distributed in many countries. Nicaragua implemented an AIDS education program in 1987. Despite some cultural attitudes of homophobia there, Nicaragua has actively included gays and lesbians in the development of the program. Health educators are conducting safer sex workshops, and explicit safer sex information is being printed in the newspapers. Because there are no funds for blood testing, the extent of HIV infection in Nicaragua is largely unknown. However, similar intensive AIDS education programs in San Francisco have reduced the rate of new infection among gay men to less than 1 percent.

For intravenous drug users, one route of infection is the sharing of blood-contaminated drug injection equipment. Logically, an AIDS prevention program that supplies condoms, and bleach for needle cleaning, would also provide clean injection equipment. The Netherlands, Australia, Norway, Sweden, Great Britain, Canada, and most recently, Warsaw, Poland have instituted needle exchange programs as a part of an AIDS prevention program. There is evidence from many programs that needle exchange has reduced the sharing of contaminated syringes and prevented transmission of HIV and other blood-borne diseases. Yet, in the United States, 33 states have laws that make it a crime to possess a needle without a prescription. This does not block access to needles by IVDUs, only access to sterile ones. In states with legal obstacles to needle exchange, several "unsanctioned" needle exchanges, where a IVDU can exchange a used syringe for a sterile one, have started. Needle exchange is not a crime in the face of a fatal epidemic.

While it is not realistic to assume that we can easily affect the international, global response to AIDS, we can and must exert ourselves to change what we can in our own communities. There are many local issues in this global emergency. Our own government is responsible for dragging its feet through the first eight years of the epidemic because those primarily affected were stigmatized populations. Volunteerism and private initiative, while necessary and commendable, cannot possibly address an epidemic of this magnitude. The tax dollars that should have been directed to compassionate public health efforts have instead financed our military expansion. The government must change its priorities and policies. AIDS is an epidemic that has been fueled largely by lies and a deadly silence. This silence must be broken.

"Silence = Death, Action = Life"

ACT-UP

ACTION*

Individual Actions. Create an atmosphere of openness in which you and your friends can talk about safer sex and drug use. Don't assume that your friends who use IV drugs are going to stop—non-judgmentally encourage them to use good needle hygiene. Always include young people in your conversations about AIDS.

- Keep a bowl of condoms in your bathroom. Suggest to the management of your favorite restaurant that they install a condom vending machine in *both* the men's and women's restrooms.

- Volunteer to be a practical or emotional support person for someone with AIDS. Cooking dinner for someone once a week can mean a lot.

Letter Campaigns. Write to your representatives, House of Representatives, Washington, DC 20515, and Senators, Senate, Washington, DC 20515, urging them to:

- Provide as part of foreign aid, funding for AIDS education and prevention materials and supplies.

- Institute a national health care system, one that will guarantee access to health care for all, including HIV-affected individuals.

- Write legislation that prohibits discrimination against those who are HIV positive in employment, insurance, housing, education, and health care.

- Provide experimental treatment and drugs to *all* HIV-affected individuals who desire them, provided full disclosure of potential risks and the experimental nature of the treatment has been made.

- End all placebo trials (experiments where some get potentially life-saving treatments and some don't).

- Provide sufficient funding for drug treatment programs so that drug treatment on demand is available to anyone who desires it.

- Take responsibility for and fund a national comprehensive program that will reduce HIV transmission by

* Action section by Patricia Case

needle-sharing—a program that includes education, needle exchange, outreach programs and treatment on demand. These programs must be culturally appropriate and accessible to IV drug users.

- Urge them to repeal needle possession laws and to oppose quarantine measures for any group.

- Write to the editor of your newspaper any time a story appears that attempts to target any group—gays, IV drug users, prostitutes—for the "spread" of AIDS or that talks about "innocent victims" or the "general population." Language such as this perpetuates fear and prejudice.

Generate Popular Support/Direct Action. Start a food bank, housework group, or other practical support service for persons with AIDS.

- Join an AIDS activist group, such as ACT UP, or start one. Participate in demonstrations and civil disobedience actions that will force change in prevailing attitudes, laws, and funding policies.

- Time is of the essence. If local authorities are dragging their feet on necessary programs, do direct action. If your community doesn't have a needle exchange program, start one and demand the Public Health Department take it over.

RESOURCES

Organizations

AIDS Coalition to Unleash Power (ACT UP)
2300 Market Street, Suite 68
San Francisco, CA 94114
(415) 563-0724

Activist-oriented coalition of people working for the rights of those infected with AIDS and AIDS-related diseases. They endorse and organize actions such as "die-ins" (to publicize the lack of government spending on AIDS research), provide networking for individuals working on the issues of treatment, housing and government spending. They publish a newsletter and participate in local gay-awareness events.

ACT NOW (AIDS Coalition to Network, Organize and Win)
2300 Market Street, Suite 87
San Francisco, CA 94114
(415) 861-7505

A national network of approximately 40 AIDS action organizations in the US. Educates, agitates and organizes to fight to end the epidemic and empower people living with AIDS. To receive their national newsletter contact: ACT-UP, LA, P.O. Box 26601, Los Angeles, CA 90026.

Center on Budget and Policy Priorities
236 Massachusetts Avenue NE, Suite 305
Washington, DC 20002
(202) 544-0591

Puts out frequent reports on the national budget, poverty data and other topics of special interest to the poor. A reliable source of information and analysis about what is happening in Washington to poverty programs.

Clearinghouse on Homelessness Among Mentally Ill People (CHAMP)
8630 Fenton Street, Suite 300
Silver Spring, MD 20910
(301) 588-5484

Clearinghouse of information about the segment of the homeless population that suffers from chronic mental illness.

Community for Creative Non-Violence
1345 Euclid Street NW
Washington, DC 20009
(202) 393-4409

A religiously based group that focuses on direct service to the homeless, along with public education and political activism. Homeless advocate Mitch Snyder is an active member of CCNV.

Co-op America
2100 M Street NW, Suite 310
Washington, DC 20063
(202) 872-5307

A member-controlled and worker-managed association linking socially responsible businesses and consumers in a national alternative marketplace. Services include an insurance program, travel program and boycott information. Their publication is Building Economic Alternatives.

Credit Union National Association
5710 Mineral Point Road
Madison, WI 53705
(608) 231-4000

A national trade association for the credit union movement in the US, representing 91 percent of all credit unions in the nation. They provide lobbying and legislative representation in Washington, public relations assistance, publications, education and training in economics and business. The CUNA has publications on credit, investment and money management for the layperson. They publish the monthly Credit Union Magazine *and the weekly* Credit Union Newswatch. *The quarterly* Everybody's Money *is intended for credit union members and provides money management tips and financial and consumer advice.*

Interfaith Action on Economic Justice
110 Maryland Avenue NE
Washington, DC 20010
(202) 543-2800 or (800) 424-7292

A Washington-based organization of Protestant, Jewish, Roman Catholic and other national religious agencies working to secure just and effective US food and agriculture, health and human services, and development and economic policies for the world's poor and hungry. It selects and sets public policy goals in these areas and develops and implements strategies to realize those goals. Currently, Interfaith is working with American farmers caught in the farm crisis. Their newsletter is Policy Notes.

Interfaith Center on Corporate Responsibility
475 Riverside Drive
New York, NY 10027
(212) 870-2293

An association of religious institutional investors who use their investments to hold US corporations responsible for their actions. They publish 10 issues a year of their periodical, Corporate Examiner. *Subscriptions are $35/year.*

International Labor Rights Education and Research Fund
110 Maryland Avenue NE
Washington, DC 20002
(202) 546-4304

A non-profit organization founded in 1986 to protect and promote the rights of workers around the world. Subscriptions to Labor Rights News *are $15 for individuals and $25 for organizations.*

Low Income Housing Information Service
1012 14th Street NW, Suite 1006
Washington, DC 20005
(202) 662-1530

Dedicated to research, education and technical assistance to end the low-income housing crisis. LIHIS's mission is to empower low-income people and organizations representing them.

National Association of Community Action Agency

1775 T Street NW
Washington, DC 20001
(202) 265-7546

Networks over 900 community action committees, providing self-help for low-income individuals in the form of training, technical assistance and professional development. They hold an annual conference and publish a newsletter.

National Association of Housing Cooperatives

1614 King Street
Alexandria, VA 22314
(703) 549-5201

A national federation of housing co-ops, private individuals and professional organizers promoting the institution of co-op housing communities. It is the only organization of its kind, and publishes the bimonthly Co-op Housing Bulletin *and the annual* Co-op Housing Journal.

National Association of People with AIDS

2025 I Street NW Suite 1118
Washington, DC 20006
(202) 429-2856

Provides technical assistance and information to affiliate groups and local coalitions organizing for local people with AIDS. Supports development of food banks, housing and AIDS litigation.

National Coalition for the Homeless

1439 Rhode Island Avenue
Washington, DC 20002
(202) 659-3310

Involved in research, education, legislative advocacy and litigation. Works in close cooperation with dozens of homeless programs across the country and can refer you to a local program. Publishes a monthly newsletter, Safety Network.

National Housing Task Force

1625 I Street NW, Suite 1015
Washington, DC 20006
(202) 964-1230

The NHTF was founded by James Rouse, a former real estate developer who has devoted his retirement years to the construction of low- and moderate-income housing. The task force has published A Decent Place to Live, *outlining a systematic approach to the housing crisis, building on the successes of the liberal approach to the problem.*

National Volunteer Clearinghouse for the Homeless

1310 Emerson Street NW
Washington, DC 20011

National center that matches volunteers with local providers who need assistance in providing food and shelter.

North American Students of Cooperation

P.O. Box 7715
Ann Arbor, MI 48107
(313) 663-0889

Promotes co-op housing for college students, as well as other types of co-ops on college campuses. Runs education and career programs for students seeking careers as co-op administrators. Their monthly newsletter, Newsbriefs, *is free for co-op members, and $35 to others.*

PACE of Philadelphia, Inc.

2100 Chestnut Street, 2nd Floor
Philadelphia, PA 19103
(215) 561-7079

A non-profit consulting firm providing legal, business and organizational development and other technical assistance services for the creation of employee-owned businesses and community-controlled organiza-

tions. Write for a publications list. Provides services throughout the US and Canada.

The Society For Women and AIDS in Africa

Dr. Fathia Mahmoud
P.O. Box 1598
Khartoum, Sudan

The society promotes health education and HIV prevention strategies for women in Africa.

Worker Owned Network

50 South Court Street
Athens, OH 45701
(614) 592-3854

A grassroots organization established to help organize and support businesses owned and operated by workers. WON provides services including computer sharing, and training in cooperative skills. It is developing a "Business Incubator," offering the fledgling business the above training opportunities as well as operating space at a reduced rate. They publish Network News *three times a year (available for a donation), and offer two training packets—an introduction to the worker-owned business, and a compendium of their training programs. These are available for $2 each.*

World Health Organization

Global Programme on AIDS, CH-1211
Geneva 27, Switzerland.

The United Nations agency that coordinates mobilization on AIDS, with 176 nations involved in the global AIDS reporting network, provides assistance to countries in establishing national AIDS programs, produces policy statements on topics such as breastfeeding and HIV and coordinates global AIDS research.

Periodicals

Cooperative Grocer
c/o WorkerOwned Network
50 South Court Street
Athens, OH 45701
(614) 592-3854

A bi-monthly trade journal for US food co-ops. Offers tips on everything from how to organize the floor plan of a co-op to how to serve on a board of directors.

Workplace Democracy
111 Draper Hall
University of Massachusetts
Amherst, MA 01003
(413) 545-4875

Provides a comprehensive overview of US trends in worker participation and ownership, and a forum for speaking on the issues.

Books

AIDS and the Third World. Renee Sabatier. Philadelphia, PA: New Society Publishers, 1989.

An excellent overview of the global dimensions of AIDS, and highly recommended as an introduction to those seeking an international viewpoint. Chapters on the scope of the pandemic, blame and prejudice, AIDS and the development dollar, and humanitarian issues.

AIDS: Cultural Analysis, Cultural Activism. Douglas Crimp, ed. Cambridge, MA: MIT Press, 1988.

Thought-provoking collection of essays on the meaning of AIDS, the assumptions about AIDS that have arisen, the language and images used in describing the epidemic. Useful to any AIDS activist thinking about issues beyond medical facts.

Blaming Others: Prejudice, Race and Worldwide AIDS. Renee Sabatier. London: Panos Publications, 1988.

A myth-busting book about fear, stigma and blame. Looks at virus origin theories, AIDS and race, and the importance of culturally appropriate prevention messages.

Corporate Crime and Violence: Big Business Power and the Abuse of the Public Trust. Russell Mokhiber. San Francisco: Sierra Club Books, 1988.

Includes short chapters describing corporate crimes including: Dow Chemical's Agent Orange, Union Carbide's incident at Bhopal and their dumping overseas of products banned in the US, and the tobacco companies' intensive advertising of a drug that is known to cause over a million deaths a year worldwide. The author proposes over 50 concrete ideas to make corporations more responsible to citizens and the environment, such as: prohibiting companies with criminal records from getting government contracts, licenses and grants; establishing stiffer penalties for convicted corporate executives; and keeping the press free of corporate control so as to avoid occurrences like GE's purchase of NBC.

Growing Beyond Prejudices. David Shields. Mystic, CT: Twenty-Third Publications, 1986.

Designed to help the educator, especially the religious educator, implement programs to address the prejudices of students. May be used effectively to overcome prejudices against the homeless.

Homelessness in America: A Forced March to Nowhere. Mary Ellen Hombs and Mitch Snyder. Washington, DC: Community for Creative Nonviolence, 1986.

A good, brief summary of the problems and roots of homelessness, together with proposals for eliminating it. Includes a state-by-state directory of organizations working with the homeless.

The Politics of AIDS. Nancy Krieger and Rose Appleman. Oakland, CA: Frontline, 1987.

Well-researched, lucid 60-page pamphlet on the politics of AIDS. Grounded in the United States, but includes an analysis of the international situation. ($4.80 post paid from Frontline Pamphlets, P.O. Box 2729, Oakland, CA 94602.)

Rachel and Her Children. Jonathan Kozol. New York: Crown Publishers, 1988.

A moving book that tells the story of a former nurse and mother of two who couldn't meet the mortgage and lost everything. Contains a helpful list of books and documents dealing with homelessness.

The Right to Housing: A Blueprint for Housing the Nation. The IPS Working Group on Housing with Dick Cluster. Washington, DC: Institute for Policy Studies, 1987.

Outlines a radical housing alternative to end homelessness, based on the creation of a "social housing" sector that would operate on a non-profit basis.

The Unsheltered Woman: Women and Housing in the 80's. Eugenie Ladner Birch, ed. New Brunswick, NJ: Center for Urban Policy Research, 1985.

Addresses the difficulties encountered by homeless women.

We the Homeless: Portraits of America's Displaced People. Stephenie Hollyman. New York: Philosophical Library, 1988.

A compelling collection of photographs by award-winning photojournalist Stephenie Hollyman.

The Big Boys.   Ralph Nader and William Taylor. New York: Pantheon Books, 1986.

The values and life stories of the chief executives of some major US corporations. A window into how these men choose to run their businesses and how their choices are shaped by the corporate culture and personal values. Profiles include Thomas Jones of Northrop, Whitney MacMillan of Cargill (who has a better and more extensive spy network than the CIA, which he uses to make money on grain trading, storing, and transporting), and William Norris of Control Data (who receives tax breaks for building factories in slums to employ the unemployed).

PART FIVE

HEALING THE EARTH

Rights for All Species
MIKE ROSELLE

"We are not frightened by the spectre of imprisonment in Siberia. We are frightened by the vision of a sterile ocean and a barren land, an Earth devoid of non-human life, an Earth without the songs of the whale and the birds, the trumpet of the elephant, the howl of the wolf and the sigh of the redwood in the wind.

"We are not scared of the Japanese exploding harpoons or the potshots of ignorant whalers armed with rifles. We are scared of doing nothing, of being apathetic, complacent and being guilty of ignoring the cries of mother Earth as she is raped, tortured, mutilated and wasted."

—PAUL WATSON, SEA SHEPHERD SOCIETY

---

1. **A legal right is recognized as such by law and is thereby protected from infringement.**

2. **The entity holding the right can seek legal protection on its own behalf.**

3. **The assertion of the rights should protect the entity from injury.**

4. **The relief the law provides should directly compensate the holder of the right.**

5. **Incapacity on the part of the holder of the right does not preclude a representative from protecting the best interests of the holder of the right.**

A SHIFT IN AWARENESS and perception has led many of us to the inevitable conclusion that justice solely for humans is a perverse distortion of any meaningful concept of justice. For those of us who see the world as a seamless web of life, the notion of legal rights for non-humans is hardly a far-fetched one. While the right of the natural world to continue three-and-a-half billion years of evolution without reckless interference may seem obvious, many ecologists and legal authorities today are expressing some doubts over the concept of giving legal rights to other species. This is due more to a failure to understand the evolving nature of legal institutions and a

"Grizzly" being read his rights at a Yellowstone action protesting development in grizzly habitat. DAVID CROSS, 1985

reluctance to break with conventional wisdom than with the limitations of the law itself.

When modern law speaks of rights, of course, it is speaking of human rights. Since most people don't extend their sense of community to include non-human life-forms, they think it preposterous to assume that bugs have rights just as they do. But modern *Homo sapiens,* like their predecessors the hunter-gatherer bands who populated the early Pleistocene landscape, are members of a broader community that includes all forms of life. Understanding fully our dependence on the entire biotic community for our livelihood is essential if the law is to do what it was created to do: protect the rights of all community members.

As every lawyer knows, personhood is a prerequisite to the conferring of legal rights. The significance of the efforts to identify "personhood" is that in actuality it represents an effort to separate human beings from the rest of the natural world. But even today, personhood is not exclusively bestowed on humans. Ships and corporations are now given standing as legal persons with the accompanying legal rights.

It may seem absurd to assume that legal rights for non-humans could be protected by a human jury and judge. Think about it in terms of the civil rights struggle in the American South: a black defendant could not expect equality or justice in the courtrooms of this country from a white jury, so how can a snail darter or a Furbish lousewort expect a fair trial in a human court? But if we broaden our definition of the law beyond it's current interpretation by the courts, we may draw some important conclusions as to the legality of a system that is unable to address the current mass extinction of non-human life, and about our responsibilities as citizens of the global and biological community to arrest this problem, which now threatens all life on Earth.

When we discuss "the law" here, we are simply talking about a shared system of beliefs and taboos that are codified within an accepted system of justice. Any legal system derives its legitimacy from the acceptance of those who come under its real or imagined authority. In this respect, all human societies have laws, and it could be argued that plants and animals do as well.

Although there also is arguably a "natural law," for the purpose of this discussion we should assume that we humans may never learn what it is or if it is possible to codify it or conform to it. Attempts to incorporate natural law into modern law are usually in themselves anthropocentric, and have given rise to such misguided political philosophies as "social Darwinism" and even influenced the disastrous National Socialism movement in post-war Germany. All we as humans can ever hope to understand with any certainty is human law, and we have a great deal of difficulty even with that. For relevant examples we must examine the three million plus years of human law, how it evolved and what it is today. The older established traditional law accepts that the Earth does not belong to the people, but rather the people belong to the Earth. The people, in this case, are not limited to humans.

Modern legal systems are human-centered, and reflect the worldview that humans exist apart from nature. It doesn't matter if you go back to Hammurabi, Plato, Cicero, Confucius, the Magna Charta, Thomas Jefferson or John Mitchell. Modern law accepts a basically Judeo-Christian view of the world, in which an omnipotent god created the Earth for man to use, a concept sometimes described as "stewardship." The driving principle here is man as the crowning achievement of evolution, and rightful heir to the planet, which he may use to satisfy all his needs and desires, so long as he does right by his fellow man.

It is in this way that modern law sees all non-human life as well as all material objects as property. This concept clearly has its roots in the development of earlier economic systems heavily dependent on agriculture. One need only to read Chief Seattle's great speech to see that this modern concept is by no means universal even today. And it represents the most profound difference between traditional law and modern law.

Older, traditional laws are still used today in various forms by the many tribal peoples now living in the more remote and unspoiled parts of this ravaged planet. It is an orally codified, highly specialized and extremely sophisticated legal system that has existed for over millions of years. It is effective and just. The highest penalty for any crime under this system is banishment from the tribe or band. Imprisonment is unheard of as a means of punishment, yet societies that use this system have extremely low crime rates by our standards. Respect for the Earth and all non-human life is a common thread that runs through all traditional legal institutions. Currently there are an estimated 200 million tribal people who live according to traditional or customary law.

Modern law is not a static concept. Rather, it is a dynamic process through which we seek justice. The case that legal rights for all living things are not spelled out specifically anywhere in the Constitution today is no argument that they do not exist. Recall that blacks and Native Americans were long denied full legal protection under the law by nearly every court in the United States. They were denied personhood, or standing, and were even considered sub-human. It has now been determined that those courts had acted illegally in denying any US citizen full protection under the law.

In other words, the US Supreme Court did not magnanimously award blacks and Native Americans rights that they did not already possess. Rather, they merely recognized the rights blacks and Native Americans already held but which had been denied to them in other courts. The principle here is what has become known as the "evolving concept of liberty" and is central to our constitutional system of law.

This principle is addressed clearly in the Ninth Amendment, where "unenumerated rights" are discussed. Although today some conservatives still insist this reference is only to unenumerated states rights, a big issue of the day, the framers of the constitution undoubtedly recognized that they may have missed something in writing the Bill of Rights. In the Ninth Amendment the framers state plainly that simply because certain rights had been enumerated and recognized as inalienable, they were making no claims that additional inalienable rights did not also exist. Thanks to this amendment we today enjoy the right to vote, the right to travel and the much-discussed right to privacy.

But the Ninth Amendment also says something else. It is an admission that the law is not, and never can be, perfect. This is why the framers of the Constitution included the statement, "We hold these truths to be self evident." By choosing these words they were stating clearly that everyone should be able to grasp the concepts upon which all US law is based. Just because a law has been written and approved by Congress, signed by the President and has survived challenges in the Supreme Court does not mean that it is unquestionably legitimate. The Ninth Amendment recognizes that the law itself exists somewhere outside the institutions designed to protect it, and is not a product of those institutions. The ultimate authority on the principles of the law are the individuals who live under, or according to, the legal system in question.

Modern law has mistakenly upheld as legal many actions that have disgraced what we sometimes refer to as civilized society. Many governments have supported or carried out policies of genocide, war and plunder that were justified at the time as being within the law, even though later courts determined that the actions undertaken were illegal under the existing domestic and/or international laws. Legal systems are not infallible, and like other social institutions, are constantly evolving and changing.

Today, all international and common law recognizes the existence of a "higher law" and a community's responsibility to uphold contemporary moral principles. That is why juries are composed of one's peers, and are instructed to let their conscience be their guide. They may even disregard the judge's instructions and the weight of the evidence if they see the need to let

higher legal and moral responsibilities influence their decision.

A "necessity" or "choice of evils" defense is allowed in modern legal systems when the intentions of the law are not clear, or are seemingly in conflict with the best interests of society. When the system fails, and everyone admits that it does occasionally, an individual has only his or her conscience to consult for guidance. If you as an individual decide to break the established law to uphold what you believe to be a higher principle, you have a right to do so, providing the crime you seek to prevent is greater than the crime you are committing, that other legal remedies have been exhausted and that your actions have a reasonable chance in preventing the crime. You have the right to intervene in the commission of a crime. You can even use force if necessary. You may legally break a window, enter a locked building and physically subdue a person who you believe is assaulting a person inside.

It has been said that an injustice to one is an injustice to all, and that no man or woman can be free until all men and women are free. But if we cannot stand alone in the universe, one species among 10 to 50 million, and live as human beings, then we must accept that the otherness of the natural world is just an illusion, and that real freedom cannot exist on this planet until the other life forms are free from unprincipled exploitation and extermination as well.

This is not a question of aesthetics; it is the burning question of survival. The snail darter has a right to exist because its survival can be linked directly to our survival. By "our survival" we mean not merely human survival, but that of the entire community of life on Earth. The natural world does have a legal right to exist, and if we don't soon recognize this, we could be guilty of complicity in the most horrible holocaust imaginable—the willful destruction of the entire biosphere, all life on Earth, for short-term profits.

Recognizing the rights of all living things can also mean accepting and experiencing the natural world as "self." This recognition is based on two key principles: first, that we are all citizens of a global biotic community, each having the same right to fulfill the unknown measure of our own existence; and second, that membership in a community is not meaningful if there are no rights or responsibilities.

By this reasoning, non-humans are fully protected under a common or community law, and any action that unfairly or unnecessarily threatens other community members is both immoral and illegal, whether the Justice Department or the Department of the Interior think so or not.

If non-humans have legal rights under modern law that are being violated, as we have argued, then the current war against the Earth is an illegal war. So, then, what are our legal responsibilities in this regard?

To answer this question we can consult the Nuremburg Principles, which were adopted by the US at the Nazi war crime trials after World War II. The US, in adopting the principles, accepted them as the highest law of the land, and although there is no official mechanism for enforcement, violation of international law is a crime, and violators can be prosecuted and sentenced in the courts of international justice. Enforcement is then possible through voluntary sanctions against offending nations by the world community. Thus international law is not powerless.

Judges in this country have been reluctant to implement the Nuremburg Principles, or even allow the arguments upon which they are based into the courtroom. The necessity defense has been disallowed in many cases involving protesters attempting to protect old growth forests and endangered species, and expert testimony on larger ecological questions has been banned from the courtroom. Until we gain a fair trial, this defense may go largely untested. It is up to us to bring this miscarriage of justice to the attention of the public by confronting the legal system with sound legal arguments to support our claims, both inside and outside the courtroom.

Today, environmental law—whether it be derived from the National Environmental Policy Act, Endangered Species Act or any other legislation, and whether it be civil or criminal—is inherently human-centered, or anthropocentric. This, as we stated earlier, is due solely to the existing legal concept of community. So the principal goal of any biocentric legal strategy is to expand the legal concept of community, or, as US Supreme Court Justice William O. Douglass argued in his minority opinion in *Sierra Club v. Rodgers Morton,* the well known "Mineral King" lawsuit, to give "standing" to the non-human community.

When any case comes before the court today, the plaintiff, or the party bringing the charges of illegal conduct before the court, must be a legal person with standing, and must be able to prove damages to his/her rights in order to prevail against the defendant. The notion that "personhood" is a prerequisite to the conferring of legal rights is a common theme in all law. The significance of the concept of "personhood" in modern law is that it is an attempt to separate the rights of certain human beings from the rights of others, and of the rest of the living world.

For example, in a case involving the pollution of a stream by industries upstream, a human defendant would have a legitimate claim only by proving that his/her drinking water was made unsafe for human consumption; or that fisheries were harmed, causing him/her economic hardship; or that by threatening the fish with extinction, the industries violated the Endangered Species Act, which was enacted to protect the human environment. The party is prevented from bringing suit against the polluters on behalf of the fish, or even the stream itself, which many people throughout the ages have seen as a living entity with certain rights.

Since this principle of a trans-human community is fundamental to any deep ecological system of jurisprudence, then we must make it central to any legal actions we take on behalf of the endangered Earth. We do not simply defend the grizzly bear, we defend the right of the grizzly bear to live in his/her natural habitat. The grizzly bear is thus not simply the property of the Game and Fish Department, but a legal person, or plaintiff, and should be listed as such on any claims against the government, or any other institution or person who infringes on these inalienable rights.

By this reasoning, a lawsuit would not be called *Earth First! v. Chevron Oil*, but *Ursus horribilis, et al. v. Chevron Oil*. In one case, Gerry Spence, a well-known US trial lawyer *(Silkwood v. Kerr McGee)* went one step further, seeking to halt plans to develop an oilfield in the Little Granite Creek watershed in northwestern Wyoming, listed the rocks and lichens as plaintiffs. The courts predictably rejected legal standing for Mr. Spence's clients, but this was an attempt to expand the legal community into the biotic community. Such decisions need to be appealed to higher courts, if only to bring our claim to the attention of the public in our attempt to establish precedents.

Some favorable precedents have already been established. Laws against animal cruelty have been an important step toward actual "animal rights"; the growing animal rights movement sees these laws as establishing legal rights for non-humans, even if in a limited sense. This right to freedom from cruel and unusual treatment must be seen as a right of the animal and not of any human party that may find such treatment offensive, however, for it to be viewed as a real step toward standing in a courtroom.

New laws are usually enacted to deal with activities that are seen as threatening to the basic well-being of society, or in anticipation of those activities. They are a reaction to a threat to life, liberty or justice, whether it be real or imagined. But new rights are not bestowed; they can only be recognized by a society as already existing. They are inalienable.

Our society is now gravely threatened by the prevalence of a relatively recent perception of the natural world. We are bound by the overriding principles of communal self-defense to take effective action. We must accept the urgency of adopting legal principles and institutions that seek to remedy the failure of the new worldview to address the legitimate needs of the whole global community. This will necessitate the delegitimization of the now-dominant paradigm that sees humanity as existing apart from nature. For those seeking to defend the Earth, traditional law as practiced by the hunting tribes that once exclusively peopled the natural landscape is a system that is well equipped to deal with the complex legal issues facing us today.

ACTION*

1. Endangered Species

"On the average, one new species of mammal, three birds and 100 plants are discovered every year. Between 50 and 100 species become extinct every day."
—FRIENDS OF THE EARTH, UK

The number one cause of species extinction is habitat destruction. It is necessary not only to ensure that wilderness exists but that it is defended from misuse and pollution. Poaching, and accidental killing of non-target animals in the nets of fishing fleets, also cause extinction. There is a strong tradition of successful intervention on behalf of wilderness and endangered species: Save the Whales, the Chipko Movement in India, the Penan in Malaysia, and Old Growth activists in Northern California and the Pacific Northwest. In many cases this intervention has been symbolic but has had a profound effect on public opinion.

- **Locate and identify key wilderness areas in your region.** Become familiar with various species of wildlife that live there.

- **Identify threats and who's responsible.** Find out if the land is under federal, state, or local administration, or if it is privately owned. Determine whether it is classified as wildlife habitat and is being mismanaged or if it needs to be reclassified as habitat. Current threats to wilderness include logging, mining and mineral exploration, hydroelectric projects large and small, cattle grazing, toxic

runoff from agriculture, road building (sometimes done under the guise of recreation), off-road recreational vehicle and motorized vehicle abuse, and poaching and collecting.

2. Intervene on behalf of the wilderness and the species living within it.

- **Appeal at the administrative level** if the area is public land. Usually there will be a public land policy that is either not being enforced or needs to be strengthened in order to protect the habitat effectively. Legislation may be necessary if appeals fail.

- **Organize a campaign** to include letter writing, demonstrations and direct actions.

- **Form or join a local working group to take action.** There are a spectrum of groups that have local chapters, including the Sierra Club, the more radical Earth First! and Sea Shepherd Society. Some of these groups have blocked logging roads by burying themselves in the road, have staged tree sittings, and engaged in other types of physical interference. Those interested in stronger methods should consult Dave Foreman's *Ecodefense.*

3. Animal Rights

"Results of tests on one species cannot be accurately applied to other species . . . . Fifteen thousand children were born with severe deformities because Thalidomide, a sedative prescribed to pregnant women, was found 'safe' after extensive animal testing. More sophisticated non-animal tests showed Thalidomide dangerous to

*Action section by Mike Roselle

the development of the fetus . . . . Many alternatives, such as highly developed computer and mathematical models, cell and tissue cultures, already exist."

—PEOPLE FOR THE ETHICAL
TREATMENT OF ANIMALS

The evidence is in that not only is animal testing cruel and unnecessary but is also unreliable and unsafe for humans. There is a strong grassroots movement for animal rights in the US today, with well-developed strategies and tactics, some of them listed below.

- **Reduce your consumption of meat and dairy products.** Conditions on factory farms where the majority of "food animals" are raised are inhumane. Reducing meat production also encourages more efficient land use, making more food available in a hungry world and leaving more land as habitat for other species.

- **Boycott cosmetics, apparel and other goods that are tested on animals or contain animal remains.** Let companies know you are boycotting their products and ask them to use alternatives. For a list of cruelty free products, write to People for the Ethical Treatment of Animals (see resource list at the end of this section).

- **Discourage friends and neighbors from destructive or cruel types of hunting and trapping.** Leghold traps are among the cruelest devices, leaving the animal to suffer for days or even causing it to chew off its own leg in order to free itself. Hunting and trapping can also jeopardize humans, non-target animals and the environment. Lead buckshot poisons fresh water habitats, killing many organisms upon which larger animals feed and causing widespread water contamination.

- **Protest animal experimentation at high schools, universities or research labs.** If you are a student, refuse to participate in academic experiments that cause animals pain or fear. Suggest curriculum alternatives such as films, computer demonstrations and non-animal models.

Defending the Rainforests

RANDY HAYES

"We will hug the trees and dare them to let their axes fall on our backs."
—CHIPKO MOVEMENT, INDIA

RAINFORESTS ONCE OCCUPIED 14 percent of the land mass of the planet. Now it is less than 7 percent. An area the size of the state of Pennsylvania is being destroyed every year. All remaining rainforests could be destroyed in less than one person's lifespan. We are the last generation to have the chance to save the rainforests. These ancient forests, unscarred by past ice ages, support many of the remaining tribal peoples. Rainforests are also the home for woolly spider monkeys, golden lion tamarins, ocelots, jaguars, Sumatran rhinoceroses, harpy eagles, macaws, parrots, exotic orchids and much more. All of these creatures are endangered and need your help.

We are connected to the tropical rainforests by more than a fantasy for jungle adventure. The burning of the rainforests contributes to the global warming trend and the ensuant heat waves and droughts. Modern agriculture depends on fresh supplies of genetic stock from the rainforest to fortify basic food staples such as corn and rice against new breeds of insect pests and viruses. Rainforest ecosystems provide genetic material for new foods and medicines. Twenty-five percent of our pharmaceutical drugs are derived from plants; most of the plants being studied for anti-cancer curative properties occur only in tropical rainforests. Rainforests regulate rainfall. Their rivers supply clean water for millions of people. The forests moderate the Earth's hydrologic cycles and air currents. When vast forests are destroyed, major populations suffer from dislocation and starvation. These disasters destabilize political systems in the Third World and enable repressive military regimes to come into power. The security of neighboring nations is threatened and the world economic order becomes more fragile.

Randy Hayes is the Director of the Rainforest Action Network, which confronts transnational banks and corporations whose policies destroy tropical rainforests.

"We will hug the trees and dare them to let the axes fall on our backs." CHIPKO MOVEMENT, INDIA

Some of the Causes of Rainforest Destruction:

- Development projects destroy rainforests with funding from the US Agency for International Development, the World Bank, InterAmerican Development Bank and other lending institutions. Your tax dollars have funded rainforest-destroying hydroelectric dams in the Amazon. These are the dams that flooded tribal peoples' ancestral homelands and enriched corrupt military regimes while saddling the rest of Brazil with debt. This development aid has been referred to as the "false generosity of the oppressor" because it places political, economic and cultural decision-making power outside of the hands of the affected local population.

- US-based corporations such as dam builders, road builders, mining companies, timber companies and oil companies that trade or operate in the tropics contribute to deforestation. It is not a desire for environmental protection, justice, nutrition or land reform that motivates them; it is the vicious, unrelenting drive for profit and personal fortune. Responsible companies are few and far between.

- Consumer demand for tropical timber and cheap beef to supply fast food chains are two major causes of rainforest destruction. Nigeria has lost 90 percent of its rainforests, mostly from timber extraction. In the US, fast food restaurants' demand for cheap beef has caused species' extinction and permanent destruction to once productive forests. Not only does this process destroy rainforest, but it is less productive than other forms of food production. One acre of land can produce 20,000 pounds of potatoes but only 165 pounds of beef.

- Sheer poverty and landlessness resulting from grossly unequal distribution of land and resources force marginalized people to exploit the rainforest for firewood and slash-and-burn agriculture. Without land reform and the development of national agricultural programs that de-emphasize export crop production and re-emphasize the nutritional needs of national populations, this form of rainforest destruction will continue.

We need to ask ourselves some crucial questions about this life-threatening situation. Are we going to let this unparalleled destruction continue? As it stands, the tax dollars and investment capital of the rich nations are destroying the future of Third World peoples and countless other species on the Earth. Out of ignorance, greed and racism, the early settlers of this country nearly destroyed the tribal peoples of this continent. We are still losing at least one tribe per year—forever. Are we going to stand by and let this happen?

As US citizens we need to understand the limits to our control, influence and moral authority. Is it correct simply to *tell* Brazil and Indonesia to stop cutting down their forests when US forests are in such bad shape? It is better that we first tell our own governments, local store owners, and ourselves not to buy tropical timber cut from virgin rainforests. We in the industrial North need to focus more on what needs to be done here at home rather than "down there." Once we bring our own consumption down to sustainable and globally equitable levels, then we are ready to participate cooperatively with our international partners in preventing further rainforest destruction.

"The World Bank's call of action for tropical forests is inconsistent with the socio-ecological imperative of sustainability and survival in the tropics. It threatens to create new forms of poverty for the poor, and new forms of ecological destabilization in the tropics, even while the World Bank's forestry projects are legitimized on environmental grounds and grounds of poverty alleviation. But legitimization and packaging is not the same as content. In content, all forestry programs, all the tropical forestry action plans are created in World Bank's vision of the theology of the market in which neither the poor nor nature have any role except as victims."

—Vandana Shiva

*ACTION**

We need structural changes in government policies and purchasing. The US government, including its military, is one of the biggest purchasers on Earth. It's time to apply criteria to these purchases to encompass: Low/no toxicity, no beef imports, etc., and to limit technology, i.e., the number, size and use of bulldozers and chainsaws. While we think big about the overall conditions determining the fate of rainforests and strategize creative and positive alternatives there are a number of other steps we can take:

1. **Consumer Intervention**

   Boycott fast food burgers, beef tacos and processed beef products. The US currently imports 130 million pounds of beef raised on deforested land in Central America. The beef is not labeled with the country

of origin, so once it enters the US, it is difficult to track. We know it does go to fast food and processed products, so boycott them all to be on the safe side. What is needed is a beef labeling law which identifies the country of origin and biological region. If you're a vegetarian you've already saved one acre of tropical rainforest per year.

   Don't buy tropical wood products such as teak and mahogany used in furniture. Refrain from using disposable chopsticks (bring your own). If you're a carpenter or contractor, don't buy plywood made from timber clearcut from rainforests.

2. **Letter Campaigns**

*Action section by Randy Hayes

Write to your Congressional representative and senators, urging them to support legislation that ties funding of institutions such as the World Bank to the implementation of strong human rights and environmental practices.

Write to the Treasury Secretary (US Treasury, Washington, DC 20220), whose department is responsible for US/Bank relations.

Write to World Bank President Barber Conable (1818 H Street NW, Washington, DC 20433), demanding cancellation of the Botswana-Livestock III, Brazil-Carajas Iron Ore Program, China-Three Gorges Dam, India-Narmada Dams and the Indonesia-Transmigration projects. Insist that programs be instituted to restore the land and native peoples' rights.

Urge them to support small-scale development.

The Rainforest Action Network's *Action Alerts* (see address in resource list below) provides additional officials to write to, and updates on issues and campaigns. And don't forget to write letters to the editor in your own community.

3. **Generate Popular Support**

Form a grassroots Rainforest Action Group, which can act as a local catalyst educating others about rainforest destruction. (Contact the Rainforest Action Network, below, for information.)

Initiate community education projects such as a lecture series, conference or school curricula on rainforest issues.

Organize media events, issue press releases and public service announcements.

Organize a petition drive.

Why Blacks Should Be Environmentalists

CARL ANTHONY

W HEN MARTIN LUTHER KING de-
cided to raise his voice in opposition to the war in Vietnam,
many of his critics told him he ought to stick
to domestic issues. He should concentrate
on securing civil rights of Blacks in the
South, and leave foreign policy to the
professionals who knew best. But King de-
cided to oppose the war because he knew it
was morally wrong, and because he understood the link between the brutal exploitation and destruction of the Vietnamese people, and the struggle of Blacks and others
for justice and freedom in our own land.

Today Black leadership, and the Black
community face a similar challenge. Every
day the newspapers carry stories about the
changing atmosphere and climate, threats
to the world's water supply, threats to the
biodiversity of the rainforest, and the crisis
of populations of poor nations growing too
fast to be supported by the carrying capacity

of their lands. Some environmentalists suggest that in the near future, we will be unable to feed the world's population without
radical changes in land ownership, distribution of wealth, and new community decisions about crops and diets. Can Blacks
afford to view the social and economic
problems of Black American communities
in isolation from these global trends?

The modern civil rights movement came
into being when southern Black organizations, frustrated by Southern intransigence,
challenged racist laws and practices restrict-
ing the rights of Blacks to public accomo-
dations. Thirty years ago, at Montgomery,
Alabama, Blacks won the right to ride in the
front of the bus. Today, African Americans
must ask where the bus is going.

Since the late 1960's, African American
economic and political gains in the United
States have suffered erosion, as legislation
and social programs have been cut from fed-

Carl Anthony is an architect and urban planner. His work has focused on planning and designing facilities for
meeting basic needs in urban communities. He has served on the Faculty of the Columbia University Graduate
School of Architecture and Planning, and the U.C. Berkeley College of Environmental Design. With Karl
Linn, he is co-founder of the Urban Habitat Program at Earth Island Institute. He is working on a book, *The
Landscape of Freedom*, which will describe connections between the Afro-American struggle for human
rights and changing American attitudes toward the land in the decade following the Civil War.

eral and local budgets. During this period, the environmental movement has developed new insights about the connections that join people, community and land. It has also come a long way from its conservative, apolitical origins to become a major force for progressive social change. An environmental perspective could provide much needed focus for a new generation of Black Americans. Indeed, Blacks may have a great deal to gain by forging closer bonds with existing environmental organizations working to save the planet.

I. Developing New Visions

Blacks could benefit from expanding their vision to include greater environmental awareness. For example, a recent study of deteriorating conditions called young Black males in America an endangered species. "This description," the author suggests, "applies in a metaphorical sense, to the current status of young black males in contemporary society." The study, edited by Jewelle Taylor Gibbs, presents a comprehensive interdisciplinary perspective of the social and economic problems of these young people. It provides valuable statistics on high school drop out rates, work skills and attitudes, unemployment, robbery, rape, homicide and aggravated assault, drug addiction and teenage parenthood. But Gibbs makes no mention of the utter alienation of these young people from the natural environment, which is, after all, the source of Earth's abundance and well being. The loss of this contact with living and growing things, even rudimentary knowledge of where food and water comes from, must have serious consequences that we yet have no way of measuring.

The study says nothing of the difficult days ahead as American society seeks to make the transition from its current levels of consumption of resources to more sustainable patterns of the future. Developing an environmental perspective within the Black community could help smooth this transition in several ways:

- by promoting greater understanding of the productive assets of society, including land, water and natural resources.

- by strengthening collaboration with groups seeking to redirect public investment and economic development away from wasteful exploitation of nature toward urban restoration and meeting basic human needs.

- by gaining access to information and resources that enhance the potential of community survival.

- by developing new knowledge and skills to be shared by groups of people who live in the city.

- by strengthening social and political organization and creating new opportunities for leadership within the community.

Environmental organizations in the United States should also modify practices to expand their constituency to include Blacks and members of other minority groups as participants in shaping and building public support for environmental policies. With the exception of limited collaboration between environmentalists and Native Americans groups, and anti-toxic campaigns, there has been little communication between environmentalists and non-European minority groups within the US. Critical issues such as population control, limiting human intervention in the ecosystem, or rebuilding our cities in balance with nature have been discussed almost entirely from a European, and often elitist perspective.

Environmental organizations have taught us to appreciate the diversity of non-human species and to recognize the fundamental interdependency of human and non-human life on the planet. Such a perspective affirms the importance of a fundamental link between human societies and the ecosystem that sustains them: the air, the water, the minerals and fossil fuels, the soil and diversity of life forms that are the source of bountifulness and health. Appreciation of the ecological web, of season, setting, climate and nature, can guide us toward greater knowledge and skills for survival and success.

Respect for ecological diversity implies respect for human diversity. Thus far, however, the environmental movement, despite its highlighting crises in underdeveloped countries, has tended to be racially exclusive, expressing the point of view of the middle- and upper-income strata of European ethnic groups in developed countries. It has reproduced within its ranks prevailing patterns of social relations. Until recently there has been little concern for the environmental needs and rights of historically disadvantaged groups in developed countries. Few efforts to mobilize such groups in addressing environmental needs of Third and Fourth world communities have been made. If environmentalists hope to have credibility as the voice of a grassroots planetary perspective, this pattern will have to change. Black Americans can play an important role in this shift of strategy and consciousness.

II. Environmental Justice

The principle of social justice, however, must be at the heart of any effort aimed at bringing Blacks into the mainstream of environmental organizations in the United States. Such a vision must offer an alterna-

ANTON VAN DALEN, 1988

tive to the romantic view of the wilderness without people as being the only concern of environmentalists. Advocates of environmental justice would join efforts to conserve species diversity, living natural resources—plants, animals, microorganisms and ecosystems of tropical regions. They would question, however, a view of the tropical rainforest as a private laboratory for European pharmaceutical companies ignoring the needs of indigenous populations. Advocates of environmental justice seek to avoid distortion of environmental information as a way of rationalizing the economic status quo. They would challenge us not to misuse concern for endangered species as a way of diluting our collective responsibility for meeting basic human needs for health care, food and shelter. Environmentalists should not manipulate legitimate concerns about population growth as strategies for preserving racial dominance and purity.

To be useful for Black Americans, an environmental perspective must acknowledge that institutional violence and oppression do exist, and that capital accumulation by a small, privileged elite is at the heart of the global ecological crisis. Environmental protection, therefore, must be understood as intimately connected to efforts to eradicate injustice. Solutions must offer a practical guide for goals that can be accomplished in the short run as we seek a path toward a more sustainable future.

III. Jobs vs. Environment

The principle of environmental justice can provide for more than a symbolic coalition between environmental organizations and Black political leadership addressing the needs of separate constituencies. It can be the basis for functional collaboration in a new environmental and economic agenda.

A big issue is jobs. In 1955, for example, the Black and White employment rates among teenagers were about equal (52 percent for each); by 1980 a 26 percent gap had opened up between them as the employment rate for Blacks fell to 27 percent, and that of Whites rose slightly to 53 percent. One half of the male teenage unemployment is concentrated among 7 percent of the youth population. Without intervention, structural and institutional changes will lead to greater losses among population groups least able to afford these losses.

Undoubtedly even larger changes will be needed to make the transition from industrial society to more sustainable patterns.

Environmental organizations can no longer afford to take the view that they are unconcerned about who benefits and who loses from restrictions on economic growth. Shifting resources away from projects that are damaging to the ecosystem toward programs and projects that meet basic human needs must become the highest priority for the environmental movement.

Environmentalists suggest that global restoration can create new work. They have argued that programs such as mandatory refillable container legislation, recycling and pollution abatement, reforestation and increased use of public transportation can stimulate creation of new jobs. Social expenditures on health, education, welfare and the arts, they point out, have few negative environmental impacts. Finally, some environmentalists argue that, in a steady state economy, work can be redistributed, sharing on an equitable basis opportunities with all who wish to work. Thus a commitment to full employment and environmental protection is possible.

If these proposals are to be taken seriously, however, Blacks, other minority groups, and blue collar workers must be active participants in an environmental movement that places a high priority on their needs. Organizations such as the National Association for the Advancement of Colored People (NAACP) and the National Urban League have a real stake in the outcome of such environmental policies. They should be invited to participate in the dialogue establishing public environmental priorities. New organizations and perspectives are also needed.

IV. Environmental Restoration and the Drug Epidemic

It is not likely that major allocations of funding for urban restoration can be made available unless such programs can solve multiple urban problems. An example of these conflicting needs occurred recently when the financially strapped City of Berkeley turned down a modest request to fund a feasibility study for a popular restoration project: the opening up of Strawberry Creek as a central element in revitalizing the downtown. The City was under pressure to allocate $500,000 to fight the drug wars in the predominantly Black flatlands neighborhood of South Berkeley.

The fiscal bind of the City underscores a connection between social and environmental problems. Drug abuse in the inner city is approaching epidemic proportions. Recent studies of drug use among young Blacks confirms high correlation to low school achievement, delinquency and accidental death, the newest threat being the specter of AIDS which is rapidly increasing among intravenous drug users in the inner city.

These connections are likely even deeper than they appear. The inner city drug crisis is, perhaps, an inevitable outcome of an unhealthy separation between communities and their surroundings. Drug lords and law enforcement agencies battle for control over inner city neighborhoods, while fearful residents look on in dismay or resignation. The people who live in crack-infested neighborhoods have little control over their environment. Often ownership of property is held by absentee landlords. Discussing the mass migration of Blacks from the South to northern cities, Wendell Berry has correctly observed:

> The move from country to the city, deprived (Blacks) of their competence in doing for themselves. It is no exaggeration to say that, in the country, most blacks were skilled in the arts of make do and subsistence. If most of them were poor, they were at least competently poor; they could do for themselves and for each other. They knew how to grow and harvest and prepare food. They knew how to gather wild fruits, nuts and herbs. They knew how to hunt and fish. . . . In the cities, all of this know how was suddenly of no value, and they became abjectly and dependently poor as they had never been before. In the country, they possessed a certain freedom in their ability to *do*

things, but once they were in the city freedom was inescapably associated with the ability to *buy* things.

Without blaming the victims, or suggesting the clock be turned back, these remarks nevertheless give some idea of the damage of excessive urban dependency.

The link between environmental dependency and the drug epidemic points to a relationship between urban restoration and progress in eradicating drug abuse. "Never do anything for only one reason," says Dan Hemenway, author of a book on permaculture, a new approach to agriculture that emphasizes humans living within constraints of natural systems. How can environmental perspectives help fight drug abuse?

There are many connections between what we ingest—whether intravenous drugs or healthy food—how we feel, our bodies and the Earth. Emphasis on these connections, including disciplines of preventive medicine, diet and exercise are central to the new environmental ethic. Measures of self esteem such as social merit, skill, artistry, effort and integrity, rather than conspicuous consumption are environmental values related to an emerging global consciousness. This consciousness can be an important resource for inner-city communities, providing a practical context for new citizen initiatives on a scale with the drug crisis.

Grassroots neighborhoods have been organizing to fight drug abuse. Courageous individuals in many such neighborhoods have become vulnerable to attack by threatened drug dealers. Support of internationally vibrant environmental organizations can be targeted to such grassroots organizations. New networks can be established. Collaboration with environmental organizations can lead to greater wilderness exposure for inner-city kids, within the city, within the region or even in international exchange programs. The challenge of mountain climbing, exposure to geological formations of the Grand Canyon, the discipline of sailing, the quietness of the forest floor, and new human friendships can be compelling alternatives to the adventure of dealing drugs, if such challenges are available on a sustained basis. The mysteries of the universe can stimulate young minds before they become cynical.

Environmental scientists, such as toxicologists and epidemiologists, can work with community organizations, public officials and urban planners to find ways of integrating the wilderness experience and drug treatment facilities. Such collaboration can also lead to sustainable new urban habitats for re-entry of those who have completed treatment programs. Grassroots organizations could benefit greatly from the broader base political support such programs would engender.

V. Inner City as Damaged Land

The American inner city was once a wilderness. Today, islands, estuaries, forests, riparian habitats that once existed in these privileged locations have been replaced by asphalt, concrete, barbed wire fences, boarded up stores, crack houses, abandoned factories, landfills, and pollution. After generations of isolation and broken promises, exploitation and manipulation, the people who live in these places rarely pause to remember what it once was, or to speculate on what it might become.

Isolation of Blacks from stewardship of the environment has deep historic roots. It is hard to keep the faith. The Black population migrated to the cities to escape the four centuries of exploitation on plantations, crop farms, and coal mines of the south. Displacement of Blacks from the rural countryside is parallel to experiences of others in the Third World. Understanding of these experiences, however painful, is an important resource as we seek a path toward sustainable development.

For two decades, American central cities have been shrinking in population as those more fortunate have been fleeing to the suburbs in search of a better life. Suburban development continues the destruction of fragile agricultural lands. Can we afford a new round of urban expansion and abandonment as the Black population seeks to realize its legitimate aspirations as a part of the American dream? Will the suburbs become new ghettos isolated from new work in the information age? Should we encourage urban gentrification while ignoring the underclass trapped in American ghettos? None of these alternatives is an adequate reconciliation of economic growth and the integrity of the environment. If we are to restore damaged inner cities, we must also invest in the future of the people who live there.

VI. Developing Urban Environmental Leadership

In the next decade, important decisions about the future of cities, and surrounding agricultural land will have consequences affecting millions of people. The deteriorated infrastructure of urban areas must be rebuilt. There are hidden rewards for undertaking a program of rebuilding our urban cores in tune with nature. The investment of billions of dollars which will be required offer opportunities for fresh approaches to affordable housing, public services, recycling of resources and waste. There is room for small projects and bringing wilderness back into the city. Restoration of inner city neighborhoods should be a high priority for environmentalists. But investment in education and social organization of the existing inner-city population is needed if this population is to have a stake in the outcome.

Within this same time period, new urban environmental leadership must be developed. The belief that human societies ought to be established on a more sustainable technical and physical basis creates an opening for increased growth and maturity for Black and other minority groups in the city. In ten years, hundreds of geologists, biologists, artists and writers, agricultural economists, political scientists, epidemiologists, and resource and population specialists who make up the leadership of the environmental movement could be Black Americans. These new environmentalists could provide guidance to hundreds of thousands of people in society at large and in their own communities, making the difficult transition from industrial to more sustainable patterns of urban life.

Building new bridges could help Blacks resolve age old conflicts between desire for separation and integration. A global, rather than an isolationist view, and a new respect for diversity offers encouragement to rethink relationships between neighbors, communities, past and future possibilities. An extended time horizon, concern about the future of the planet, challenges all of us to visualize renewed communities of diverse population groups living together without racism.

VII. Earth Island Institute Urban Habitat Program

In order to meet responsibilities for citizenship, Blacks and other minorities must have opportunities to experience the fullness of the healing powers of nature, and to play a greater role in creating environmental projects that benefit all members of the community. We must find new ways to bridge the gap between minorities and advocates of the environment. The Urban Habitat Program at Earth Island Institute is an example of an organization set up to contribute to these objectives. It will serve as a clearinghouse emphasizing access by community based organizations to global, regional and neighborhood environmental resources. Initial efforts will focus on African American communities in the San Francisco Bay Area. As the program evolves, parallel efforts will be made in Hispanic, Asian and other minority communities. Priority will be placed on strengthening the human potential within these communities for environmental awareness, discipline and action. The program is a modest beginning in an effort long overdue. Hopefully, its elements can be replicated in other urban communities.

ACTION*

1. Arrange presentations to groups with substantial minority membership by existing environmental organizations and individual resource persons.

2. Develop outreach programs by organizations like the Sierra Club to promote active learning and exposure to the wilderness experience by minority youth.

3. Create networks among minority based organizations, environmental groups, public schools, community colleges and institutions of higher learning to expand educational opportunities for minorities in environmental science and related fields.

4. Work specifically with inner-city organizations fighting drug abuse to develop environmentally related projects such as tree planting, restoration, urban farming, horticultural therapy, international exchanges, etc., reinforcing neighborhood-initiated efforts at law enforcement, prevention and treatment of drug abuse.

5. Build coalitions with environmental groups, labor and minority organizations promoting creation of new jobs compatible with environmental restoration.

6. Develop new legislative initiatives linking environmental restoration and inner city needs.

*Action section by Carl Anthony

Barnraising for
Community and Peace

KARL LINN

It is in the nature of all human species, all people, to be able to deal with
environment, hence also to fashion the spaces they require, adequately and
beautifully, the way all people are given to communicate with each other
adequately and beautifully through language, speech, which, like making
spaces, belongs to our primordial equipment.

—ALDO VAN EYCK, COMMENCEMENT SPEECH, 1979
NEW JERSEY INSTITUTE OF TECHNOLOGY

ALL CREATURES INNATELY engage in habitat building. Traditionally, people have shaped their dwellings to suit their lifestyles. Constructing their houses themselves instills in the builders-in-residence a sense of accomplishment, pride, mastery and self-confidence. Molding their homes, gardens and neighborhoods with their hands imparts a personal, human touch to the fabric of their immediate physical surroundings and generates a deepened sense of belonging to a place.

The Armoring of Habitat

Today labor-displacing technologies are creating impersonal and alienating building structures and public spaces untouched by human hands. Massive, regimented apartment and office complexes intimidate their occupants, reducing them to passive spectators in their own living and working environments.

Over the centuries the architecture of buildings and open spaces and the planning

Karl Linn is a landscape architect, psychotherapist and community resource planner. Adopting a "barnraising" process, he has engaged students, volunteers and neighborhood residents across the United States and abroad in envisioning, designing and constructing spaces they share in common as celebrations of community. Linn has taught at the Massachusetts Institute of Technology, the New Jersey Institute of Technology and the University of Pennsylvania. A founding member of Architects/Designers/Planners for Social Responsibility, during the 1960's he established the Neighborhood Commons Non-profit Corporations, the first pilot community design centers, created in eight US cities. Currently, he works with Earth Island Institute developing its Urban Habitat Program with Carl Anthony.

of entire cities has evolved as a professional service to the privileged few. The accumulation of capital enabled private patrons, established institutions and governments to create physical settings designed to protect their bounty and strengthen their empire. Like the military triangle, the private and corporate patrons, the architects and the building contractors reinforce each other in constructing big and ostentatious structures for their own profit and ego gratification. The resultant sky-penetrating high-rise buildings provide regimented social hives for ever-growing masses of people. These narcissistic sculptural contrivances which compete for attention fast transform our cities into an aesthetically disgraceful display of architectural cacophony.

At present more than 70% of the world's population inhabit urban areas. Each day newcomers migrate from rural regions where they are unable to sustain a livelihood and are forced to leave behind their supportive network of extended family and village life. The majority of urban dwellers live in declining neighborhoods, substandard public housing and shantytowns. Many struggle to survive despite abject poverty, unemployment and no prospects for change. Many succumb to despair and escape into drugs and violence.

At the same time the affluent minority lives in the expanding gentrified quarters of cities, saturated with extravagant consumer offerings adjacent, but in blatant contrast, to the others. As the social stratification widens and the frustrations, especially of disengaged black and Hispanic youth, flare up more frequently into violence, city lives become less and less bearable. Adding to the environmental ills of cities are the polluted air and waterways, the adverse climate and

exorbitant waste production. Our cities are indeed in a state of crisis. In the words of Lester Pearson, past Prime Minister of Canada,

No planet can survive half slave and half free, half engulfed in misery, half careening along toward unlimited consumption. Neither ecology nor morality can survive such contrasts.

Alternative Mass Societies— Community and Collectives

The ever growing masses of people forced to live in anonymity and isolation in their crowded regimented housing cubicles become easy prey to the proselytizing of charismatic and authoritarian leaders. Hierarchical corporate employment structures, spectator sports, passive TV viewing and consumer conditioning propel the urban masses further into collective mass existence. Martin Buber poetically contrasts the two possible forms of mass organization, which can evolve in the urban context, in his juxtaposition of collectives* and community.

Collectivity is not a binding but a bundling together, individuals packed together, armed and equipped in common, with only as much life from man to man as will inflame the marching step. But community, growing community, is the being no longer side by side but with one another of a multitude of persons. And this multitude, though it also moves towards one goal, yet experiences everywhere a turning to, a dynamic facing of the other, a flowing from *I* to Thou. Collectivity is based on an organized atrophy of person-

*The Buberian critique of collectives refers to alienating mass organizations, not to the small dynamic groups that call themselves collectives.

al existence, community on its increase and confirmation in life lived towards one another.

—MARTIN BUBER,
BETWEEN MEN AND MEN

To prevent the degeneration of urban mass societies into marching regiments or roving stampedes of fanatics, meaningful and functionally constructive relationships must evolve among people. Masses of people need to *experience* their human poten-

tial for cooperation. To talk or moralize about the virtues of cooperation is not enough.

Especially today, masses of people must be awakened and mobilized on behalf of life to assure the survival of our green planet. Since many ecological and social systems have lost their resilience and are in a state of crisis, the campaign to restore the earth must turn the tide of destruction and disintegration in the very short time span of a few decades.

ACTION*

Barnraising: Building Community with Environment

Despite the degeneration of human habitat making into a function of capital investment, building traditions that engender cooperative mass participation and community are still alive. The old American tradition of barnraising occupies a special place in the minds and hearts of citizens because of the cooperative spirit and sense of community it generates. A farmer alone is unable to carry the long heavy beams on his shoulders. In order to survive, farmers have to engage in mutual aid and erect each barn as a cooperative effort. As they work together they experience their interdependence, appreciating everyone for holding up their part.

Our disintegrating urban habitats with their multitudes of unemployed and homeless people have become the new frontiers for restoration. Restoration efforts aspiring

towards ecologically, economically and socially sustainable development at the grassroots level can be staged as inspiring urban barnraising celebrations, enabling large numbers of people to work together cooperatively in interdependence, maintaining a high level of personal and communal creativity.

Such community dynamics will respect the autonomy of the participants, support their initiatives and facilitate the growth of mutual trust—these are the three mainsprings for generating human creativity.

The compelling vision and commitment to a restored green planet, the respect for personal skill and talent, and the rigorous and objective demands of the restoration work provide a work-democratic discipline that will safeguard the mass participatory process from degenerating into collective regimentation or fanaticism. In fact restoration efforts engaging masses of people, if properly staged, should overshadow the pseudo-glamor of militarism and provide a vitally inspiring moral alternative to war.

*Action section by Karl Linn

Restoration: the new frontier. KARL LINN

Community Design Service

Since standard construction technologies for buildings and open spaces require considerable fiscal resources and a skilled labor force, progressive social movements, especially in their fledgling phases of growth, have paid little attention to their physical surroundings. Yet the spaces in which we live and act affect our spirit and actions much more deeply than we realize. How often have unflattering flickering fluorescent lights stressed and demoralized an evening gathering of people who after a long day of hard work are meeting voluntarily in the service of social responsibility?

Only during the last three decades has environmental design in the service of community begun to explore socially responsible approaches to the development of human habitat. By the early 60's urban renewal had just eradicated its first ethnic neighborhood, Boston's Italian North End. Protest against such federal bulldozing and the dissecting of metropolitan areas by highway construction catalyzed many neighborhood organizations throughout the country. Throughout the 1960's networks of community design centers were established all over the US. Volunteers were recruited to serve as advocates of disenfranchised populations. These centers promoted activities such as neighborhood preservation, self-help housing rehabilitation and community gardening. The emphasis on restoration of ethnic neighborhoods dovetailed with a maturation in American society as it began to acknowledge and affirm its diverse roots, replacing the metaphor of the melting pot with images of cultural pluralism.

Participatory planning, design and construction methods were developed to democratize the system of human habitat building. Today affordable housing and counter-gentrification strategies occupy the minds of socially responsible environmental designers, who aspire to prevent the repeated dislocation of the less affluent segment of the population.

More recently, since 1982, environmental designers have begun to counter the arms race, particularly the nuclear arms race. Architects/Designers/Planners for Social Responsibility was established as an umbrella organization in 1984 with about a dozen chapters throughout the US; while the International Architects/Designers/Planners for Prevention of Nuclear War was created in 1987 with about 50 nation members. ADPSR exposed the farcical claims of nuclear air raid shelter protection and prepared posters, which graphically compared the cost of military equipment with that of schools, hospitals and homes that could be built instead. Creating places for peacemaking has been the subject of many workshops. The first US/USSR Peace Park was constructed during the summer of 1988 in Tashkent, the sister city of Seattle. Two hundred fifty volunteers from Seattle brought 10,000 tiles made by the schoolchildren of that city. Currently a design competition is taking place for the first National Peace Garden in Washington, DC.

Disarming the System of Habitat Building

During the last 30 years of working with social movements dedicated to ecology, social justice, human potential, religious libera-

tion, women's rights and peace, environmental designers had to learn to work with highly inspired but often unskilled volunteers and little money. The labor-intensive and capital-restricted reality of social movements inspired innovations in environmental craft technology. For example, the architect Neil Mitchel's barnraising invention of the light-weight concrete beam for use in South America enables two people to carry a reinforced beam spanning the whole length of a house on their shoulders, bypassing the need for expensive construction equipment. New machines need to be invented that perform the backbreaking work, freeing human hands to leave their imprints on urban habitats.

To enable these social movements to tackle the restoration of urban habitat effectively, the sponsoring organizations must

Tree-planting brigade in Nicaragua. Under the Sandinista administration, the country has implemented a number of progressive ecological programs unique in the region. Many US citizens have joined in the restoration efforts. NICARAGUA NETWORK

not tax their human and material resources unrealistically. To overtax or underutilize the energies of people will cause exhaustion or boredom. On the other hand, the sense of satisfaction in joint accomplishment of tangible restoration work is an empowering experience that helps strengthen solidarity among the participants. The work should be laid out in such a way that each act of building will inspire the next.

Though vivid sketches drawn by environmental designers make desired restoration realistically visible, they can also easily mislead. Often, these pictures inspire people and move them into action, while in their enthusiasm they underestimate the sustainability of the energy needed to complete the task. I will always remember a drawing of an amphitheater that inspired a group of teenagers who wanted to use it for dancing. They started digging with great zest, but after the first week I often found myself standing alone in a great pit. If these young people approached me again, we would start with an improvised dance floor using recycled plywood and pallets. If a month later the dancing continues, one can put in wooden logs for sitting around the dance floor. If the dancing continues drawing more people, one can put wooden planks across and pile logs upon logs to make a makeshift amphitheater. A year later when the dancing has become a custom, one can take the planks and use them as wooden forms to pour concrete. One should never use concrete before an activity has cemented itself. Pouring concrete prematurely can easily build mausoleums.

Depending on available human and physical resources, the process of restoring urban habitat can be applied to instant spatial transformations, the creating of temporary settings and the building of permanent spaces. Instant transformations usually employ flexible and easily removable props and decorations, such as cable reels, rolls of paper, banners, candles and torches. Temporary spaces are often constructed of easily assemblable components made of surplus or salvage material creatively recycled, while permanent spaces use heavier construction material permanently embedded in the terrain.

Citywide Support Systems for Restoration

Rather than tackling urban restoration projects one by one, it is much more efficient to set up citywide support systems. For economic, ecological and aesthetic reasons, salvage and surplus building material should be creatively recycled. Demolition contractors will often be delighted to drop off a load of bricks if a municipal depot is easily accessible within city limits. The historic continuity of a city fabric is not preserved when some historic buildings are refurbished and then surrounded with oceans of new concrete. When historic building material such as cobblestones have to be removed, they should become part of a public treasury rather than being dumped or left out for private scavenging. Demolition of historic buildings, if inevitable, should also be a public act, assuring that precious salvageable historic building material be stored for future use.

Municipal nurseries, compost operations and topsoil depots could support community gardening. New York City's Green Thumb operation even provides tools and fencing. Heavy construction equipment should be provided by municipal or state agencies. Even the National Guard has often supplied neighborhoods with bulldozers and trucks for simple grading operations.

The private sector has often lent support to self-help efforts of neighborhood restoration. Telephone and electric companies have used their mechanized augers to dig tree pits in lots where demolition had left brick walls embedded in the soil.

Community-based restoration workshop-centers are another component of such a citywide support system. Here, year-round work can take place, especially in the cold regions of the country. During inclement weather, for example, personalized mosaic pavement blocks can be prefabricated to be set out with the coming of spring. These workshops would accumulate tools and equipment and could conduct research and development in creative recycling of salvage and surplus building materials in order to produce marketable products which would strengthen the economic sustainability of community-based cooperative enterprises.

The centers could also serve as training grounds for neighborhood residents and young people enrolled in summer employment and career development programs in urban restoration. In time coffee pots, radios, guitars and other instruments would find their way to the workshop, which could become a magnet in its area, a center of ongoing creative energy.

Building Commons

Barnraising of spaces can involve the transformation of existing locations into instant or temporary commons or the building of new permanent ones. The process of building commons provides an immediate context for people to engage in brainstorming or shared envisioning of the places to be. Participatory planning and design processes engage people in decision-making through consensus, and self-help construction efforts generate mutual aid.

Often community block gardens can be easily transformed into commons by adding a sociability setting composed of a light-weight shelter, a sitting area and a barbecue. Temporary commons can be simply installed in vacant lots or on side streets during farmers' market days. A few chairs and cable reels with colorful outdoor umbrellas inserted in their center holes create an immediate attractive outdoor cafe. Easily assembled outdoor play equipment made from recyclable materials such as tires can entertain children who would otherwise be dragged along by their shopping parents.

More permanent neighborhood commons built on vacant lots in the block can be constructed so that young and old can be in each other's presence but not in each other's way. Such commons reinforce extended family living based on intergenerational support and mutual aid among neighbors. A neighborhood commons could even include a solar-heated demonstration building to house daycare, a food cooperative, a block laundromat or car repair shop. Such a building could also be the seat of a community board or a neighborhood government council, decentralizing the city's governance.

People on the Move: Barnraising Social Movements

The awareness that the Earth is in urgent need of intensive care is penetrating the consciousness of people and governments the world over. Growing concern about the greenhouse effect strengthens people's sense of connectedness as global citizens. Millions of people joining the campaign to restore the Earth socially and environmentally are becoming a powerful social movement.

We have all experienced states of crisis and been surprised at the latent reservoir of courage and strength we were able to mobilize. Survival is up to every one of us. Tapping into the cumulative survival experience of the human species, its survival archetype, the restoration movement connects with an ongoing flow of creativity from the collective unconscious, the bedrock of shared human psyche.

The patronage of most established institutions entrenched in their self interest usually generates massive bulwarks for their perpetuation. In contrast, this vital and compassionate social movement, dedicated to the preservation of life, provides the foundation for the conception and construction of a functional, disarming and humane habitat, which will shelter but not overpower it.

People on the move, whether on marches or in demonstrations, are shoots that can grow and mature into social movements or new and vital institutions. Through their bodily presence the demonstrators are putting themselves on the line and making a forceful, tangible and symbolic statement of commitment to their cause. Even in such a charged social atmosphere, simple environmental improvements can empower people. For example, since the hands of marchers are occupied carrying signs, posters or banners, they can easily get discouraged or sick from wet and cold on rainy days and, when attacked, be unable to defend themselves. A specially designed umbrella that can be attached to people's backs would free their hands. And imagine, if these umbrellas were also framed with velcro, soon they would join and become a moving canopy as people move in close to one another, a rudimentary expression of an architecture of social movement.

The spaces through which marchers move can be instantly transformed into ceremonial corridors. The route can be decorated with banners or torches. Even the posters people carry can be sequenced as a mobile exhibit and ultimately placed in an outdoor or indoor public gallery.

As the restoration movement gains strength and more sustained energies and resources become available, temporary structures can be built through self-help efforts. There is always a need for billboards, kiosks, soap and sand boxes. Flexible tent structures or parachutes can be easily raised to shelter teach-ins. Even temporary housing of infinite variety can be created through an easily assembled system of plywood components as was designed for Tent City in Washington, DC, when masses of Black protesters assembled during the late sixties.

Despite the fact that lack of financial resources often diminishes the effectiveness of social movements, for environmental design it can often be a blessing in disguise, leaving no room for frills and contrived extravagances. We delight in and are inspired by the exquisiteness and authenticity of indigenous architecture that evolves out of an economic and functional relationship to existing building materials and the existential urgencies of daily survival.

The worldwide reaction against the homogenizing of people and their habitat by centralized governments is gaining strength. Affirmation of cultural pluralism and grassroots struggles is beginning to transform the image of urban neighborhoods. Ethnic, lifestyle and religious diversity are becoming impressively visible through large murals, shapes and colors of buildings and public open spaces. With the passage of time the colorful richness of human nuances can imbue the fabric of people's habitat with the vibrant spectrum of the rainbow.

Creating Green Cities

PETER BERG

"Portion of all land in downtown Los Angeles used for driving, parking or servicing cars: 2/3."

—NEW PERSPECTIVES IN TRANSPORTATION RESEARCH

URBAN LIVING, the ordinary daily way of life of city people, has become a major ecological threat to the bioregions where cities are located, and consequently to the planetary biosphere as a whole. Yet cities continue to grow in both size and number. By the year 2000, close to 80 percent of North Americans will live in urban areas of 25,000 people or more, and over half of the entire world's population will reside in cities, making them the primary site of human habitation for the first time in history.

Cities are generally in decline and often prove to be more injurious than beneficial to the people who live in them. Air and water quality steadily worsen in spite of efforts to keep these necessities of life from becoming poisons for millions of people. Crowding, noise, traffic, alienation, the potential for accidents, and the threat of violence can create so much stress in people's lives that simple physical and mental survival becomes an overriding concern.

The effect that cities have on regional natural systems is particularly devastating. Garbage landfills ooze pollutants into water tables and soil. Bays, rivers and creeks are dumping places for everything from sewage to chemical wastes. Burgeoning housing de-

A founder of the concept of bioregions and the bioregional movement, **Peter Berg** is the director of the Planet Drum Foundation, a non-profit educational organization founded in 1974 to pursue research, organize workshops, create forums and publish information about the relationship between human culture and the natural processes of bioregions and the planetary biosphere. Peter is the director of a bioregional symposium, "Listening to the Earth: The Bioregional Basis of Community Consciousness," a co-sponsor of the North American Bioregional Congress and a founder of the Frisco Bay Mussel Group. He lectures at a number of universities and associations, and has authored or edited numerous articles and books, including *A Green City Program for San Francisco Bay Area Cities and Towns*.

A.v.D.'88

For more than a century New York City's Lower East Side has made major contributions to the social and political progress of American life in the areas of labor, housing, childcare, women's rights and others. This stencil celebrates the neighborhood public gardens developed on the lots of torn-down, burned-out buildings. ANTON VAN DALEN, 1988

velopments on the urban fringes cover over irreplaceable farm land. Wildlife habitats are constantly being destroyed or encroached upon. At a time when cities must become more self-reliant to handle rapidly growing populations, Nature's methods of promoting self-reliance are being subverted at a faster rate than ever before.

If we as a society are going to face and deal with the overwhelming plethora of urban problems, there needs to be a profound shift in the premises and activities of city living. Urban dwellers will have to adopt conserver values and carry out more responsible practices in a great variety of realms of daily life. Municipal governments need to restructure their priorities so that long-term sustainability can become a feasible goal. Cities need to become "green" in the broadest sense: they must be transformed into places that are life-enhancing and regenerative.

In order to facilitate the scale of urban greening that is actually needed, a new, overarching program of changes must be developed to help coalesce the efforts of existing single-issue groups, and to introduce and explore other concerns. This "umbrella" approach also has the advantage of being sensitive to many fronts at once, so that single issue programs, once developed, can withstand onslaughts from unexpected directions. The clean air issue, for example, can be seen as related not only to automobile smog controls, but also to many other aspects of urban life, such as the reduction of traffic in general, the creation of pedestrian malls in place of downtown streets and the rewriting of zoning laws so businesses can operate within walking distances of residential areas.

ACTION*

Planet Drum Foundation's *A Green City Program for San Francisco Bay Area Cities and Towns* was conceived as a prescription for the looming problems of the principal metropolitan center in the Shasta Bioregion (Northern California). It was developed through a series of highly participatory, democratically facilitated meetings on different issues of urban sustainability that were attended by representatives of activist groups, city agencies, businesses and citizen organizations. The recycling and re-use ses-

* Action section by Peter Berg

sion, for example, included people involved with small re-use businesses, large municipal garbage companies, city recycling departments, youth employment organizations and ecology groups. Other meetings addressed renewable energy, smart transportation, urban wild habitat, sustainable planning, urban planting, neighborhood character and empowerment, socially responsible small business, and celebrating life-place vitality.

The proposals that resulted from these wide-open "citizen planner" meetings are much stronger than the palliatives that are timidly discussed by city governments. This illustrates that people who work in areas of urban sustainability with the public are in general more aware of urban problems and more eager for change than are their designated local leaders. Here are some specific eco-conscious urban planning ideas:

- Cities should institute full-scale curbside recycling programs and point the way to greater re-use by buying recycled products whenever possible.

- All city buildings should be retrofitted to make use of some source of renewable energy.

- Single-passenger automobile use should be heavily discouraged through increased tolls; new municipal gasoline taxes should be imposed to pay for more public transit; downtown streets should be closed to private automobiles.

- City Departments of Natural Life should be established around the country to protect and restore wildlife and habitats.

- Planning decisions should be framed around residents' interest in preserving neighborhood livability; a share of city taxes should be allocated to neighbor-

hood councils for the maintenance and expansion of immediate local services.

- Natural features, native plants and animals, seasonal changes and other bioregional features that exist within cities should be taught at all school grade levels, emphasized in public information programs and celebrated through public art, festivals and holidays.

This is only a sampling of *A Green City's* proposals for re-thinking practices of urban life and city government policies. Some of the recommendations are already being actualized in a few communities, such as the restoration of Strawberry Creek in Berkeley, California. When many more of them are adopted and developed in urban environment, there will be a radical change in the way our cities look, feel and are regarded by the people who live in them.

Developing a program for each community is the first step toward creating a Green City. Once a "green print" has been developed, it can become a basis for starting Green City Centers and environmentally oriented activities that inform residents about sustainable practices. The final goal is to unite the groups that develop the program with the people who use the Centers. Together they can form the core of a large public constituency that can bring about municipal government policy changes by circulating petitions, lobbying elected officials, endorsing candidates and campaigning for public initiatives.

Today's cities face and generate problems that are already huge and can become even larger as their urban populations continue to grow. Creating a model for tomorrow's Green Cities conference is an important new priority that can fulfill the goal of fitting an increasingly urbanized majority of the world's human population back into Nature.

───────── RESOURCES ─────────

Organizations

Animal Liberation Front
Support Group
P.O. Box 915 Station F
Toronto, Ontario M4Y 2N9
Canada

Supports direct action, such as physically liberating animals from research labs. Frontline News ($10/year) reports on international actions and accomplishments of the animal rights movement, presents a radical social/political analysis of the issue and makes links with environmental issues, world hunger and native peoples' rights.

Architects, Designers and Planners for Social Responsibility
225 Lafayette Street
New York, NY 10012
(212) 334-8104

Works to integrate environmental and social issues into the planning process.

Center for Plant Conservation
125 Arbor Way
Jamaica Plain, MA 02130-3520
(617) 524-6988

A national network of programs at leading botanical gardens, dedicated to the preservation and study of all endangered American plants. Their goal is to create a systematic, comprehensive national program of plant conservation, research and education within existing institutions, to supplement and reinforce the preservation of genetic diversity through habitat protection. They intend to create a comprehensive collection of all the seeds of endangered native American plants. The center also organizes a network of botanic gardens and propagates seeds and cuttings. They publish a quarterly available for a non-obligatory $25

donation and offer a video entitled "The Garland of Generations."

Cultural Survival
11 Divinity Avenue
Cambridge, MA 02138

An essential resource for rainforest activists working to support indigenous peoples. Their scope is worldwide with a focus on Latin America and especially the Amazon. Cultural Survival Quarterly, available with a contribution of $20 or more, gives in-depth and authoritative coverage.

Earth First!
P.O. Box 5871
Tucson, AZ 85703
(602) 622-1371

Earth First! has no members; it consists of local groups and individuals who decide their own agenda and tactics under the banner of "No Compromise in Defense of Mother Earth." Earth First! groups stage tree sittings, block roads by self-burial and engage in "monkeywrenching," the disabling of the instruments of enviromental destruction. Earth First! Journal ($10/year) reports on national and international deep ecology activism and includes a lively discussion of the issues, strategies and tactics of defending the Earth.

Earth Island Institute
300 Broadway, Suite 28
San Francisco, CA 94133
(415) 788-3666

Initiates and supports internationally oriented action projects for peace, justice and the protection and restoration of the environment. Earth Island supports environmental brigades to Nicaragua, works with environmentalists in the Soviet Union and Japan, works in solidarity with activists in the Third World and organizes direct actions, public education and international *conferences. A $25 membership includes the quarterly* Earth Island Journal, *which reports on environmental action worldwide and makes explicit ties between politics, economics, social justice and ecology.*

Eco-home Network
4344 Russell Avenue
Los Angeles, CA 90027
(213) 662-5507

Maintains a model home to demonstrate environmentally sound living, including water conservation, recycling and a home orchard. Their newsletter is Ecolution.

Ecology Center
1403 Addison Street
Berkeley, CA 94702
(415) 548-2220

Has provided information to citizens for 20 years on ecological issues, including gardening, recycling and alternatives to fossil fuels. Offers classes and workshops, and publishes the monthly Ecology Center Newsletter.

Environmental and Developmental Group
CUSO Program in New Brunswick
180 St. John Street
Fredericton, NB E2B 489
Canada

CUSO has developed a model for sustainability in New Brunswick, exploring crucial issues for the province and illustrating a different kind of development—for social, environmental, and economic sustainability. Their booklet As If We Plan to Stay *outlines the environmental problems affecting both New Brunswick and the world at large. It is intended as a basic reference on green cities, energy consumption, water quality, forests, farming practices, peace, economy, labor, consumer awareness, ecology and indigenous peoples.*

Friends of the Earth-UK
26-28 Underwood Street,
London N1 7JQ
United Kingdom

Works closely with other European groups on a regionwide timber campaign. Their work is covered regularly in the World Rainforest Report *(available from RAN) or in* Tropical Rainforest Times *($30/year).*

Friends of the Urban Forest
512 2nd Street, 4th floor
San Francisco, CA 94107
(415) 543-5000

Plants trees in San Francisco and neighboring areas (as well as other countries). Their goal is to plant 2 million trees by the year 2000. They help neighborhoods, schools and other neighborhood groups plant and care for trees. Their periodical Treescapes, *available with $25 membership, provides information about tree-planting events and includes other articles of interest. The book* Trees for San Francisco *lists the best trees to plant in the area and is available for $6 postpaid.*

Global ReLeaf Program
American Forestry Association
P.O. Box 2000
Washington, DC 20013
(800) 368-5748

Aims to aid in the planting of over 100 million trees in the United States by 1992. They can put you in touch with a state coordinator who can help you set up a tree planting project of your own.

Green Belt Movement
P.O. Box 67545
Nairobi, Kenya

Founded by the National Council of Women of Kenya, an indigenous grassroots environmental campaign focused on tree planting. Relies on local expertise and organization, promotes public education and the involvement of women in the local envi-

ronmental and restoration process, and has established over 1000 tree nurseries to date. Invites donations.

Green Committees of Correspondence
P.O. Box 30208
Kansas City, MO 64112
(816) 931-9366

An organizing vehicle for the international Green movement in the US. Works on solutions to social and environmental problems through a decision-making process that is not hierarchal—a grassroots democracy of self-governing, humanly scaled, bioregionally integrated communities. It is a network of more than 200 local communities organized into 28 bioregions that are integrated at the national level. They have three publications: Green Letter, Green Synthesis and In Search of Greener Times. A membership is $10 for a person active in a local green group, $25 for a supporting membership.

Institute for Local Self-Reliance
2425 18th Street NW
Washington, DC 20009
(202) 232-4108

Encourages cities to utilize human, natural and financial resources to promote self-reliance and democratically controlled economic development. A resource on issues of solid waste management, recycling, and green cities. ILSR provides technical assistance, applied research and policy analysis.

Learning Alliance Bioregional Skills Network
494 Broadway
New York, NY 10012
(212) 226-7171

The BSN was designed out of the last Bioregional Congress to help those concerned identify and better utilize resources inside their bioregion. It covers bioregional education, mapping, publishing, culture and art, economics, people of color, native peo-

ples, green cities, watershed restoration, permaculture and food systems, and ecofeminism.

Mennonite Central Committee
12 South 12th Street
Akron, PA 17501
(717) 859-1151

Works on grassroots development, providing opportunities in over 50 countries for volunteers in agriculture, health, education, social services and community development. You must be an active member of a Christian church, and share their vision to participate. Their newsletter, Contact, includes human interest stories, volunteer experiences and MCC news.

The Nature Conservancy
1815 North Lynn Street
Arlington, VA 22209
(703) 841-5300

Purchases land that is habitat to endangered species and forms public access preserves. They have preserved hundreds of thousands of acres of diverse habitats worldwide, and support restoration projects on many of their preserves. They publish The Nature Conservancy Magazine bimonthly.

New Alchemy Institute
237 Hatchville Road
East Falmouth, MA 02536
(508) 564-6301

A research group focusing on small scale agriculture. They have designed a model home that processes nitrates, run a program where interns work in market gardens and participate in a children's program. The New Alchemy Quarterly, includes organizational news and environmental education.

Ocean Arks International
1 Locust Street
Falmouth, MA 02540
(508) 540-6801

Incorporated in 1982, OAI dissemi-nates the ideas and practice of ecological sustainability throughout the world. Currently, they are involved in development of solar aquatic waste treatment plants.

People for the Ethical Treatment of Animals (PETA)
P.O. Box 42516
Washington, DC 20015
(202) 726-0156

An educational and activist group opposed to all forms of animal oppression and exploitation. Their activities include activist workshops, lecture and film series, legislation, picketing and street theater. Call or write for their information packet.

Planet Drum
P.O. Box 31251
San Francisco, CA 94131
(415) 285-6556

A membership organization working towards urban sustainability and a clearinghouse for bioregional publications. They have recently published a practical guidebook, Green City Program for the San Francisco Bay Area Cities and Towns. *Their periodical is* Raise the Stakes.

Planners' Network
Institute for Policy Studies
1601 Connecticut Avenue NW
Washington, DC 20009
(202) 234-9382

Works to integrate environmental concerns into the planning process.

Rainforest Action Network
301 Broadway, Suite A
San Francisco, CA 94133
(415) 398-4404

To protect rainforests from destruction, RAN works with environmental and indigenous people's organizations in rainforest countries, and is building a grassroots movement in the US. RAN seeks to promote a better understanding of tropical defores-tation through education and direct action. For a $25 yearly membership you get monthly Action Alerts, *as well as the quarterly* World Rainforest Report.

Restoring the Earth
1713 C Martin Luther King, Jr. Way
Berkeley, CA 94709
(415) 843-2645 or 843-2928

An educational organization focusing on restoration ecology. Currently in the works is a handbook entitled Restoring the Earth.

Sahabat Alam Malaysia
(Friends of the Earth)
43 Salween Road
Penang 10050
Malaysia

Addresses issues affecting the rainforest and its peoples such as industrial invasion, toxic wastes, agribusiness, mining, timber extraction, cattle ranching and racism. The group publishes Suara Sam, *Malaysia's leading environmental newspaper ($23 airmail).*

Sea Shepherd Conservation Society
P.O. Box 7000 S, Dept. A
Redondo Beach, CA 90277
(213) 373-6979

Through non-violent confrontation and ecotage, the SSCS physically defends endangered wildlife from whalers, sealers, wolf hunters and others. They are committed to respect for life and, when neccessary, destroy the instruments of killing, with the conviction that life is more valuable than property. Over 300 volunteers have crewed on Sea Shepherd ships. They have sunk five pirate whaling ships, two of them by ramming on the high seas. (No one has ever been injured in a Sea Shepherd action.) Donations help maintain their two ships.

The Society for Ecological Restoration and Management
The University of Wisconsin Arboretum
1207 Seminole Highway
Madison, WI 53711
(608) 263-7889

Works to develop grassroots public support for the restoration and sound management of natural areas in urban, rural and wilderness areas. The society publishes the SERM Newsletter, *containing bulletins from members, updates on forthcoming meetings, job openings, news of society affairs and other events. They also publish* Restoration and Management Notes, *devoted to native ecological communities.*

Tree People–California Conservation Project
12601 Mulholland
Beverly Hills, CA 90210
(818) 769-2663

A volunteer-based organization dealing with environmental education and urban and mountain reforestation. The Seedling News, *a four-page newsletter, updates members on events and reforestation efforts. Tree People has also published* Planter's Guide to the Urban Forest *($12).*

Turtle Island Office
1333 Overhulse Road NE
Olympia, WA 98502
(206) 866-1046

A clearinghouse for many bioregional groups, providing information and news of events.

Volunteers in Technical Assistance
1815 North Lynn Street
Arlington, VA 22209
(703) 276-1800

A worldwide citizen corps of 4,500 private technical volunteers in science, engineering, construction, agriculture, informa-

tion systems and education. They provide service in the field and answer technical inquiries. Their newsletter, VITA News, *features articles on development, information about specific projects and volunteer experiences.*

The Women's Environmental Network
287 City Road
London, EC1V1LA
England

Examines issues of women, environment and development, redefining "development" to mean a process of change that safeguards the environment, facilitates women's self-empowerment and balances social and economic needs. WEN's resource materials reflect strong Third World participation and perspective.

Worldwatch Institute
1776 Massachusetts Avenue NW
Washington, DC 20036
(202) 452-1999

An independent non-profit research organization established to alert decision-makers and the general public to emerging trends in the availability and management of resources, both global and natural. They publish a yearly report, State of the World, *and a bimonthly magazine,* World Watch.

World Rainforest Movement
87 Cantonment Road
Penang 10250
Malaysia

A growing worldwide network of activists and concerned citizens working to crystallize public concern and devise campaigns to stem the destruction of tropical rainforests. Patterned after the Chipko Movement, it is attempting to form a broad-based coalition of human rights, consumer action, environmental, religious and labor groups to protect the rainforests and tribal peoples.

The Forest . . . a peculiar organism of unlimited kindness and benevolence that makes no demands for its sustenance and extends generously the products of its life activity: it affords protection to all beings, offering shade even to the axeman who destroys it.

—BUDDHA

Periodicals

Animals Agenda
P.O. Box 6809
Syracuse, NY 13217
Lively and informative monthly of the Animal Rights Network. $18 per year.

The Ecologist
Worthyvale Manor Farm
Camelford, Cornwall
PL32 9TT
England
A magazine critical of international institutions such as the World Bank, with tough coverage of the issues worldwide and a focus on the rainforest. The Ecologist is seeking one million signatures calling for a special United Nations session on tropical rainforests. Six issues, $28 ($40 airmail).

Books

All Their Own: People and the Places They Build. Jan Wampler. New York: Oxford University Press, 1978.
A collection of innovative environments and homes people designed and built for themselves.

And on the Eighth Day We Bulldozed It; Building the Rainforest Movement. Richard Grossman. San Francisco: Rainforest Action Network, 1988.

A challenge to take a hard, critical look at the US, its history, and present geopolitical behavior. Can we save the rainforests without addressing the problems of war, hunger, overpopulation and the denial of basic human rights? Citizens support the corporations that build the chainsaws, supply the gasoline and build the bulldozers that destroy the rainforests. Grossman asserts that the rainforest movement has the potential to influence other international campaigns profoundly. 20-page booklet, available from RAN for $2.

The Death and Life of Great American Cities. Jane Jacobs. New York: Vintage Press, 1961.
The drama of people living in neighborhoods neglected and destroyed by federal urban renewal programs.

Deep Ecology. Bill Devall and George Sessions. Salt Lake City: Gibbs M. Smith, Inc., 1985.
Argues that all human action should be based on a profound identification with the natural world. Contrasts biocentrism to anthropocentrism, and dissolves ethical distinctions between the value of human life and the value of other life forms.

Design for the Real World: Human Ecology and Social Change. Victor Papanek. New York: Van Nostrand Reinhold, 1984.
Approaches industrial design from a human point of view. Through his design work, the author has brought about a closer understanding between the poor and disadvantaged people of the Third World and rich and powerful people of the over-developed world.

Ecodefense. Dave Foreman. Tucson: Ned Ludd Books, 1985.
The complete guide to monkeywrenching in defense of the Earth. These tactics

may violate local and national laws but pro-vide the activist with methods for enforcing international moral and biological law.

Ecology as Politics.   Andre Gorz. Boston: South End Press, 1980.

A compelling historical analysis show-ing that ecology can never be considered apart from politics and economics. Argues that there are only two political directions that can save the Earth; one, towards a cen-tralized and undemocratic eco-facism where capital consolidates its power for sustaina-ble global exploitation; the other, towards a decentralized eco-socialism where economic justice complements sustainable environ-mental practices.

Ecology for Beginners.   Stephen Croall and William Rankin. New York: Pantheon Books, 1981.

An informational and fact-filled intro-duction to the principles of ecology, incor-porating a global analysis of the political and economic forces at work in the destruc-tion of the environment.

Endangered Species Handbook.   Greta Nilsson. Washington, DC: The Animal Wel-fare Institute, 1983.

A sourcebook on endangered species, with detailed descriptions of species. Ex-plains how extinction occurs through devel-opment, the fur and reptile trades, hunting and pesticide use. Especially good for teach-ers, it lists things you can do and a variety of class projects, films, books and slideshows.

In the Rainforest.   Catherine Caufield. Chicago: University of Chicago Press, 1984.

A highly readable book on tropical for-est destruction.

Life Above the Jungle Floor.   Donald Per-ry. New York: Simon and Schuster, 1986.

An intriguing look into life in the tropi-cal forest canopy. Written by one of the pi-oneering biologists in canopy studies, it

brings the reader up into the trees for a view of the biologist's life and the lives under his observation.

The Man Who Planted Trees.   Jean Giono. Chelsea, VT: Chelsea Green Publishing Company, 1985.

The true story of a man who planted 100 acorns a day for 30 years, converting thousands of acres of dry, bare, eroded hill-sides into lush, moist valleys full of wildlife. This book is compact and inspirational.

Our Common Future.   World Commis-sion on Environment and Development. New York: Oxford University Press, 1987.

An independent body at the UN headed by Norway's Prime Minister re-examines critical environmental and development problems and attempts to formulate realis-tic proposals to solve them. Serves notice to governments around the world that the time has come for a marriage of ecology and economy.

The Primary Source.   Norman Meyers. New York: W.W. Norton, 1984.

Probably the best book to begin one's education about tropical forests. Particu-larly useful in illustrating the connections between tropical forests and the industrial economies of the US and Europe. Full of useful examples and handy facts.

The Rise of Urbanization and the Decline of Citizenship.   Murray Bookchin. San Francisco: Sierra Club Books, 1987.

Defines a new and imaginative politics to help recover the power of the individual, restore the positive values and quality of ur-ban life and reclaim the ideal city as an in-spiring force in our civilization.

Sacred Cows at the Public Trough. Denzel and Nancy Ferguson. Bend, OR: Maverick Publications, 1983.

Describes clearly and graphically how public lands are being destroyed by over-

grazing. Describes how wildlife refuges and other public lands are doused with pesticides, filled with predator traps and overgrazed until the water table drops, the native plants are gone and the birds and waterfowl leave.

A Sand County Almanac. Aldo Leopold. San Francisco: Sierra Club/Ballantine, 1966.

The classic statement of the joy and beauty of a lifestyle in harmony with natural regions and rhythms.

The Scope of Social Architecture. C. Richard Hatch, ed. New York: Van Nostrand Reinhold Co., 1984.

Descriptions of 26 projects from 12 countries, continuing the international debate on the goals, methods and scope of social architecture, transforming the environment and the people who live in it.

Should Trees Have Standing? Christopher Stone. Los Altos, CA: William Kaufman, Inc., 1972.

A brilliant essay proposing that trees, mountains, rivers and lakes should—like corporations—have legal rights. The Supreme Court's opinions in the controversial Mineral King–Disney–Sierra Club suit are included in full.

Taking Part. Lawrence Halprin and Jim Burns. Cambridge, MA: MIT Press, 1974.

A work-study approach to collective creativity, encompassing environmental design, participatory planning and design.

Tools for Conviviality. Ivan Illich. New York: Harper and Row, 1973.

An indispensable framework for development of appropriate technology. Illich's far-reaching analysis of our decaying technological society attempts to define the border at which technology or "tools" infringe on individual liberties. It is an "ethics of energy"—a book filled with brilliant ideas.

A Wilderness Bill of Rights. William O. Douglass. Boston: Little, Brown & Company, 1965.

Associate US Supreme Court Justice Douglass sets forth his argument for recognizing the legal rights of natural entities.

PART SIX

MAKING WAR OBSOLETE

Nonviolence

S. BRIAN WILLSON

"If they can shed their fear of destruction, if they disarm themselves, they will automatically help the rest to regain their sanity. But then these great powers will have to give up their imperialistic ambitions and their exploitation of the so-called uncivilized or semi-civilized nations of the Earth and revise their mode of life. It means a complete revolution."

—GANDHI, SPEAKING ABOUT
NONVIOLENCE IN THE LARGE
NATIONS OF THE WORLD

I EXPERIENCED THE BEGINNINGS of awareness shortly after participating with the US military in 1969, in the incomprehensible marauding of Vietnam. I realized just how culturally conditioned we were to be violent in the name of good. The Vietnamese, "slopeheads" as we called them, our evil "enemies," became, strangely it seemed, like brothers and sisters and I felt a deep connection with them. Where did that feeling come from? I was not aware that it came from my training or education. I believe I was experiencing the real Brian Willson, a more authentic self, my humanity screaming for expression in a dehumanizing and violent setting produced by my culture and government. I believe this was the beginning of my nonviolent journey, even though I didn't have a name for it then. The fact is that I am still conditioned in violence but I

S. Brian Willson was brought up in a strict Baptist household. He once wrote a letter supporting the bombing of North Vietnam to stop the spread of communism. He enlisted in the US Air Force and served from 1966 to 1970. While in Vietnam he began speaking out against the war. Sensing another Vietnam War was unfolding in Central America, Brian went to Nicaragua to see for himself. During his nearly two-month visit, contras attacked nearby targets, killing eleven civilians—compelling Brian to act. After returning home, he joined three other US war veterans in a Veteran's Fast for Life on the steps of the US Capitol that ultimately lasted 47 days. In 1987, Brian helped organize Nuremberg Actions to protest US weapons shipments to Central America from the Concord, California Naval Weapons Station. Escalating his participation in the Nuremberg Actions, he planned a 40-day fast on the tracks at the Concord Naval Weapons Station beginning September

am far more aware of another more profound dimension of my nature that I call love or nonviolence.

Shortly after my term of duty in Vietnam I became a seeker of peace. I began reading about the history of justice and anti-war struggles, and became interested in nonviolence as an alternative *concept* to violence and militarism. This interest tended to distract me from seeking a comfortable career path. Even so, I was reasonably successful in my various pursuits, while possessing what I believed to be politically "correct" views. Throughout the 1970's and early 1980's, however, I experienced a problem that interfered with feeling peace within myself.

My problem was that I harbored hatred for my father. I had conveniently focused my feelings of betrayal and rage since Vietnam onto him. After all, he had been a significant teacher of my values and, I believed, of lies and of my ignorance. My developing thoughts about a new society based on justice in a global context were being actively blocked by my unhealthy inner psyche. Hatred is like poison. I had not yet learned the essence of love and health: that love is unconditional and that forgiveness is profoundly healing. Growing up in a conservative Baptist family had provided me with the teachings of Jesus and Christianity, including at least rhetorically, the power of love and forgiveness. But as we had been led to slaughter nearly five million Southeast Asians, killing "communists" under the guise of Jesus, I had developed a personal

philosophy that rejected what seemed to me simplistic, even if inaccurately understood, biblical teachings. I had become an eclectic, listening to many sources of wisdom, including the Native Americans. I continue to evolve with this ecumenical approach.

A breakthrough came, however, not in unraveling the "correct" religious view, but as the result of therapy with an excellent, though not highly "professionally" qualified counselor. I needed to unravel myself. After much painful work over time, I was able to love my father unconditionally. Isn't this the real love? My father was not likely to change. I had to choose to change if I wanted to feel good about myself and to become an effective peace warrior. Almost unbelievably, I was able to love my father without liking him. He was no longer the "enemy." In fact my "need" for "enemies" has become much less, sometimes seeming virtually nonexistent. I could look at the world, and all its problems, and all the struggles necessary to pursue justice, without creating enemies in my analytical mind. I realized everyone is transformable! Even myself!

The calm I began to feel inside, without prescribed medicine, seemed almost miraculous. Experiencing a sacred connection with my own father, an embittered and intensely racist man, without having to accept or like any of his irritating traits and views and without requiring him to accept any of my beliefs, was the beginning of my intimate and visceral journey with nonviolence. I found a new level of integration of my

1, 1987. He notified Navy officials of his planned fast and blockade well ahead, informing them of his peaceful protest. Navy officials ignored the protester's warnings and ordered their munitions train to proceed. The train accelerated into the protesters, traveling over three times the legal speed limit. Brian was struck by the train, severing both his legs and causing severe head injuries. Despite serious injuries, Brian continues to work for peace in Central America and elsewhere, devoting his life to "waging unconditional peace through nonviolence." Brian lives with his wife Holley Rauen in San Francisco. Brian and Holley are co-founders of the Institute for the Practice of Nonviolence. The Institute promotes nonviolent action inspired by the teachings of Jesus Christ, Gandhi, Martin Luther King and others.

A massive anti-nuclear march winds its way through Tokyo in February 1988. Grassroots anti-nuclear activism has increased in Japan since the first radioactive winds from Chernobyl reached there in 1986.
KATHY GLASS

thoughts (mind) with feelings (heart), very important for inner peace and therefore health. Liberation occurs as one is able to remove distracting inner conflicts and fears.

Learning about this natural interconnectedness (through unconditional love) with the soul of my father, even in an unsentimental way, opened up a visceral consciousness that *everything* is interconnected and sacred. The visceral and intellectual came together. I began to offer my father an alternative, a nonretaliatory attitude. Internally I no longer felt the need nor the impulse to be hostile to him. This became for me a powerful new weapon that, while expressing outwardly the product of an ongoing transformational process within, was creating a new noncombative atmosphere for my father as well. Though to this day he hasn't changed any that I am aware of, our relationship is respectful, even if not intimate.

This experience helped me understand better what Gandhi meant when he said: "The virtues of mercy, nonviolence, love and truth in any man (sic) can be truly tested only when they are pitted against ruthlessness, violence, hatred and untruth." I had already experienced evil incarnate with our behavior in Vietnam. I had become an amateur student of the barbarity of the history of US foreign policy, and had learned a more authentic view of our historic domestic justice struggles. But this relatively minor, though very personal and painful, struggle with my father provided me a real visceral taste of both the challenge, and the liberation of nonviolence.

Thus, I believe nonviolence springs from an inner consciousness that understands interconnectedness. Nonviolence becomes the fruit of this inner unity and health, not a means of achieving inner peace. It becomes a powerful *force*. It is *daily* learning. This consciousness affects our attitudes and our whole way of life.

I also believe that nonviolence is based on conviction of the presence of a higher Truth. Each day we can commit to being a partner with this infinite life force, a force that Gandhi called truth force, or Satyagraha, and Martin Luther King called cosmic companionship. This commitment cannot be taken for granted, for our egos and arrogance are well developed. Gandhi and King catalyzed the most powerful nonviolent social/political change movements in the 20th century, discerning daily with this infinite wisdom. Along with moments of great clarity, there are times of anguish and uncertainty. But the path of justice is sustaining. Some call it God, or the higher self, a force far more powerful and wise than our mere cerebral dimensions. I call it the Great Spirit. But it matters not what one calls it.

Gandhi considered each day a new opportunity to experiment with the Truth.

Our truth is discerned through intuition, experience, observation, reflection, quiet listening, informed judgment, conversation and from being questioned while we question. We can choose to act each day on this wisdom, reflect upon our actions, then using this guiding process, act again.

As intimated above, nonviolence recognizes the interconnectedness of all life as the natural law of our being, and that this truth resides in each of us. It seeks to be part of this harmony, while offering it to others hoping they will be transformed by getting in touch with this higher self within them. Nonviolence knows that injustices experienced elsewhere threaten our own well being also. Everything is connected!

For me, nonviolence is like a new invention, even if it is really the authentic nature of life. It is vigorously active, the opposite of passivity. Because it is so different from the way I was raised, it is challenging, while it is empowering. Nonviolence actively resists evil in ourselves and others. It takes personal responsibility to be a part of the solution—to promote justice. Thus I have to prepare myself often for situations that may present tense confrontations with aggressors or authorities. Nonviolence non-cooperates with and actively confronts injustice. One must be prepared to transcend cowardly tendencies, through spiritual and mental preparation. In its actions nonviolence seeks to bring to light the nature of injustices and contradictions by offering a clear expression of love and truth in the face of obvious oppression and injustice. It is tough love, for when resisting injustice, it accepts sacrifice and suffering when necessary without retaliating.

When civil rights activists were desegregating lunch counters with their bodies, for example, they were subjected to extreme humiliation, if not physical beatings or death. The firm but nonviolent presence of the activists promoting something so basically just in the face of the prejudice directed against them brought to clear light the dehumanizing racism of the segregation laws. The issues became illuminated for all to see. Nonviolence takes the risks necessary, thoughtfully but forcefully, to affirm justice and sacredness, even for the oppressor. Nonviolence, therefore, seeks transformation in the oppressor. It avoids humiliating or defeating one's adversary. It seeks reconciliation and healing. It stirs conscience with militant peacefulness.

We need to continually ask whether our behavior is complicit with policies, practices and lifestyles that destroy any person, including their dignity, or any other part of the sacred ecological web of life. It we truthfully have searched for and discovered our complicity, nonviolence requires an openness to change our behavior.

Though obvious, nonviolence seeks to avoid internal violence of the spirit as well as external physical violence. As I learned with my father, we can love people without liking them. Unconditional love need not be sentimental in order to express compassion that flows from the awareness of our inherent interconnectedness. It resists while transcending evils being perpetrated at the moment. It understands that we get what we *actually* do with our lives, rather than what we intend to do. Ends and means become inseparable as to character and intrinsic nature.

In short, the ongoing process of becoming nonviolent is a revolutionary process of affirmation and transformation of consciousness. Revolution begins within the consciousness of people like you and me, and is continually refined through acting, reflecting, acting, etc.

Nonviolence provides us with the basis for a new paradigm based on justice and ecological consciousness. This pilgrimage of responsible and empowered citizenship transcends nations, states, religions, political parties and ideologies, races and sexes. It respects the uniqueness and diversity of people and cultures, while it understands our unity and interconnectedness. It daily asks the question: What does it mean to be a *human being* on the planet with millions of other species coexisting in a mysterious biological and spiritual fabric?

Our way of life in the so-called civilized, industrialized societies has developed at the expense of billions of people, millions of plant and animal species, most resources, and of the health of the planet earth herself. Our emphasis on material consumption, accumulation and waste is a lifestyle of incredible violence. We are assaulting the dignity and sovereignty of life and "resources" as if they are mere objects at our mercy and for our personal profit and comfort. We are murdering countless poor in the "Third" or "undeveloped" world because they want to live with justice rather than misery. We are killing water, air, soil, plants and animals everywhere. Our waste, a concept totally at odds with fundamental ecological principles requiring everything to be the basis for new life again, is literally going to kill us if we don't stop creating it. We intervene with overt and covert military barbarism into the sovereignty of dozens of other nations. We are marauding everything in our way, just as we did with the indigenous people who were present before Europeans landed on the continent. In the United States, with 5 percent of the world's population, we consume an extraordinarily disproportionate amount of the Earth's resources. Thus, it doesn't take much to offend the "national security" interests of the United States.

This kind of barbarism and insanity has happened, and continues to happen, only because we lack consciousness and under-standing. We have come to believe ourselves as detached from and superior to virtually all of the natural world and most "other" people. In fact, we are detached from our own nature. We have been assaulting ourselves! In our worship of money and things we have become spiritually depraved, and mentally ill.

The good news is that in our experiment with the truth, every day is a new opportunity to make choices to change, to willingly endure transformation, even though it is painful as well as liberating and joyous. As we look around we see people making profound changes everywhere. Change is in the wind—it is inherent in our natures. We can take personal responsibility for making choices based on our sense of truth. We can dare ourselves, if necessary, to "say it the way we see it," and "express it the way we feel it." We can actually live as if justice was everything, respecting the incredible fabric within which we live and upon which our lives are absolutely dependent for survival. We must examine what we buy, what we read and view, how we invest or spend our money and personal time, the method of our transportation and movement, how much we consume in resources each day, how we "make" our livelihood, etc. In looking at the whole picture are we harming or enhancing life? Our choices must respect our humble place on the planet. Every choice we make possesses social, economic and ecological implications that affect the health of all life, perhaps the survival of the planet herself, and certainly the survival of our own and many other species. Perhaps it is now time to declare: Change or Perish! The prevailing system really requires our cooperation in money, work and silence. The truth is that living "business as usual" amounts to suicide. We really do not need a system that is killing us all. This is the epitome of sheer madness. To embark upon a path of change based upon our truth, to move into revolutionary nonviolence, is to be part of hope and affirmation.

I believe that we are at a point in history when we need to remove any preconceived limitations we might possess about what is possible once we empower ourselves to act. But our challenge is a moral, not a technological, one. We in the industrialized societies must choose to join the human race as equals and defer to the ecological imperative, in effect, to the true nature of ourselves. We need to enthusiastically and vigorously resist and noncooperate with policies and practices that are at odds with what we know to be true. Boldly, but thoughtfully, we can affirm a new vision of living in inter-relationship with all other life. There are no technological fixes, only a willingness to change our consciousness, a much greater challenge. It is conceivable that in one generation the concept of bioregions and regional ecosystems (e.g. historic Indigenous sacred hunting and roaming areas where the people intimately knew their resources and limitations) will replace historic nation-states as the only reasonable manner for defining political boundaries. We will have to quickly terminate our use of fossil fuels and learn that "slow" as well as "small" may in fact be beautiful, and required. Changes in our lifestyles will be dramatic. I predict that after the initial shock we will feel relieved, and healthier.

Virtually all that we need to know in order to participate in this nonviolent revolution has been devised. We only need the will. How much do want to survive with dignity? From various appropriate technologies to numerous expressions of spiritual/political consciousness through noncooperation, boycotts and resistance campaigns, we have a profound experiential base in order to walk this new path. The Indigenous peoples of the world, including the Native Americans, have never lost their ecological consciousness—a beautiful wisdom.

We are witnessing a movement of grass roots efforts throughout the world, people empowering themselves to be part of the solution. Numerous groups and individuals are working to stop the intervention of the United States in "Third" World countries in defiance of their own US government. Similar efforts are fighting further testing and deployment of nuclear and other military weapons, not just in the US, but worldwide. The number of local, regional, national and international actions responding to the cries of Mother Earth, the Gaia, for ecological sanity is growing at a phenomenal rate. Responses to homelessness, hunger, lack of health care, the AIDS challenge, Apartheid, protecting sacred Native lands, etc., are springing from the people wherever they are feeling the pain of injustice.

Nation-state governments are generally continuing to maintain the traditional economic development and consumption model destined to kill all life, if left unchecked. But people are spontaneously, and often without knowing of other similar activities, rising up to meet the challenge of the truth as it reveals itself so clearly in front of our eyes. The choices are becoming clearer: work harder to maintain deeper denial, or affirm empowered alternatives. Tax resistance, one of the most decentralized forms of resistance, is becoming a more accepted manner of extricating oneself from complicity of literally paying for death and destruction.

The number of people involved directly in solidarity and diplomatic efforts with peoples of other nations is also increasing. In unprecedented fashion, over 100,000 US citizens have gone to Nicaragua to stand in the way of the US government's illegal determination to murder and maim an entire nation. Activities of US and other citizens working in various Latin American countries, in Africa, in the Soviet Union, among others, while Vietnam War veterans are now rebuilding health clinics in Vietnam achieving atonement with the people they once bombed, foretell a new age where people will no longer wait for governments to wage peace. People are increasingly willing to pay the price and make the sacrifices necessary in order to begin a people's worldwide nonviolent revolution of consciousness. It is the only hope left for our species and the earth.

The Vision Guide to the Practice of Nonviolence provides the reader with suggested ingredients of this practical revolution. CHANGE OR PERISH!

ACTION*

A Vision Guide To The Practice Of Nonviolence

Resistance and Noncooperation	Affirmative Alternative
1. Boycott mass media, including TV; the media monopoly regularly distorts news and images.	Support alternative information sources: community access and community owned radio and TV, alternative print media, local networking.
2. Boycott bank and stock investments; investments profit on injustice worldwide.	Invest in locally controlled banks and credit unions and in socially just funds where you know precisely what the money is being used for; Vermont State Bank now invests exclusively in local development and social services; there are many alternative funds now.
3. Phase out use of fossil fuels, especially use of private automobiles and central power plants; these two modern inventions are the largest source of pollutants destroying the ecological health.	Develop conservation of energy lifestyles; use only replenishable resources such as solar; alternative transportation such as trains, bicycles, horses and walking; massive reforestation in every local area as antidote; Amish model.

*Action section by Brian Willson

4. Boycott mass consumer items; our consumption patterns and habits furnish the basis for a world of unaccountable transnational corporations exploiting human and natural resources and thriving on waste and *our* lifestyles.

Live in locally reliant communities in harmony with local ecology; use only recyclable resources; develop economy based on local services and barter; live simply with appropriate resources and locally produced organic food; respect of land is indispensable; study practices of indigenous people.

5. Boycott payment of national taxes; they now support a military and transnational industrial complex that is literally destroying the world and ignoring human and ecological needs.

Redirect monies for the public good to local needs, peace efforts, and socially responsible efforts directly; support groups like Greenpeace, Veterans Peace Action Team, and the newly forming Peace Army, as examples.

6. Boycott military service; what happens if they prepare for wars and nobody cooperates?

Redefine responsible citizenship, contribution of our labor for justice, peace efforts, and local community human and ecological health.

7. Resistance and noncooperation with nation-state policies/values; lawlessness is rampant to maintain the 16 percent that comprise the "First World" by consuming 80 percent of the world's resources via exploitation and domination.

Develop bioregional ecosystems as bases for community definition; participate in civil obedience to international law protecting sovereignty and prohibiting aggression (Nuremberg Obligation); civil resistance to government lawlessness.

Important: Resistance is not effective without affirmative counteraction!

Addressing the Nuclear Threat

DR. HELEN CALDICOTT

T HE TROUBLE IS that the world is run by old men, some women, but mostly old men. And they're stuck in old modes of thinking. Einstein, a brilliant man (although I wish he hadn't been so brilliant as to split the atom), said that the splitting of the atom changed everything except humankind's mode of thinking. Thus we drift toward unparalleled catastrophe. The men that run the world still think of war as they did when they stood at the top of a castle wall and fought with bows and arrows. They have not understood that war now is not war, it is annihilation.

How many leaders of the world have actually seen a hydrogen bomb explode? A small number. How many have felt the heat on their faces or seen a battleship rise up in the water like a splinter and disappear? I would say none. How many leaders of the world have ever seen a baby being born? It's a miracle—out of this fat tummy comes this magnificent thing. A miracle every time a baby is born. How many leaders of the world have ever helped a child to die and helped the parents in their grief? Probably none. And that's what we're talking about-individual lives. And not just humans—what about the lions, tigers and the elephants and the whales? What about all the beautiful plants—the roses and the gardenias? And what about even the microorganisms, upon which the whole structure and pyramid of life depends?

Somehow we have to penetrate our leaders' psychic numbing.

And so what's happened to us? We have not been able to keep up with technology—most of us don't even understand it. I don't understand how a missile is fired; I've had to learn a lot about it, but I don't really understand it.

Dr. Caldicott was born in Melbourne, Australia, and earned her medical degree at Adelaide Medical School. From 1977 to 1980, she was instructor in pediatrics at Harvard Medical School. She is President Emeritus of Physicians for Social Responsibility and the founder of Women in Action for Nuclear Disarmament (WAND). Author of *Nuclear Madness: What You Can Do* and *Missile Envy*, Dr. Caldicott was the subject of the film *If You Love This Planet,* produced by the National Film Board of Canada. The film was labeled "political propaganda" by the Justice Department in 1983 and won the the 1983 Academy Award for Best Short Documentary.

At Greenham Common, a nuclear-equipped air force base in southern England, women established a peace camp which for several years was a center for resisting and disrupting the military activities there. RACHEL JOHNSON

Scientists stay in their ivory towers at MIT and Harvard and Johns Hopkins and Los Alamos, designing these weapons of genocide, not telling anyone about it because most of it is classified and secret. We must not know how we're going to die, it's all kept secret. It's like when we used to be very arrogant in medicine and we'd say, "Don't worry, we'll fix everything. But we won't tell you what you've got. We won't tell you that you've got a cancer so that you can adjust to the fact that you're going to die and therefore die in peace." Tremendous arrogance! And we're paying for it. We pay for it with tax dollars. The Pentagon has 1,600 lobbyists on the Hill every day. Where are the lobbyists representing the children of the world? There aren't any. That's why the politicians aren't representing us—they don't even hear from us!.

And we are prepared to continue our

lives in the same psychic numbing, not thinking about the fact that we're about to die at any time. You know, if you have rats in a cage, and you threaten them with a life-threatening situation, they run away and do something totally irrelevant from that which threatens them. It's called *displacement activity*. Isn't that what we do every day?

Let's describe a nuclear war so you understand what we're talking about. Every town and city with a population larger than 10,000 in this country and the Soviet Union and Europe is targeted with at least one bomb. There are probably 65 bombs targeted on New York alone, 60 on Moscow alone—each one bigger than the bomb dropped in Hiroshima. Nuclear war between Russia and America will take about 30 minutes to an hour to complete, because once one side presses the button, the weapons go out into space and re-enter the earth's atmosphere at 20 times the speed of sound and land pretty accurately at the targeted city. Meanwhile, the other country's satellites—and there are hundreds of satellites watching all the time—see the weapons being launched and they press their button, the weapons cross in midspace, and the whole thing is over in an hour or two.

So we're not going to have much time to prepare for it, but the Department of Civil Defense is preparing for us to relocate from risk areas to host areas out in the country. It takes eight days to evacuate cities, but they say not to worry, we'll have time. The President is planning to put little gadgets on our televisions and radio sets so that they turn on just in time to tell you that you have a quarter of an hour to say goodbye.

Out to a radius of six miles, every person would be killed, many actually vaporized. We could never do that before nuclear weapons—vaporize people. Most of the body is water and, when exposed to the heat of the sun, we just turn into gas. We've already done it, there are pictures and photographs of shadows of people from Hiroshima. Every building will be destroyed up to a radius of six miles, that's a diameter of twelve miles. Out to a radius of 20 miles, every person will be killed or lethally injured. The pressures are so great that human beings, bricks, broken glass and so forth are converted into missiles, traveling at 100 miles an hour or so until they hit the nearest solid object. Such missiles will cause severe lacerations, decapitations, and other injuries. The Pentagon has a book called *The Effects of Nuclear War,* and they work out in detail just how far a piece of broken glass, traveling 100 miles an hour, will penetrate human flesh. It's like reading a recipe for Auschwitz.

Out to a radius of 26 miles, if you're just walking along, your clothes would instantaneously ignite and you'd become a flaming torch. If you look at the flash from 40 miles away, you could be instantly blinded. There would be a firestorm from about 1,500 to 3,000 square miles, so if you go to a fallout shelter, the firestorm sucks the oxygen out and you die of asphyxiation, and the blast and heat convert the fallout shelters to crematoria.

So to talk about civil defense and fallout shelters is medically unethical. We think that within 30 days after nuclear war up to 90 percent of Americans, Russians, and Europeans will be dead. What will be the long-term effects on the world? Well, of course, those few poor people staggering about around the ruins will have to stay in their fallout shelters for two months, because the radiation fallout is so severe that it will cause vomiting, cause hair to fall out and ultimately result in death. If they come out the world will be different; everything we know will be gone. All the music—Bach, Beethoven, Handel; no more art, no more literature, no more buildings, and millions and millions of corpses. And, as the corpses decay, bacteria will multiply in the dead flesh. Insects are very resistant to radiation; cockroaches are 400 times more resistant to radiation than humans. They'll multiply by the trillions because the birds will be killed by the fallout. So there will be epidemics, like the Black Plague in the 14th century, of diseases that we now cure, such as typhoid, poliomyelitis, hepatitis and many others. We think that so much ozone that protects us from the sun will be destroyed in the upper atmosphere that every creature on the planet would be blinded by the ultraviolet radiation. That's the death of the Earth. And the ultraviolet radiation could even destroy microorganisms, and thus all life.

So we're talking about the death of the planet. How it is that it hasn't happened yet, I don't know. The computers in the Pentagon keep making mistakes; 151 errors in a 15-month period. The most serious was when someone plugged a war games tape into the fail-safe computer, and it made a mistake—it saw missiles coming from Russia. Three squadrons of planes took off with nuclear weapons heading toward the Soviet Union. At the seventh minute they had to notify the president, but they couldn't find him. Suppose he was in the bathroom or something?

We were 14 minutes away from annihilation in November, 1979. It was in the headlines in Britain, and in the *New York Times* there was a tiny item near the obituaries. Five thousand men who handle nuclear weapons are discharged from the military every year because they drink, take drugs or are mentally unstable. We had a president recently who was not mentally stable toward the end of his term. We see patients who become psychotic under severe stress.

It's stressful being a president of a superpower. There are many ways a nuclear war could start. It could start mostly by mistakes.

Ninety-two percent of the people of the world don't live in Russia or America and don't care about the petty arguments about how many bombs each side has. It really is up to us to "take the toys away from the boys." They behave like little boys in a sandbox with arrested emotional development. And we have to see that they grow up, mature or get rid of them and put in people who are mature adults. It really is up to everyone of us to save this planet. We can't just blame the president. We/I have to take the world on our shoulders like Atlas and say, "I am totally responsible for this planet and my children and the children of the world."

ACTION*

1. **Intervene in the testing, transport and manufacture of nuclear weapons.** Protest US policy and demand that the goal of arms negotiations be a 100 percent reduction of our nuclear arsenal. Protest and disrupt uranium mining. Contact the War Resisters League or a peace resource center in your region to learn of upcoming actions.

2. **Boycott General Electric, Lockheed, Sylvania, Boeing and Westinghouse.** Write to them and tell them your are boycotting all of their products and services until they cease producing nuclear weapons or components of nuclear warfare. Contact INFACT for information on the G.E. boycott.

3. **Particpate in citizen diplomacy efforts** through educational exchange, sister city programs or the various "peace walks" and other East/West friendship events.

4. **Work to free all the Plowshares and other prisoners who have done symbolic damage to warheads and missiles.** Put *them* on milk cartons.

5. **Make reparations to people and communities harmed by atomic bomb factories.** Provide alternate jobs for workers.

6. **Shut down all nuclear power plants.** Workers should get alternative jobs or salaries for life.

7. **Withhold taxes.** Work for laws establishing alternate funds for people to make tax payments to implement all of the above transitions.

*Action section by Brad Erickson

Economic Conversion

MICHAEL CLOSSON

"We have for too long been reacting to someone else's agenda. The time has come for us to establish our own. Peace and justice advocates of all persuasions have one common enemy: *war!* It is a terminal disease that drains the finances, youth, energy and intellect of nations. We must abolish war and violence as instruments of state policy and begin addressing the real national security threats: poverty, prejudice, illiteracy, disease and environmental degradation."

NATIONAL PRESIDENT, VETERANS FOR PEACE

HOW DO WE REVERSE the global arms race and build a peaceful and sustainable world? The answer lies in a strategy that effectively counters the economic momentum of militarism.

Across America, millions of workers, thousands of companies and hundreds of communities are hostages to the Pentagon. They depend upon the jobs and profits generated by military spending for their economic well-being. Indeed, many defense firms are addicted to the the Pentagon dole.

They experience the short-term high of contracts followed by the need for another "hit."

As a result of the hostage/addiction phenomenon, many Congresspeople are themselves hostages to the Pentagon. For example, Don Edwards (D-Calif.) is a staunch supporter of the Bradley Fighting Vehicle, which has been called a "lemon on tracks." Edwards says he supports the dubious system because he wants to keep our troops safe in combat. Another obvious rea-

Michael Closson is the Executive Director of the Center for Economic Conversion. He consults with military-dependent communities on economic revitalization strategies, conducts workshops on strategies for building a civilian-oriented economy and lecures and writes extensively on conversion and related topics.

*"Swords into Plowshares," the badge of un-
official East German peace groups.*
EUROPEAN NUCLEAR DISARMAMENT (END)

*Inside a US Army Recruiting Station. On
tax day, a Gray Panther demonstrates
against US military spending.*
RACHEL JOHNSON, 1987

son for his support is that over 2,000 defense workers are employed in his congressional district producing the Bradley.

Weapons spending is a giant and largely
sacrosanct jobs program. The Pentagon
picks the winning and losing technologies,
the winning and losing industrial sectors
and, to some degree, the winning and losing
sections of our country.

The other major area demanding re-
thinking is our relationship with the Earth.
Human-induced global environmental decay threatens a fate as horrific as nuclear
holocaust. Yet, it is largely a quiet crisis.
Carbon dioxide build-up and ozone depletion are not detectable by the average person. It is easy to ignore the impending catastrophe since its manifestations are currently
relatively imperceptible. But, we rapidly
need to learn to live in harmony with the
Earth if our children are to have a future on
this beautiful and fragile planet.

How do we turn this situation around?
How do we attain a condition in which military spending is justified solely on the basis
of legitimate defense needs and not on the
basis of exaggerated foreign threats or needed domestic jobs? How do we address the issues that really matter?

The answer is to engage in the process
of "economic conversion"—the systematic
redirection of resources now employed in
military activities to socially and environmentally useful endeavors.

Economic conversion includes transforming defense plants and bases to civilian
endeavors and diversifying the economies of
military-dependent areas like Los Angeles,
Connecticut and Seattle. Writ large, economic conversion means establishing new
national priorities designed to revitalize our
society, restore our environment and educate our populace.

Advance planning for conversion of military industry is very desirable both politically and economically. Congresspeople are loath to cut Pentagon spending when they know it will cause significant economic dislocation and job loss. Without advance plans for the transformation of defense industry, our legislators (and the general public) will have difficulty opposing military spending solely on its own merits. Also, without contingency plans in place, defense firms will lay off thousands of workers when Pentagon contracts are cut—just as they did when the Vietnam War was winding down. Plans for commercial production will enable a smooth transition to a "peace economy."

How do we achieve this shift? There is a saying, "People are more comfortable with a problem that is familiar than with a solution that is not." In order to overcome resistance to change, even on the part of those who recognize the need for it, we have to make the solutions familiar to people. "Star Wars lacks not from cogent critiques but from compelling rivals." To positively transform the world, we must create compelling rivals to Star Wars and the mentality it reflects.

To do this, we need to make a conceptual flip-flop. Problems confront us at every turn: acid rain, fossil fuel depletion, decaying cities, inadequate health care, eroding topsoil and malnourished children. These problems can also be viewed as opportunities to redirect our resources and talents in a positive direction.

In addition to starting to alleviate the problems of militarism, shifting our energies and talents in this manner will generate millions of socially useful jobs—three million in renewable energy development alone. Thousands of positive business ventures can be created and expanded. (Many of these jobs and business ventures will provide direct applications for workers and technologies now in the military sector.) And, given the global scope of the work before us, opportunities for multinational collaboration will abound. (Imagine a joint project involving the US, the Soviet Union and Japan, which assists African countries to develop a system of sustainable agriculture.)

The time is right to make this shift in thinking and behavior. The American public is waking up to the fact that military might cannot cure our budget deficit. It cannot prevent global warming or acid rain. And, it cannot insure that our children are well educated and healthy.

Only by shifting significant resources and talents to these problems can we start to solve them. That is what economic conversion is all about.

ACTION*

1. **Push Congress to allocate the military budget to social programs, environmental restoration and urban renewal.** Cutting the military budget 50 percent right away would be a good clean start. Insist that our tax money be used to improve living conditions instead of bankrolling the machinery of global destruction. Set up mechanisms for communites and regions to decide what they need. Suggest that military personnel be assigned to retool or dismantle weapons and other destructive technologies. Remind your elected representatives of their responsibility to our children and ask them to think about the effects of military spending on our real security. Tell them that the nuclear arms race makes you feel less, not more, secure.

2. **Protest and disrupt the activities** of Lockheed, Boeing, General Electric, weapons labs, arms manufacturers and arms transporters, using creative and vigorous methods.

3. **Withhold taxes.** Direct the money you would pay in federal income tax to community conversion funds to carry out the transitions, taking care of the needs of any workers displaced by demilitarization.

* Action section by Brad Erickson

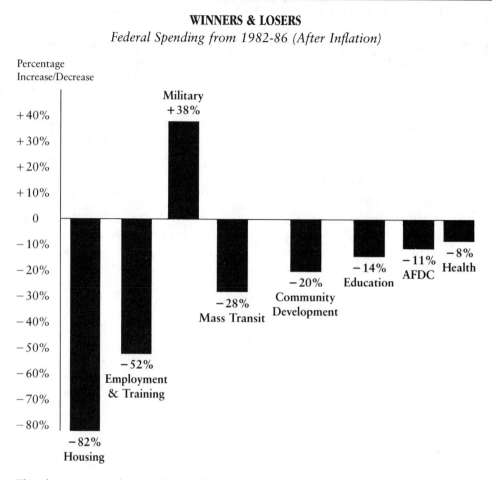

WINNERS & LOSERS

Federal Spending from 1982-86 (After Inflation)

This chart measures how much spending has changed as a result of federal budget policies from fiscal years 1982-86.

Sources: Military figure based on Department of Defense data, December 1986. Domestic program estimates, except housing, from "The Republican Record, FY 1982-86," prepared for the American Federation of State, County and Municipal Employees by Fiscal Planning Services, September 1986. All figures based on current service estimates of budget outlays. Housing figure from the Low Income Housing Information Service based on budget authority data contained in the FY 1987 Budget of the U.S. Government.

JOBS WITH PEACE CAMPAIGN

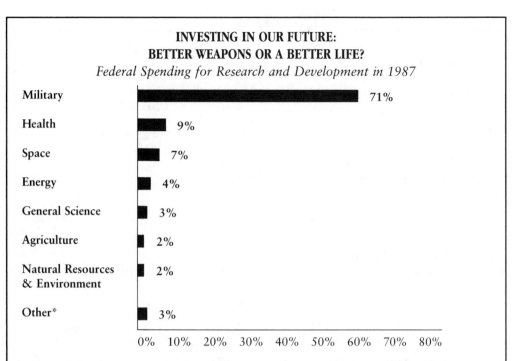

INVESTING IN OUR FUTURE:
BETTER WEAPONS OR A BETTER LIFE?
Federal Spending for Research and Development in 1987

Military — 71%
Health — 9%
Space — 7%
Energy — 4%
General Science — 3%
Agriculture — 2%
Natural Resources & Environment — 2%
Other* — 3%

0% 10% 20% 30% 40% 50% 60% 70% 80%

*Other includes Commerce (.5%), Transportation (.5%), International Affairs (.3%), Veterans (.3%), and (.9%) divided among Education and Training, Labor, Justice, Housing and Urban Development, and other Social Services.

The chart above shows how the U.S. government will spend our money for research and development (R & D)—approximately $58 billion during 1987. The lion's share is for weapons, which means that we are able to produce the world's most technologically advanced arms. Meanwhile civilian industries are losing their ability to compete because of outdated and inefficient factories.

Our international competitors, on the other hand, commit the bulk of their R & D money to civilian industries. While U.S. industrial workers are steadily losing jobs, Japan, West Germany and other trade competitors are cornering the market in steel, automobiles, textiles and electronics.

Our choice is between investing in more sophisticated weapons for the Pentagon or investing in a future that creates better and more productive lives for people.

Source: FY 1987 Enacted Budget, U.S. Office of Management and Budget; "Federal R & D Funding by Budget Function, FY 1985-87," National Science Foundation, March 1986.

Jobs with Peace Campaign

RESOURCES

Organizations

The Albert Einstein Institution
1430 Massachusetts Avenue
Cambridge, MA 02138
(617) 876-0311

Supports work on the strategic uses of nonviolent sanctions in response to political violence. Books by its president, Gene Sharp, are available from the Literature Department, Suite 600 at the above address.

Albert Einstein Peace Prize Foundation
1430 W. Wrightwood Avenue
Chicago, IL 60614
(312) 472-8832

Works toward bilateral, verifiable nuclear arms reductions. Key members meet frequently and privately with world leaders to influence policy and opinion outside the constraints of official diplomatic channels.

Center for Economic Conversion
   Peace Resource Center
222C View Street
Mountain View, CA 94041
(415) 968-8798

Promotes positive economic alternatives to military spending. CEC publishes Plowshare Press, *a journal with interviews, book reviews and reports on conversion activities, movements and trends. Another publication,* Economic Conversion Organizer's Update, *provides organizational information and reports on actual conversion activities occurring across the nation.*

Citizens Network for Common Security
Anabel Taylor Hall, Cornell University
Ithica, NY 14853
(607) 255-8276

Develops and distributes educational materials on alternative defense measures, sufficiency for all and ecological sustainability. They are organizing a "Global Walk" to

start in the fall of 1990, featuring appropriate technology, cultural celebrations and educational programs, with the goal of promoting a just, sustainable and secure world.

CISPES (Committee in Solidarity with the People of El Salvador)
P.O. Box 122056
Washington, DC 20005
(202) 265-0890

Works to stop intervention and to direct the support of people in civil disobedience, demonstrations, rallies, marches, human rights campaigns, fundraising and directory services. They publish a yearly newsletter, Alert: Focus on Central America.

Committee for US–Central American Relations
731 8th Street SE
Washington, DC 20003-2866
(202) 547-3800

Provides the media, government and public with an analysis of development policy and its relation to military intervention.

Environmental Project on Central America (EPOCA)
Earth Island Institute
300 Broadway, Suite 28
San Francisco, CA 94133
(415) 788-3666

EPOCA's Green Paper *series on Central American environmental issues informs the public about the environmental destruction caused by militarization, making connections between environment and social justice. Free samples are available and the subscription/membership rate is $15 per year. Their award-winning 30-minute video, "Environment Under Fire," costs $35 to purchase or $25 to rent. EPOCA has a speakers bureau, an internship program and co-sponsors reforestation and sea turtle conservation brigades with Nicaragua Network.*

Fellowship of Reconciliation
P.O. Box 271
523 N. Broadway
Nyack, NY 10960
(914) 358-4601

Works to abolish war, refusing to give sanction to any physical, psychological or financial preparations for war. FOR organized the National Civil Liberties Bureau (now the ACLU) in 1916 and has since been actively involved in opposing the arms race, military intervention and human rights violations.

INFACT
256 Hanover Street
Boston, MA 02113

After a successful international boycott against Nestlé corporation's sale of deadly baby formula in the Third World, this consumers' union has turned its sights on the military-industrial complex. A massive General Electric boycott seeks to force the transnational defense contractor to back off from its support for arms buildup and uranium mining. Local organizer kits are available, as is the informative INFACT Brings G.E. to Light exposé book.

Institute for Defense and Disarmament Studies
2001 Beacon Street
Brookline, MA 02146
(617) 734-4216

Conducts research on domestic policy, national security, international economics and human rights. Publishes the annual American Peace Directory, *as well as a monthly newsletter,* Arms Control Reporter *($120/year; reduced rates available).*

Institute for the Practice of Nonviolence
P.O. Box 170670
San Francisco, CA 94117
(415) 753-2882

Founded by Brian Willson and Holley Rauen, the Institute examines the history and practice of nonviolence and puts those studies to direct use, facilitating personal, economic, social and political transformation. They direct people to existing projects on nonviolence (e.g. Nuremberg Action, Big Mountain, American Peace Test), by sponsoring delegations to Central America and the Middle East, and by cooperating with Veterans' Peace Action Teams to make reparations in areas of Central America that have been destroyed by US policies.

Jobs with Peace
77 Summer Street
Boston, MA 02110
(617) 451-3389

Advocates halting the nuclear arms race and military intervention, and redirecting federal funds to meet human needs. They build grassroots support through public referenda and their annual Jobs with Peace Week.

Mobilization for Survival
853 Broadway #2109
New York, NY 10003
(212) 533-0008

A coalition of local peace, disarmament, safe energy, religious and community organizations, with affiliates throughout the US. Goals include banning nuclear weapons and nuclear power, and reversing the arms race. Assists local groups in developing organizing skills, initiates and promotes national campaigns and provides a forum for local organizations to participate in national issues and activities. Publishes the Mobilizer, *quarterly ($10/year).*

NARMIC
1501 Cherry Street
Philadelphia, PA 19102
(215) 241-7000

The research and resource group of the Peace Education Division of the American Friends Service Committee. NARMIC draws on its database of defense industry and corporate files to provide groups working for social change with education resources and action tools on US military policy, human rights and disarmament issues.

National Commission for Economic Conversion and Disarmament

P.O. Box 15025
Washington, DC 20009
(202) 544-5059

Comprised of former and current members of Congress, local elected officials, leaders of trade unions and scholars, ECD works to educate the public about conversion and disarmament. Write for their newsletter and publications list.

Nicaragua Network

2025 I Street, NW, #1117
Washington, DC 20006
(202) 223-2328

A network of 300 local committees working to stop Contra aid and provide humanitarian assistance. Co-sponsors environmental, housing and harvest brigades. Their newsletter, Nicaragua Network News *($10 per year), and quarterly magazine,* Nicaragua Perspectives *($12 per year), provide in-depth analysis and thoughtful reporting of issues affecting Nicaragua and the US peace movement.*

Nuclear Free America

325 E. 25th Street
Baltimore, MD 21218
(301) 235-3575

National clearinghouse and resource for nuclear free zones. Provides a variety of resources including tactical, logistical and legal support for local, national and international nuclear free zone campaigns. Also assists individuals and communities in start-ing such campaigns. Their monthly newsletter, New Abolitionist, *is $15/year.*

Nuclear Information and Resource Service

1424 16th Street NW, Suite 601
Washington, DC 20036
(202) 328-0002

Provides information on nuclear issues and extensive resources for influencing waste disposal and other nuclear policy decisions; recently organized a G.E. boycott. They publish a quarterly, Groundswell, *and offer other publications, including* Protecting Environmental and Nuclear Whistleblowers: A Litigation Manual *and* The Citizen's Nuclear Waste Manual, *as well as an extensive and comprehensive list of publications dealing with nuclear issues.*

Nuke Watch

315 W. Gorham
Madison, WI 53703
(608) 256-4146

A peace education organization focusing on disarmament and related environmental issues. Organizes civil disobedience, serves as a grassroots directory, and issues a quarterly newsletter.

Pacific Studies Center

222B View Street
Mountain View, CA 94041
(415) 969-1545

A non-profit, public interest information center focusing on US economic and foreign relations with Asia and the Pacific, the arms race and the electronics industry. Maintains a clipping, periodical and book library; publishes papers and books, including their monthly newsletter, Global Electronics Information Newsletter *($5/year), and* Pacific Research, *a quarterly ($5/year).*

Physicians for Social Responsibility

639 Massachusetts Avenue
Cambridge, MA 02139
(617) 491-2754

A non-profit, non-partisan group that educates the public on the consequences of nuclear war, nuclear war preparedness and the buildup of nuclear weapons. Membership is open. Their quarterly is the National PSR Newsletter *($30/year).*

Pledge of Resistance
National Office
P.O. Box 53411-3411
Washington, DC 20009-3411
(202) 328-4040

Organized around a network of local committees, the Pledge of Resistance encourages people to commit nonviolent acts of civil disobedience or legal protest in response to any significant escalation of the US war in Central America. The March, 1988, US invasion of Honduras, for example, led to national protests with tens of thousands in the streets. The group is made up almost entirely of volunteers.

Psychologists for Social Responsibility
1841 Columbia Road NW #207
Washington, DC 20009
(202) 745-7084

PsySR provides a forum for professional psychologists to speak out on nuclear issues, network among themselves in areas of research and action, and develop and distribute information on how psychological skills and expertise can be used to develop an enduring peace. Membership dues ($30/year; $10/year for students and seniors) include their quarterly newsletter.

Religious Task Force on Central America
1747 Connecticut Avenue NW
Washington, DC 20017
(202) 387-7652

Works for peace in Central America and an end to US intervention. Publishes packets of information on recent events in the region, works on legislation in Congress and puts out action alerts to its network in the religious community.

St. Louis Pledge of Resistance
438 North Skinker
St Louis, MO 63130

The St. Louis Pledge carries out POR's nationwide campaign against intervention. Additionally, their project and newsletter, The National Guard Update, *provides news about state defense forces and discusses strategies to prevent the creation of a police state in the US.*

Union of Concerned Scientists
26 Church Street
Cambridge, MA 02238
(617) 547-5552

An organization of scientists, engineers and other professionals concerned about the impact of advanced technology. Sponsors convocations on nuclear war, advocates no-first-use policy, publishes books and reports and litigates on nuclear reactor safety. Their newsletter, Nucleus, *is free to sponsors.*

Veterans Vietnam Restoration Project
P.O. Box 69
Garberville, CA 95440
(707) 923-3357

Works for the non-governmental normalization of relations between the United States and Vietnam and psychological healing of Americans and Vietnamese. One of their projects is building a rural health clinic in Vietnam.

War Resisters League
339 Lafayette Street
New York, 10012
(212) 228-0450

Believes "war is a crime against humanity. We therefore are determined not to support any kind of war, international or civil, and to strive nonviolently for the removal of all causes of war." Members must agree to the above statement. Principal activities include organizing demonstrations, working in coalitions for national actions, promoting draft resistance and the non-payment of war taxes, training for civil disobedience, and developing other campaigns. Also provides a training program for organizers. The WRL News *is bi-monthly and free.*

Washington Peace Center
2111 Florida Avenue NW
Washington, DC 20008
(202) 234-2000

An affiliate of the National Mobilization for Survival, this 25-year-old group functions as a clearinghouse for local peace organizations. Provides a variety of support services to local peace and activist groups, publishes the monthly Washington Peace Letter *and sponsors several interns.*

Women's Action for Nuclear Disarmament
New Town Station, Box 153
Boston, MA 02258
(617) 643-6740

A grassroots women's organization (founded by Helen Caldicott) that raises public awareness about nuclear issues, monitors legislative activities on nuclear weapons policy and organizes grassroots lobbying campaigns around Congressional votes on nuclear weapons systems. WAND sponsors a political action committee, speakers' training, voter registration drives and media outreach programs. Membership is open to all women (minimum dues are $5/year) and includes the quarterly WAND Bulletin.

Women's International League for Peace and Freedom
1213 Race Street
Philadelphia, PA 19107
(215) 563-7110

An international women's organization that works nonviolently to establish the political, social and psychological conditions for peace, freedom, and justice. Publishes Peace and Freedom *(monthly, $4/year) and* WILPF Legislative Bulletin *and* Alerts *(monthly, $8/year).*

Women Strike for Peace
145 S. 13th Street
Philadelphia, PA 19107
(215) 923–0861

An activist group of women of all races, creeds and various political persuasions, determined to end the arms race and military intervention and to bring about disarmament. Lobbying, leafletting and demonstrations are primary activities. Branches exercise autonomy in developing programs and adapting national actions to local communities. Membership is open to women for $25/year, and includes the newsletter Peacelines. *WSP also publishes the* Legislative Alert *($10/year).*

World Peace Through Law Center
1000 Connecticut Avenue NW, Suite 800
Washington, DC 20036
(202) 466-5428

An international venture combining the efforts of judges, lawyers, law professors, law students and others to foster peace through international law. Publishes a newsletter, The World Jurist.

World Without War Council
1730 Grove Street
Berkeley, CA 94709
(415) 845-1992

Provides information and education on arms control and disarmament, war and peace, and human rights. Publishes a quarterly newsletter, World Without War Bookstore Newsletter.

Books

Civilian Resistance as a National Defense. Adam Roberts, ed. Harrisburg: Stackpole Books, 1968. British title: *The Strategy of Civilian Defense.* London: Faber, 1967.

Deadly Defense: Military Radioactive Landfills. Dana Coyle and others. New York: Radioactive Waste Campaign, 1988.

Describes the radioactive and chemical pollution caused by nuclear weapons plants, the health risks from radiation and grassroots efforts to clean up toxic wastes at nuclear weapons plants.

Fire in the Lake: The Vietnamese and the Americans in Vietnam. Frances Fitz-Gerald. New York: Vintage Books, 1972.

A vivid introduction to the hidden history of the US war in Southeast Asia and what it meant to the people affected by it. An important antidote to historical amnesia.

National Security Through Civilian-Based Defense. Gene Sharp. Omaha: Association for Transarmament Studies, 1985.

An introduction to defense through massive nonviolent noncooperation and defiance against invasions and internal coups. Available from The Albert Einstein Institution Literature Department (see listing above).

The Politics of Nonviolent Action. Gene Sharp. Boston: Porter Sargent, 1973-74. Paperback in three volumes: *Power and Struggle; The Methods of Nonviolent Action; The Dynamics of Nonviolent Action.*

Stop Nuclear War! A Handbook. David Barash and Judith Lipton. New York: Grove Press, 1982.

A description of the forces propelling us toward nuclear war and the actions we can take to prevent it. A hopeful how-to-book, with lists of organizations, sources of information, positive and creative steps that individuals can take, steps the US can take, history of the arms race, information about the physical effects of a nuclear war and the ongoing negative consequences of the arms race. Includes a cogent and compelling plea to act.

War Without Weapons. Anders Boserup and Andrew Mack. New York: Schocken, 1975. London: Francis Pinter, 1974.

PART SEVEN

MEDIA AND EDUCATION

Defeating Disinformation

LARRY BENSKY

ANYONE WHO HOPES to have an impact on how the world is run (or ruined) sooner or later has to deal with the concept of information dissemination.

Getting one's issues covered by the media is essential whether exposing environmental destruction, aggressive foreign policy, human rights violations or making visible the plight of the homeless and hungry. Since these issues are not critically examined in the mainstream media or in the schools, there is a vast amount of catch-up to do.

Beyond education, or lack of it, there are powerful private and governmental interests at work to preserve their profits through the passive, or active, promotion of individual and collective ignorance.

The challenge, therefore, is daunting. But there can be no victory without progress in information dissemination.

The most serious threat is not false information—though that can play a critical role at times—but the setting of a media agenda which excludes, devalues or under-reports perspectives which oppose the dominant policy or practice.

The first challenge is to *get the topic on the agenda*. Progressive lesson plans and textbooks need to be developed for schools at all levels. The histories of other cultures need to be presented in their own words. War and conquest must be de-romanticized and slavery and colonization must be critically examined with their connections to current racism and economic inequality. "Nature study" and biology classes must be reformulated to include concepts of stewardship and collective understanding of the relation between the "natural," economic and political worlds.

As for the media, there needs to be *constant* pressure on newspapers and local radio and television stations (the networks are hopelessly barricaded dinosaurs, for the most part) to increase coverage of movement issues and perspectives.

It has been a long-time cliche of journalism that all news is local. The construction of housing on the site of a former gas

Larry Bensky is the National Affairs Correspondent for listener-supported Pacifica Radio and sits on the board of directors of Media Alliance. He recently received the George Polk Award for his coverage of the Congressional Iran-contra hearings.

Billboard against toxic-substance labeling measure with revealing additional information added by Earth First!. DAVID CROSS

station down the block without adequate environmental assessment is more important to almost everyone in your community than the plight of a disappearing species of bird in Armenia. Therefore, *activists must know their local problems, and who the bad guys are, thoroughly and irrefutably.* Then and only then will we earn enough respect to make global issues relevant at home.

It is not enough, however, to research matters thoroughly. *It is important to have the ability to present accurate, coherently written (or spoken) statements* to the media. Spokespeople need to be *legitimized.*

In educating students and in keeping the general public better informed, organized pressure is of utmost importance. School curricula change slowly, if at all (though individual teachers may prove sympathetic and effective). News organizations have built-in structures and ideological fil-

Warning labels now required in state of California after measure passed despite industry disinformation. DAVID CROSS

ters whose net effect is to shut out unpleasant truths . . . and many modern truths *are* unpleasant, since they tend to point out the fragility of our individual existences, and our seeming collective powerlessness to change things.

To defeat disinformation is relatively easy—we have the truth on our side, and with persistence and intelligent organization, it can creep up to, and eventually surpass lies. Abortion rights, US intervention, ozone depletion and pesticide contamination are just a few formerly arcane issues that are now very much under public discussion.

More difficult is to defeat non-information. This can only be done by changing the often trivial and sensationalized data that blasts urban audiences relentlessly, in the guise of "news." As we work to advance our causes we must let our broader community know what we are doing and why we are doing it. As one San Francisco radio announcer concludes his newscast, "If you don't like the news, go out and make some of your own."

ACTION*

1. **Be creative.** Activists like the late Abbie Hoffman often got extensive free media coverage by staging media stunts. In 1989, to protest and draw attention to US policy on El Salvador, anti-intervention groups across the country replaced the front page of tens of thousands of morning papers with their own versions presenting the real story on El Salvador. The targeted papers fumed and threatened lawsuits but other papers and TV newscasters widely and gleefully reported the switch.

2. **Think of progressive/alternative angles to ongoing newsworthy topics.** "Traffic," for example, is not only about transportation. The "weather" does not consist only of temperature and precipitation. "Food" is a wider topic than just cost and taste. Get *your* angle on these and other topics in the news, by thinking of visual adaptations for television, sound for radio, unusual details for print.

3. **Remember that news organizations** usually like to cover what they think of as "human" angles to any story. Statistics, economics and especially politics make them nervous.

4. **Create media monitoring committees** to study printed and broadcast sources for the frequency and nature of environmental coverage. Present the results to the media organizations themselves, at an executive level, and then ask for negotiations. Then, if necessary (and it almost always will be!), begin to exert further outside pressure through letter writing, talk shows, advertisements, phone calls, etc.

5. **Legitimize activists within your community** by presenting them frequently in public appearances and making them accessible to news media. Frequently, government and business spokespeople appear over and over because your side has not reached sufficient "standing" in a newsroom to be called and quoted.

*Action section by Larry Bensky

6. **Be a pain in the ass, if necessary.**
   Or have a designated pain in the ass,
   and another gentler person, who approach news executives alternately. Get
   inside line phone numbers for media
   organizations, and use them discreetly.
   *Let them know someone is out there
   watching, reading and listening!*

7. **Unmask how institutions** like the Heritage Foundation "orchestrate" coverage and the evolution of certain issues

as "problems." Expose the rewriting of
history.

8. **Redefine certain terms and phrases
   that de-emphasize, trivialize or mislead.** Change "nuclear safety" to "nuclear danger," "polluting" to "poisoning," "Department of Defense" to
   "Department of Destruction," "Bureau
   of Land Management" to "Bureau of
   Land Ravishment," etc.

Education for Social Change

JOHN HURST

"The more learners work at storing the deposits entrusted to them, the less they develop the critical consciousness which would result from their intervention in the world as transformers of that world. The more completely they accept the passive role imposed on them, the more they tend to simply adapt to the world as it is and to the fragmented view of reality deposited in them . . .

"It is only when the oppressed find the oppressor out and become involved in the organized struggle for liberation that they begin to believe in themselves. This discovery cannot be purely intellectual but must involve action; nor can it be limited to mere activism, it must also include serious reflection—only then will it be praxis. Critical and liberating dialogue, which presupposes action, must be carried on with the oppressed at every stage of their struggle for liberation."

—PAULO FREIRE
PEDAGOGY OF THE OPPRESSED

S TARKLY PUT, EDUCATION can either serve to domesticate or liberate. Which it shall be is ultimately our choice, as individuals and as a society. In face of the mounting crises confronting our global community—ecological deterioration, injustice, poverty and war—the familiar admonition of Albert Einstein, "The splitting of the atom [high-technology] has changed everything, except our mode of thinking, and thus we drift toward unparalleled catastrophe," rings ever more true. An

John Hurst is a founder of the Undergraduate Programs for Conservation and Resource Studies, and for Peace and Conflict Studies at the University of California at Berkeley. He has studied education's role in political revolutions and has worked to develop a theory of its role in the democratic transformation of society. John was a founder of Minnesota Outward Bound and the National Outdoor Leadership School.

Market women learning to read and write—Managua, Nicaragua. After US-backed Somoza dictatorship was overthrown, the new government established a nationwide literacy program for citizens of all ages. SUSAN MEISELAS, MAGNUM PHOTOS, INC.

education that empowers and enables people to collectively seek ways to overcome current destructive trends will be a critical component of any successful strategy for achieving a just, peaceful and healthy future. Certainly, our formal education institutions—kindergarten through Ph.D.—and their knowledge base will in the long run require fundamental restructuring if we are to reach and maintain our common goals; however, this issue is largely beyond the scope of this handbook.

Activists in popular movements for social change have increasingly come to realize that education is a key task if they are to engage ever greater numbers of people. And getting people engaged in a struggle for the public good is facilitated by education that empowers. Such education requires far more of the educator than the mere imparting of information. We are fortunate to have

inspiring examples of "popular education" to guide us in the creation of educational experiences for adults. The Folk High School movement in Scandinavia is over 200 years old and has contributed much to the continuing humane evolution of the Northern European societies that are at the forefront of the struggle to create a better world. The Highlander Research and Education Center in Tennessee, initially influenced by the Scandanavian Folk Schools, has played a seminal role in the Southern United States for over 50 years. It was the educational heart of the Southern civil rights movement in the 1950's and 60's and is currently a leader in the grassroots efforts to end the toxic abuse of our environment. The justly celebrated Nicaraguan Literary Crusade of 1980 and the adult education program it gave birth to is further testimony to the transformative potential of education. Finally, in the repressive conditions of Chile in the mid-1980's, a network of centers for population and democracy bloomed: the "Red de Centros de Desarrollo Local," which have brought hope, dignity, progress and a voice to thousands of poor Chileans struggling for democracy and their lives.

All of these efforts are linked together in a horizontal association of free organizations coordinated by the International Council for Adult Education, with offices in Toronto. The remarkable accomplishments of these educational programs, and the degree of democratic collaboration between them, is little known in the United States. This is no accident, for through example they pose a fundamental threat to the educational status quo: the system of schooling, the creation of knowledge and the flow of information in our society today.

> "The most important education is action, the most important action is the struggle for justice."
>
> —MYLES HORTON, CO-FOUNDER
> THE HIGHLANDER CENTER

Education in the United States

In order to better understand why the institutions described above have been so successful we must briefly examine the educational experiences that virtually all Americans have undergone. It is a comfortable myth that *public education* in the US was created in a burst of humanitarian zeal as an outgrowth of working-class aspirations to further the democratic ideals of our new nation. We are still told that the public schools are where young people come to understand and value democracy, and to accept and exercise their essential responsibilities as citizens. However, a careful reading of history reveals that the preparation of cit-izens committed to democratic ideals, who will be informed about and fully participate in the political decisions affecting their lives, has never been the dominant purpose of the public education in our country. Rather, public education and educational reform have been more typically molded by the threat of social explosions and by the desire of powerful persons for domestic tranquility and a docile workforce that will respond to arbitrary authority. How else can we fully grasp the pitifully low and still declining portion of the electorate that exercises the most rudimentary of all democratic rights— the right to vote? The evidence is clear: formal education in the US has largely served to domesticate young people and reproduce the status quo through a rigid hierarchical structure and a banking model of education (i.e. depositing information in the heads of learners). By contrast, liberatory education strives to empower individuals through authentic problem-posing and dialogue among equals; it is dedicated to developing knowledgeable, committed, engaged and vital democrats. A democratic society demands a democratic education if it is to creatively meet the global challenges we are confronted with today.

Tragically, *higher education*, provides few exceptions to the patterns we observe in public and private primary and secondary schools. Our public and private colleges and universities help maintain the status quo by fostering and legitimizing an elite whose principal commitments are to the interests of the powerful and not to those of the common good. This, in spite of the fact that the large state land grant universities, like the University of California, were explicitly founded to serve the common woman and man and the public interest (the Morrill Act, 1862; the Hatch Act, 1887).

Within the universities the fragmentation of knowledge into ever-smaller divisions (e.g. disciplines, sub-disciplines, etc.)

has made it increasingly difficult to address the complex problems in our environment and society that invariably transcend narrow disciplinary boundaries. A very critical question that we must ask is to what extent do our universities share responsibility for our current state of affairs because of how they define knowledge and what is likely to be researched and taught in them? One only has to probe the tragedy of the "Green Revolution" to understand the importance of the nature of the questions that are asked and the breadth of the context within which they are explored.

Educational and research programs in major universities that take a systemic approach tend to be marginal, embattled and chronically underfunded. Programs focusing on the environment, peace and justice, women's issues, and race and ethnic issues systematically address the central issues that will decide our common fate. If we are to accelerate the creation of essential knowledge, and the education and training of dedicated professionals, these programs must grow.

While minimal attention is given to solving global problems from the perspective of the common good, we find that the public resources of our universities are increasingly dedicated to serving private corporations and the Department of Defense. This is especially true in the sciences, but not limited to them. A blatant example is biotechnology: research funded by private corporations is conducted by university faculty in public facilities (i.e. laboratories on campus) and the corporations get proprietary rights to any discoveries or inventions resulting from the research. Similar relationships have long existed between colleges of natural resources and colleges of agriculture, on the one hand, and agribusiness and agrichemical corporations, on the other. The resulting "advances" generally come at the expense of small family farmers, farm workers, and the environment (e.g. pesticides and mechanical tomato harvesters).

We must gain improved public control of research and science policy and research funding, and public access to the fruits of publicly funded research. Quite simply, publicly funded research ought to serve the common good, bringing talent and resources to our efforts to solve our immense environmental and social problems.

Adult education. While there are many rich and diverse non-formal educational opportunities available for adults, it is the rare institution, or specific offering, whose intent is to empower and enable adults to become actively engaged in the struggle to solve major societal problems in the public interest. We need to encourage more institutions and efforts like those presented at the beginning of this chapter.

ACTION*

"The people need to *see themselves* experimenting in democratic forms."

—LAWRENCE GOODWYN
THE POPULIST MOVEMENT

We quite simply need to put in place, every place, an education that liberates and empowers—an education that is quintessentially democratic.

How do we do it? With commitment, difficulty, patience and above all compassion. A democratic education that empowers is more a commitment to a set of democratic principles and values—the development of productive social relations rooted in equity—and a state of being, than it is the mastering of a set of techniques. This does not mean one can't learn to educate democratically, only that it can't be learned in the traditional ways most of us are familiar with. Nor should one confuse a laissez faire, "do your own thing" approach with authentic democratic education. The decades, indeed centuries, of experience and reflection we find in the institutions highlighted at the beginning of the chapter have yielded a fairly consistent set of conditions associated with successful democratic or popular education. The philosophy, theory and experience that underlie them, as well as how they have been applied in various contexts, is treated extensively in the materials cited in the resource section at the end of the chapter. Organizations that offer opportunities to experience and learn a more democratic approach to education are also listed. The most critical conditions that have been honed from experience and theory are briefly described below:

*Action section by John Hurst

Conditions to strive for:

1. **Participation.** People must be full participants in the educational process, must construct their educational experience and make the critical decisions that shape it. People need to experience themselves as "equally worthy" in the group, especially in relationship to the educator. Democratic education is optimally conducted in an unbroken circle.

2. **Critical Consciousness.** People must engage in a "problem posing" experience where issues are engaged critically through dialogue (seeking to develop mutual understanding) without a fixed outcome being mandated. This is the opposite of the traditional "banking" approach, where information is simply deposited in the student.

3. **Action Orientation.** The educational process must presuppose action beyond being engaged in the educational experience itself. The knowing sought; neither thought nor action alone but a synthesis of the two. In this manner citizens are not passive consumers of education, but become producers and hence transformers of themselves and of reality. Citizens can come to see themselves as makers of history, rather than flotsam in historical currents.

4. **Praxis.** This is the process of reflecting on our actions and revising our understanding (or theory) as a result of this critical reflection. From this revised understanding new actions (or practice) are crafted. These cycles of action and reflection are continued for as long as is appropriate. It is a dialectical process continued over time through dialogue.

5. Public Interest. The purpose of popular education is to serve the common good through the liberation of people's creative potential and the mobilization of human resources to solve social problems with a utopian vision of the future in mind.

6. Love. This condition is referred to in many different ways, but it is basic. Great educators speak about honoring others as individuals, or about a generosity of spirit, or of care and passion. What is clear is that the educator must strive to create an environment of warmth, care and acceptance where each person is free to realize her or his richest potentials. We are speaking of a state of being that educators seek to realize and maintain in their own lives, not a technique one learns to apply in a specific educational situation.

"Education shall be directed to the full development of the human personality and to the strengthening of respect for human rights and fundamental freedoms. It shall promote understanding, tolerance and friendship among all nations, racial or religious groups, and shall further the activities of the United Nations for the maintenance of peace."

—UNITED NATIONS UNIVERSAL
DECLARATION OF HUMAN RIGHTS

RESOURCES

Organizations

Action for Children's Television
20 University Road
Cambridge, MA 02138-5723
(617) 876-6620

Promotes diversity in children's programming and combats abusive commercials targeted at young audiences.

Association of Community Based Education
1806 Vernon Street NW
Washington, DC 20009

An organization composed of community-based organizations engaged in popular education. They support community-based education projects nationwide, with a particular emphasis on literacy programs and economic development projects. ACBE has a team of trainers that will work with community educators to help develop programs. There is an annual convention.

Centro El Canelo de Nos
Av. Portales 3020, Paradero 6
Casilla 2-D
San Bernardo, Chile

Through popular education and democratic participation, El Canelo works to build a future democratic order. The center acts as a hub for seven regional grassroots development centers that form the "Red de Centros de Desarrollo Local." They publish an outstanding journal and a wealth of other excellent material in Spanish.

Communication Consortium
1333 H Street NW, 11th floor
Washington, DC 20005
(202) 682-1270

The Communications Consortium Media Center was established to enhance the public interest community's use of communications technology and strategic media planning as essential tools in public education and policy change. The Consortium draws together issue experts, policy analysts and constituent organizations to design media strategies for groups of non-profit organizations. Family and work issues, energy and the environment, reproductive health and women's rights are prime focuses. Write or phone for more information and a list of services.

Data Center
464 19th Street
Oakland, CA 94612
(415) 835-4692

Public interest library providing information on US relations with Latin America, corporate responsibility, the environment and the press. Publishes the Corporate Responsibility Monitor.

Democratic Socialists of America
15 Dutch Street, Room 500
New York, NY 10273
(212) 962-0390

An organization with 40 local groups throughout the US working towards reform of laws dealing with reproductive rights, environmental protection and minimum wage. They believes the economy should be run democratically to benefit all instead of a few. Publishes a bi-monthly newsletter, Democratic Left, *available with membership ($35; $15 low-income or student).*

Education/Democracy
1300 Connecticut Avenue NW
Washington, DC 20036
(312) 645-6014

Political citizens' organization, focusing on energy issues and global warming. Provides directory services for organizing, and publishes Citizens Action News *quarterly.*

Educators For Social Responsibility
23 Garden Street
Cambridge, MA 02138
(617) 492-1764

A national membership organization that offers curricula and professional development addressing the controversies of the nuclear age. Through an active network of local chapters, a growing professional development program, and innovative publications and materials, ESR is teaching students at all grade levels to think clearly and independently about security in the nuclear age, human rights, US-Soviet relations and citizens' role in a global community. They publish a bimonthly magazine, Nuclear Times *($21/year); ESR Journal, an annual; and* Forum, *issued three times a year.*

Evergreen State College
Olympia, WA 98505
(206) 866-6000

This school has established a national reputation for high-quality environmental studies and training programs at both the undergraduate and the graduate levels. Combines rigorous scientific methods with social, economic and ecological responsibility, and hands-on field experience.

Grassroots Leadership
P.O. Box 9586
Charlotte, NC 28299

A team of black and white organizers who provide people, communities and organizations throughout the Southern US with organizing and strategy assistance to confront challenges in health care, housing, the environment, discrimination, civil rights, justice and peace.

The Highlander Research and Education Center
Box 370, RFD #3
New Market, TN 37820

For over 50 years a world pioneer in empowering and democratic education. Since its inception the school has been at the forefront of every social change movement in the South: labor, civil rights and environmental and occupational health. It holds residential workshops of various lengths, some initiated by the Center's staff and others by contract with groups that share their philosophy. They have issued books, records and films about their work, and have an extensive library.

International Council on Adult Education
720 Bathurst Street, Suite 500
Toronto, Ontario M5S 2R4
Canada

With affiliate organizations in every region and virtually every nation in the world, ICAE is a powerful network for popular educators, providing resources and support. It also sustains a number of topic networks such as Participatory Research and Peace, Education, and Women, that are coordinated by individuals or groups in various locations throughout the world. ICAE publishes an excellent journal, Convergence *($25 a year).*

Learning Alliance
494 Broadway
New York, NY 10022
(212) 226-7171

An educational organization that focuses on community and local issues, and provides people with tools needed for social and public policy change. Recently they organized local panels on coastal ecosystems, hunting, urban open space, ocean policy and urban ecological principles. The Alliance also organized a symposium between "deep" and "social" ecologists, and it has an available on-site reference department. While their activities are limited to local issues, they are assisting the development of other independent local education advocacy groups based on their model.

Meadow Creek Project
Fox, Arkansas 72051

A small center dedicated to furthering alternative visions of organizing society, especially from an environmental perspective. They have focused on alternative economic and agricultural systems, and appropriate technology in the North American context. They sponsor educational programs and publish a newsletter.

Media Action Research Center
475 Riverside Drive
New York, NY 10115
(212) 865-6690

A TV viewers' advocacy organization that facilitates critical analysis of television programming, and provides guidance for "talking back" to TV and changing it through community action. For their quarterly resource magazine, Media and Values, *contact 1962 S. Shenandoah, Los Angeles, CA 90034, (213)559-2944. It provides in-depth coverage, analysis, reflection and action. Each issue is devoted to one topic.*

Media Alliance
Building D, Fort Mason
San Francisco, CA 94123
(415) 441-2557

A media-watch and advocacy organization devoted to defeating disinformation, and specifically to instilling in mainstream media legitimate issues and viewpoints that are currently marginalized. Its publications include People Behind the News *and the* Media How-To Notebook. *The Alliance publishes the bi-monthly* Media File.

Midwest Academy
600 W. Fullerton Avenue
Chicago, IL 60614

Offers training programs of varying lengths to help community activists become better organizers and leaders. Publishes the well-known Midwest Academy Organizing Manual.

New College of California
50 Fell Street
San Francisco, CA
(415) 626-1694

New College is composed of three independent schools: undergraduate humanities, graduate psychology and public interest law. All are guided by a critical, progressive ideology that places academic study in the context of social responsibility in the real world. The undergraduate humanities program offers opportunities for applied learning ("practicum" courses) such as the Earth Island environmental ecology and activism internship program. Students may also design their own practicum courses of study.

Public Interest Video Network
2309 18th Street NW
Washington, DC 20009
(202) 797-8997

Provides video and radio services at below-market prices for non-profit organizations.

University of California at Berkeley
Environmental Science Department
Berkeley, CA 94720
(415) 642-2628

A small but growing department, featuring an undergraduate major in interdisciplinary physical, biological and social studies. The major was designed to prepare students to understand environmental problems and design solutions for them. Undergraduate internships and job experience are encouraged as steps toward employment after graduation.

Women's Institute for Freedom of Press
3306 Ross Plaza NW
Washington, DC 20008

Publishes Directory of Women's Media, *which lists 702 women's periodicals, 111 women's presses and publishers, 11 women's news services, 39 regular programs on television and radio, video and film, speakers bureaus, 93 women's bookstores, 518 women in media. $15/year.*

"Establishing lasting peace is the work of education; all politics can do is keep us out of war."

—MARIA MONTESSORI

Periodicals

Children's Advocate
1700 Broadway, #300
Oakland, CA 94612
(415) 444-7136

Recognized for its excellence by the American Bar Association and twice awarded the Gavel Award, Children's Advocate *is a newspaper for parents, teachers, health, professionals and others concerned with children's issues and a quality future. Limited free distribution is available to childcare centers, schools, libraries, bookstores and community centers in the San Francisco Bay Area. Elsewhere, $18 per year. Current circulation is 10,000.*

Convergence
International Council for Adult Education
720 Bathhurst Street, Suite 500
Toronto, Ontario M5S 2R4
Canada

The seminal journal in the worldwide dialogue about popular education, empowerment education and participatory research, with contributors from every corner of the globe. Published in English with synopses of each article in French and Spanish. Quarterly; $25 a year.

Extra! The Newsletter of Fairness and Accuracy in Reporting
c/o FAIR
666 Broadway, Suite 400
New York, NY 10012
   Bi-monthly; $24/year.

Mediafile
Media Alliance
Building D, Fort Mason
San Francisco, CA 94123
   A $40 membership in Media Alliance includes the cost of Medialife, *a bi-monthly publication.*

The Nation
Box 1953
Marion, OH 43305
   An internationally respected weekly which bills itself as "a radical solution to disinformation." Known for reporting and editorials with depth, an independent perspective and a critical spirit. $36/year; $64/2 years.

Propaganda Review
Media Alliance
Building D, Fort Mason
San Francisco, CA 94123
   Propaganda Review *costs $20/year and is a quarterly.*

Radical Teacher
P.O. Box 102
Kendall Square Post Office
Cambridge, MA 02114
   A lively socialist and feminist journal on the theory and practice of teaching, published by the Boston Women's Teachers' Group. Explores all aspects and levels of formal education (kindergarten through Ph.D.) from a democratic socialist perspective. Concerned with justice and the empowerment of students and teachers. It frequently publishes a "cluster" of articles on a topic (e.g. Christianity, politics and education). $8 for three issues a year ($4 parttime workers, unemployed and retired persons).

Zeta Magazine
150 West Canton Street
Boston, MA 02118
(617) 236-5878
   An independent monthly of critical thinking on political, cultural, social and economic life in the United States. Views the racial, sexual, class and political dimensions of personal life as fundamental to understanding and improving contemporary circumstances; aims to assist activist efforts to attain a better future. $24/year.

Books

Between Struggle and Hope: The Nicaraguan Literacy Crusade. Valerie Miller. Boulder, CO: Westview Press, 1985.
   A detailed evaluation of the most successful large-scale literacy campaign in history. A moving, fully-documented story of how, through imagination, commitment and hard work, popular education can make a major contribution to the transformation of a whole society in a relatively short period of time.

Cry of the People. Penny Lernoux. New York: Penguin Books, 1980.
   The compelling story of the Catholic church's participation in the struggle for human rights in South America. Describes the "base communities" in thousands of parishes—small groups of people, largely poor, who gather to study the Bible, develop critical consciousness and devise actions to solve the immense social problems in their communities. This movement, of hundreds of thousands of small popular education groups, is slowly changing the face of societies throughout Latin America, particularly in Brazil. It is the heartbeat of the liberation theology movement.

Four Arguments for the Elimination of Television. Jerry Mander. New York: Morrow, 1978.

Explains how TV hypnotizes viewers through its pulsing image, inducing a drug-like state similar to schizophrenia. He asserts that television gives the public the false impression that they know things because they are familiar with their images, and points out the dangers of this pattern. Mander also discusses how TV time is accessible only to the wealthy and powerful, because of the high costs of advertising and programming. A wonderfully upsetting book that inspires many to put away their TVs.

The New Politics of Science. David Dickson. New York: Pantheon Books, 1984.

Examines corporate penetration of public universities and how science policy is formulated at the national level. Advocates the democratization of science policy-making to ensure that public funds and science policy are directed toward the public good rather than private interests.

Participation and Democratic Theory. Carole Pateman. Cambridge, England: Cambridge University Press, 1970.

An excellent introduction to democratic theory and the question of citizen participation. Historical shifts in meaning are particularly noteworthy.

Pedagogy of the Oppressed. Paulo Freire. New York: Seabury Press, 1968.

Probably the most influential education book to appear in the second half of the 20th century. It has been translated into 18 languages and has sold several million copies; in some Third World countries, people have been arrested for possessing Pedagogy. This critical work lays the theoretical groundwork for a liberating and empowering education and provides a sustained example of practice: a literacy campaign in northeast Brazil during the early 1960's. It is a work of love for humanity that has inspired education transformations in practice from Switzerland to South Africa, and from Canada to Chile.

Theory and Resistance in Education: A Pedagogy for the Opposition. Henry A. Giroux. South Hadley, MA: Bergin & Garvey Publishers, 1983.

This book does for public education (K–12) what Pedagogy of the Oppressed does for educating the oppressed. It is a penetrating theoretical critique of education in the US, counterposed with a radical pedagogy. Paulo Freire describes it as "a book of great importance ... [that]should be read by anyone interested in education, social theory and critical practice." One will not view education in our country through the same eyes after reading this book.

Unearthing Seeds of Fire: The Idea of Highlander. Frank Adams with Myles Horton. Winston Salem, NC: John F. Blair, 1975.

The engaging story of the Highlander Center and its work to empower the disenfranchised people of the Southern US, black and white, from the beginnings of organized labor in the South in the 1930's and 40's, through the civil rights movement in the 50's and 60's, to its current work in Appalachia, focusing on environmental and occupational health. (Andrew Young, called Highlander the "cradle of the civil rights movement" and nominated Highlander for the Nobel Peace Prize in 1983.) Many view Highlander as the most effective and influential popular education center in the world, epitomizing the strength and possibilities of a genuinely democratic education.

The Whole World Is Watching: Mass Media and the Making and Unmaking of the New Left. Todd Gitlin. Berkeley: University of California Press, 1980.

PART EIGHT
POISON AND POWER

The Export of Irresponsibility
THE HONORABLE JOHN CONYERS, JR.

S INCE THE TRAGEDY of Love Canal highlighted the dangers of hazardous waste disposal, we have struggled as a nation with the overproduction of wastes and the desire to keep them as far away from "our backyards" as possible. In 1988, the "not in my backyard" approach became visible with an eruption of hazardous waste export efforts to the Third World.

Research advances during World War II brought the petrochemical industry to new levels of production following the war. Petroleum-based fertilizers, chemicals and plastics manufacturing all boomed, along with their toxic by-products.

But it was not until 30 years later that Love Canal brought the real dangers of hazardous waste to the forefront. Ticking toxic time bombs began to explode across America as hundreds of communities became at risk from toxics, threatened groundwater and cancers and genetic defects in children.

A horrified nation prompted Congress to pass, among other laws, the Resource Conservation and Recovery Act (RCRA), which dictated "cradle to grave" vigilance over our wastes and recommended a strict reduction in the generation of waste as the first line of defense against toxic hazards.

Unfortunately, loopholes in RCRA still remain. A handful of unscrupulous businesspeople discovered that cheap disposal could take place without the scrutiny of environmental regulators. They found they could carry out their deeds absolutely legally, sending wastes around the globe to nearly any continent.

In the last five years, domestic wastes have been sent to Haiti, Guinea and Zimbabwe, while major dumpsites were planned for Guinea-Bissau, Guyana, Panama, the Congo, Guatemala, Sierra Leone and the Bahamas, among other nations.

In Guinea, West Africa, children play on mounds of Philadelphia incinerator ash. The ash contains heavy metals and dioxin,

During more than two decades in Congress, **John Conyers** has struggled for social justice and economic opportunity. He is the author of proposed legislation to prohibit the export of toxic waste; in the 100th Congress, Congressman Conyers introduced legislation on public housing, civil and constitutional rights, family farmers, voter rights, economic and community development, foreign affairs, defense contracting and criminal justice. He authored and spearheaded the drive for passage of the Martin Luther King Holiday Bill and is one of the founders of the Congressional Black Caucus.

La géographie ça sert, d'abord, a faire la guerre
(Geography = War)

Africa is rapidly becoming the dumping ground for millions of tons of toxic industrial waste from the so-called developed *countries. This* new *development is the modern version of the slave trade: although the traffic is still one way, the direction has changed. This new state of things in international affairs should come as no surprise. Boundaries from* Here *to* There *disappeared a long time ago, and this is probably the final and ultimate proof. Needless to say, boundaries from* There *to* Here *are stronger than ever, and we keep opening new doors only to close them.*

LA GÉOGRAPHIE ÇA SERT, D'ABORD, A FAIRE LA GUERRE
—ALFREDO JAAR

which can cause learning disabilities, cancer and congenital defects. More Philadelphia ash sits on the the shores of Haiti despite a vigorous outcry from the citizenry.

Unfortunately, acceptance of toxics by debt-ridden countries is tempting where waste deals can attract much-needed currency. When a Detroit lawyer approached the tiny country of Guinea-Bissau to accept millions of tons of waste, he offered them triple their $200 million national debt. With no strong industry, and a poor population, the deal was attractive. The result, however, could have been tragic.

The problem is more complex than offering poor nations the choice between poverty or poison. Toxics have been misrepresented as brick-making material, road fill and fertilizer. Moreover, corrupt officials

can be easy payoff targets for exporters seeking cheap outlets for their toxic wares.

Leaders in Africa and the Caribbean have risen to condemn the latest trend in waste disposal. The Organization of African Unity has called waste exports "a crime against Africa and its people." "Stop using us a a dumping ground" was the impassioned plea of one Third World leader on the UN floor.

Even in the US, where we have established standards for safe handling of wastes, we have been faced with disaster when wastes have caused illness and premature death, and communities have become ghost towns. There is little chance we can honestly expect safe handling of highly toxic wastes in countries with inadequate port facilities, with substandard roads shared by children and farm animals, and where there may be little understanding of the danger of these substances.

For too long, we placed a premium on consumption, and neglected the pollution pricetag that accompanied the growth. Toxics, and household garbage, continue to be produced at a spiraling pace, despite the intentions of policy-makers.

For every man, woman and child in this nation, we produce more than two tons of hazardous waste a year. And every day, each individual produces three to four pounds of household garbage. Packaging is the key culprit and much of it merely a marketing tool, but the societal costs are great.

There is hope. The Congressional Office of Technological Assessment found that today, by implementing cost-effective and achievable strategies, we could reduce our generation of waste by 50 percent.

Yet, if we continue to allow the uncontrolled export of waste, we undermine incentives for industry and citizens to reduce waste generation.

A ban on waste exports is the only way to ensure that our waste does not enter the precious drinking water of drought-stricken countries, that children do not play on barrels of cancerous and lethal hazardous waste, that we do not give birth to a new generation of problems in the Third World and that we do not keep "passing the buck."

We should move forcefully and boldly to restrict the practice before our exports become overseas Love Canals. Exporting waste abroad is the export of irresponsibility, the thorough implementation of "anywhere but in my backyard." It is the wrong answer.

The answer to our toxic waste problem is not dumping in countries wholly unprepared to deal with them. Rather it is the implementation of careful controls for disposal here, the creation of waste reduction technologies that save not only the environment but money as well, and the enforcement of criminal laws banning irresponsible waste disposal. We must tackle the problem of hazardous waste head-on, not hide it abroad.

ACTION*

1. **Stop toxic production.** The essence of "toxic waste" is toxic production. We must shift the focus from waste management to stopping the use and production of materials and processes that are deadly. Put the burden of proof on the producers.

2. **Ban toxic exports.** Make each country, state, and city keep its own waste. Establish international standards making governments and industries responsible for making reparations to poisoned people and environments and preventing any further harm. Put the

burden of reparations on the producers.

3. **Work to limit the damage and destruction at current waste sites;** treat and assist people and places affected by them.

4. **Join with workers, communities and environmentalists to take on toxic producers.** Workers and communities are vulnerable if not supported. There needs to be greater societal involvement in determining what's produced and how.

*Action section by Brad Erickson

Toxics and Minority Communities

SOMINI SENGUPTA

I. Poison in our Backyards: An Overview

Lowndes County, Alabama. When Harriet Means first learned about a proposed hazardous waste landfill in her hometown, Whitehall, she wasn't surprised. The site chosen by Browning Ferris Industries (BFI), one of the largest waste disposal companies in the country, was in Lowndes County—the third poorest county in the country, located in the heart of Alabama's Black Belt, where almost half the residents are on public assistance. To Harriet, BFI's choice was based on certain predictable considerations: "This is a rural community, and the people here are poor, low-educated and black," she says. "They think they can get away with murder here."

That America's most popular dumping grounds all share certain key features—that they are rural, poor communities of color—is not coincidental. A 1984 study commis-sioned by the California Waste Management Board highlights the demographic characteristics of neighborhoods *most* and *least resistant* to hazardous waste facilities in their backyards. Prepared by Cerrell & Associates and widely circulated in the toxics industry, the report confirms that the easiest targets for new sites are in fact the most vulnerable communities.

Although racial demographics are glaringly absent from the Cerrell report, a study conducted by the Commission for Racial Justice of the United Church of Christ found race to be the most significant variable in determining the location of toxic waste sites. The study concluded:

- three out of every five African Americans and Latinos lived in areas with uncontrolled toxic waste sites;

- three of the five largest commercial hazardous waste landfills were located in African American or Latino communities; and

Somini Sengupta is a freelance writer based in Oakland. She has served as a research intern at the Center for Third World Organizing, and is currently working with the Hotel and Restaurant Employees International Union. Most of her research and writing focuses on labor and immigration issues.

The Great Louisiana Toxics March. "*By the year 2000 chemical manufacturing as we know it will be looked on as one of the most anti-social activities in industrial history,*" *professes Pat Bryant, Black leader and march organizer. Noting that Blacks and whites joined together in the protest, Bryant adds,* "*We are using each other to build a movement to crush the profiteers of our suffering.*" SAM KITNER 1988, GREENPEACE

■ communities with the most facilities had the highest percentage of minority residents: where there was (at least) one commercial hazardous waste facility, the average minority percentage of the population was twice that of communities with no such facilities.

For the waste industry, the most coveted areas are those where land costs are low and where nearby residents have little political clout. As Reverend Mac Legerton of Robeson County Clergy and Laity Concerned says, "You take a poor rural county, add a high minority population . . . and you have the corporate formula for locating the majority of hazardous waste sites in the country."

The cases of Emelle, Alabama, and Gore, Oklahoma, illustrate this trend.

Emelle, Alabama. Emelle is a majority Black community with 32 percent of its residents living below the poverty line.

For over a decade, a 2,400-acre site run by the world's largest waste disposal company, Chemical Waste Management, has taken in 500,000 tons of hazardous wastes a year.

Despite Waste Management's assurances, the Emelle site has been leaking pesticides and volatile solvents, traces of which have appeared in local wells and brought about serious health problems in the surrounding communities.

Gore, Oklahoma. It is here, in the heart of Cherokee country, that Kerr-McGee Corporation built its uranium conversion facilities in 1970. Not until 1985—15 years after

Sequoia Fuels had been in operation—did local residents find out that uranium dust had drifted into the surrounding neighborhoods and that liquid wastes were being dumped directly into the nearby rivers, contaminating fish, wildlife and vegetation.

In 1986, Gore residents were in for another surprise. A fuel cylinder ruptured at the plant, killing one worker and sending over 100 others to the hospital. For days after the accident, recalls Pat Moss of Native Americans for a Clean Environment, a yellowish gas cloud covered over 15 miles of rural Oklahoma. Soon afterward, two-thirds of the residents within a 10-mile radius were diagnosed with cancer—half of whom have reportedly died since. The surrounding community also suffers from severe liver and kidney problems, and Indian children there have been born with gross deformities since the mid-1970's.

Native lands are hot spots for corporate waste producers for the added reason that they are not subject to federal or state environmental laws and regulations, Moreover, as Pat Moss points out, Native American territories are often on mineral-rich land. "If you poison the people who live there," he says, "you can come right in there, say it's 'uninhabitable,' and claim it for yourself."

Confronted by the growing strength of local movements against toxics, and having to justify building dumps in certain areas, industry spokespeople argue that some communities must make the sacrifice for the larger public good. Toxics projects come packaged in candy-coated promises of donations and jobs, and many economically-depressed areas are hard-pressed to turn down these short-term gains.

In a further effort to bottleneck community regulation of waste site placement, industry lobbyists are trying to introduce into law a policy of "pre-emption," which would effectively let the state decide if and where sites are located. This measure would do away with all community involvement and dismantle the hard-won right to vote and veto proposed hazardous waste facilities in states such as Kentucky, Tennesee and Oklahoma.

In addition to this legislative strategy, the toxics industry has also been buying off local officials. For example, in Sumter County, South Carolina, a new GSX Services Inc., landfill is now managed by four ex-staff members of the state regulatory agency—the same agency that approved the GSX dump in the first place.

If the "velvet glove" of donations, tax revenues, job swapping and pre-emptive legislation doesn't work, there are always the "iron fist" approaches for which the toxics industry is famous. In the South, for instance, Black families vocal in their opposition to proposed dumps have been singled out, threatened and intimidated, and in some cases, have had their houses mysteriously burned down during the peak of community protests.

II. Taking on the Polluters

Government regulations of hazardous wastes, nonexistent until 1976, are dismal today. Superfund, the only federally funded program to clean up high risk dumpsites, is famous for its "musical barrels" act—moving leaking barrels of toxic waste from one unsafe site to another, the largest portion of them in low-income communities of color.

The success of organizers against the slick new tactics of the industry is largely due to strategies that target toxic waste and toxic use reductions at the source of the pollution. A far cry from the waste management approach dominant in both the private sector and in government regulatory agencies, this approach of confronting the industry directly, rather than negotiating through state agencies, is what distinguishes toxics organizing as one of the most radical movements today.

For instance, the West Contra Costa County Toxics Coalition, organizing against the Chevron oil refinery in Richmond, California, follows what it calls "KIN," a three-part model based on the right to Know, the right to Inspect and the right to Negotiate:

> *The Right to Know* what is produced, how it is produced and what the potential hazards are—now and in the future.

> *The Right to Inspect* factory or site operations with community members and their own technical experts, in order to determine whether production safety measures are being utilized and whether the plant is being operated in the safety interests of the neighborhood and the workers.

> *The Right to Negotiate* directly with the company's top management for changes and concessions in production practices and for assistance with toxics-related health problems in the surrounding community.

Richmond residents who have lived under the shadow of the Chevron refinery since 1957 say enough is enough. "This community has been used as a dumping ground for much too long," says Henry Clark. "We have carried our weight . . . and we have declared a moratorium on chemical pollutants. We are going to organize, and we are going to enforce that."

What distinguishes toxics organizing is precisely this ability to identify a corporate target and directly go after it. It allows ordinary people to confront the polluter and bypass the intermediary power of the state.

Toxics organizing is unique in that it opens up the possibility of broad-based coalitions of labor unions, churches and community groups, and in particular, has the potential to build strong multi-racial organizations that would be unthinkable otherwise. As Clay Carter of CCHW, Birmingham says, community action against toxics in the South has "brought together people who would most likely not be in the same room were it not for the common threat to their communities."

But there are also barriers. "Although the toxics issue lends itself well to multi-racial organizing," Carter points out, "it is still a major challenge for people to rise above ingrained racial tensions that have existed for so long. The potential is great but there's still a long way to go."

---

*ACTION**

1. **Make the links between economic and ecological justice.** These links speak to the heart of what the environmental movement is for and open possibilties for broad-based coalitions. Are well-off environmentalists ready to scale down to become creditable with the poisoned rather than with the poisoners?

*Action section by Brad Erickson

2. **Support re-aligning relations** between owners and workers, owners and communities and banks and communities. The Berlin Wall was nothing compared to the invisible walls separating benefitters and sufferers in the global industrial economy. Respectful and sensitive multicultural alliance building is central to bringing down our own Berlin Walls.

3. **Learn about and fight overt and subtle forms of racism.** Education, economics, production, community, health—all aspects of society need to be reexamined and transformed to overcome centuries of cultural and racial inequality. Learning about the histories of the diverse cultures that make up our society and learning to listen to the views of individuals with cultural backgrounds different from our own is a prerequisite to achieving this transformation.

4. **Join or start a community anti-toxics group in your area.** If there are no groups in your area, contact one of the national organizations listed in the resource section for help and information.

Breaking Pesticide Addiction:
The Global Circle of Poison

MONICA MOORE

T HE MODERN PESTICIDE era began when research into chemical warfare agents during World War II also led to discoveries of chemicals that kill insects, weeds and other life forms. Pesticides were first seen as a precise, almost miraculous way to save crops and livestock, help feed the world, and eliminate dreaded diseases. Since then, pesticide use has intensified until over four billion pounds of pesticides are applied, almost a pound a day for every person on earth. Modern intensive agriculture has become dependent on enormous applications of chemical pesticides.

As in most cases of chemical dependence, recognition of pesticide dependence is frequently masked by denial. This denial takes several familiar forms. The pesticide industry and many government regulators tell us that introducing tons of these poisons into the food chain and environment is simply not a serious problem. Others assert that world food supplies can only be secured with continued massive use of pesticides and other chemical inputs.

These false claims ignore the profound short and longer term consequences of continued dependence on synthetic pesticides. In fact, pesticide use has become a serious threat to human and environmental health. United Nations agency estimates of pesticide poisoning cases range from one to two million per year, with between 20,000 and 40,000 fatalities. Most of the poisonings and nearly all fatalities take place in developing countries. Long term effects of pesticides on people and other species include cancer, reproductive effects, and neurological problems.

Moreover, in stark contrast to the cornucopia promised by the "Green Revolution," pesticide dependence actually erodes agricultural productivity and sustainability. Controlling pests is a legitimate and necessary human activity. Continuing dependence on chemical pesticides is not only a

Monica Moore is the Executive Director of the Pesticide Action Network (PAN) North America Regional Center (formerly known as the Pesticide Education and Action Project. PAN NA RC is one of seven regional centers for PAN International, and the coordinator of PAN's "Dirty Dozen" campaign.

Farm workers exposed to crop dusting. Detail of San Francisco mural "Las Luchugueras" by Juana Alicia, an artist who herself suffered pesticide poisoning while pregnant and working in the fields. JUANA ALICIA PHOTO: WILFREDO CASTAÑO 1983

dangerous, but also a self-defeating way to control pests. Growing resistance of pests to the chemicals designed to kill them makes the point. By the end of 1986, nearly 500 insect species had become resistant to one or more of five pesticide groups, and at least 17 species were resistant to all five.

Pesticides affect all of us. Yet there are unmistakable patterns in groups that bear the highest risks. Pesticide poisonings and fatalities are disproportionally concentrated in developing countries, although they account for only a fourth of all pesticide use. Agricultural and pesticide manufacturing workers, together with rural residents generally, suffer high exposures in both industrialized and developing countries. Children, whose developing organ systems are

hit harder by toxins than those of adults, are especially vulnerable. Household and garden pesticide users often apply more pesticide per square inch to their living space, with less information about the chemicals they are using, than do agricultural users.

When we are told that pesticides are subject to extensive risk/benefit studies, it is important to ask who benefits from pesticide use—and who bears the risks. When we hear experts have identified "negligible," "acceptable" levels of cancers, reproductive and neurological effects for each pesticide, ask acceptable to whom? To deflect such questions, those who are more comfortable with the status quo have developed a jargon for those who challenge their assertion that the risks are under control, or worth it. "Chemophobia," for example, is a recently coined term to describe the "irrational fear of chemicals" (usually in critics!). Other time honored labels: over-emotional, ill-informed, misled, or even foes of modernity who would turn away from progress and endanger world food supply in the process. Don't be fooled; keep asking questions, and keep looking for alternatives. You will find many people with you, willing to share what they have learned.

Pest control decisions affect the lives and well being of people and all living things the world over. Pesticides travel in air, surface and ground water, rain, snow and fog, and are found thousands of miles from where they were used. And they are produced, used and exported all over the world, as are products pesticides are applied to. Keep in mind that although the transition to more sustainable pest control practices is in fact underway and will take time, the global pesticide trade is still a very lucrative one. Even as industrialized country markets peak, developing countries still offer booming markets to pesticide salespeople, lubricated with funds from development agencies and multi-lateral development agencies.

Fortunately, resources for recognizing and treating pesticide addiction for what it is are more available now than ever before. Citizens around the world are struggling for control over decisions that affect them and their families, and to safeguard environ-

mental integrity. In some places, the work is to break free from pesticide dependence. In others it is to protect existing sustainable systems from synthetic chemical encroachment. But we are living in a turning point, the Circle of Poison is breaking up. How long it takes and what replaces it is up to all of us.

ACTION*

Citizen Intervention:

1. **Buy certified organic produce.** If your local market does not carry certified organic food, make an appointment with the manager and urge him or her to stock it.

2. **Boycott grapes in support of the United Farm Workers Union,** whose members are asking consumers to show support for their demand for a ban of five dangerous pesticides used on grapes, and that agricultural workers be allowed to hold free and fair union elections. For more information, contact the UFW.

3. **Eliminate or minimize pesticide use** in your home, garden, on your pets, and in your kids' schools and local public buildings. Seek out alternatives-both alternative pest control methods and sources of information. Educate yourself and others about non-toxic pest control options.

Note—Coming soon to a supermarket near you: Responses to citizens' concern that continued chemical-fix pest control is not good for agriculture, global environmental health, or in their interests range from sincere to fraudulent. Among the latter, be

wary that a massive public relations campaign is starting up, financed by some supermarkets, chemical trade associations and some regulatory agencies, to convince people that pesticide residues in food are not a problem. The credibility war is on, and consumers will be hearing more conflicting claims about food safety over the coming months. So check your sources, and come to your own conclusions!

4. **Write Letters to:**

    Congress. The House Subcommittee on Energy, Environment and Natural Resources. Tell them you oppose the export of banned and unregistered pesticides and want it stopped.

    Elected officials. Federal and state governments should provide financial assistance and other incentives to farmers to help them in the transition from pesticide dependence to sustainable agricultural practices.

    World Bank. Encourages export crop production in agricultural development, including heavy use of pesticide and fertilizers. Finances hundreds of millions of dollars of pesticide purchases in developing

*Action section by Monica Moore

countries every year. Has guidelines requiring use of alternative pest control wherever possible, doesn't implement them. (A new study coming out soon of Bank's non-performance re:these guidelines, by Michael Hansen, Institute for Consumer Policy Research/Consumers Union, Mt. Vernon, NY.)

School boards, parks and recreation departments. Ask what pesticides are used at your kids' schools and in public places; tell them parents and the public have a right to know whenever they and their kids are exposed to pesticides; urge adoption of a strong integrated pest management program.

Highway transportation departments use a lot of herbicides and other pesticides on median strips, roadside rights-of-way, etc. Same message as above.

Write letters to editors about all of the above. Spread the word.

Biotechnology

MICHAEL PICKER

"As public knowledge increases about toxic side-effects, there will be an increasingly strong desire for biological products that pose no threats to the environment. There is a great opportunity for biocontrols."

—JOSEPH BOUCKAERT,
ADVANCED GENETIC SCIENCES,
OAKLAND, CA

"It's possible for the industry to describe 203 different products underway right now which are trying to produce a more environmentally acceptable technology for farmers . . . The truth is that more than half the actual research is related to herbicidal tolerance. There was a time not so long ago when plant breeders worked on pest resistance. Now they work on pesticide resistance. That allows pesticide manufacturers to increase the market area for their chemicals."

—PAT ROY MOONEY

Economic Forces Drive New Technologies

In California, for the last two decades the most lively and fastest growing industries have depended heavily on chemical processes for manufacturing. No longer do aerospace, electronics or other major portions of the industrial sector depend on heat or mechanical force to produce goods. Instead, it's the application of chemical force to manufacture high tech products that has pushed California into position as the world's sixth largest economy. In California's futuristic agriculture, it's as if the land itself has become only a convenient medium for applying chemicals to crops.

Michael Picker is the West Coast Director of the National Toxics Campaign. Formerly Deputy Assistant to the California Governor for Toxics Control, Michael taught at UCLA's Graduate School of Architecture and Urban Planning and has over 10 years experience in toxics and hazardous waste issues.

But the rate of profit increases in many sectors of the chemical economy is slowing. In order to maintain a competitive edge in the coming world economy, planners point to a new area of tremendous potential—biotechnology. This new industry will be built around a wide range of new activities, all involving the application of biological forces to produce goods.

The new biotechnologies are just beginning to enter the market place (and, eventually, the environment). And, as with the chemical industry, there may be drawbacks, as well as benefits.

California is a primary center for research and production in this new industry, the home to an estimated one-quarter to one-third of the world's biotech companies, primarily clustered around the Bay Area. Massachusetts ranks a close second. The industry is high tech; heavily dependent on the cutting edge of university research, companies with names like Calgene, Genex or Biogen cluster around prestigious centers of bioscience—UC Berkeley, Stanford, Harvard and MIT.

But, soon, there won't be 400 or 500 small biotech companies around the world, there will only be Nestles, Unilever or Phillip Morris. As the new technology gets integrated into an increasingly concentrated world economy, we'll see it directed toward creating profits, not toward meeting human needs.

Activists occupied this crane for over a week at the University of California at Berkeley to protest construction of a biotechnology lab reportedly involved in germ warfare.
DAVID CROSS 1989

And What Will Biotech Bring to Us?

Looking back, David Lilienthal, the first head of the Nuclear Regulatory Commission, says: "The atom had us bewitched. It was so gigantic, so terrible, so beyond the power of the imagination to embrace, that it seemed to be the ultimate fact. Our obsession with the atom led us to assign to it a separate and unique status in the world." The tremendous potential for the technologies enthralled those closest to it, and economic pressures to develop nuclear power distorted political institutions where other checks and balances might have applied. You can see the same forces at work in the area of biotech.

Proponents of biotech point to a brilliant soon-to-be revolution in health, food production and manufacturing processes using chemical or biological products. So far, however, few of these promises have panned out. Market analysts note a new restlessness in high tech investors as years of research and heavy investments have failed to produce expected returns. For example, Monsanto and three other companies have reportedly spent upwards of $500 million on bovine somatotropin (BST), a hormone to increase milk production. But it's still not on the market.

Although few serious negative impacts have been observed to date, this may be in part because the technologies aren't widely in use. Now is the appropriate time for a broad public evaluation of the use of these powerful new tools.

But, also because of the lack of clear threat and urgency, only a few public interest organizations have mobilized resources to consider biotechnology issues. General unfamiliarity with the new technologies hampers effective discussion and the sheer intimidation of entering a new and complex subject area deters many. What are some of the problems and issues we should be talking about?

Hazards of the New Technology

Production of biotech products will result in wastes; both hazardous and biological. The industry is and will continue to use toxic solvents and sterilizing agents, as well as radioactive elements (for tracing passage of biological material). Pathogenic organisms are of especial concern. The danger to workers is clear and undeniable.

Environmental release of genetically engineered organisms (GEO's could be bacteria and microbes, plants or animals) probably won't result in giant tomatoes eating Cleveland. But novel organisms *could* end up finding ecological niches, with the potential for the same devastating impact as other

introduced species such as the gypsy moth or kudzu.

Biowarfare is described as the "poor man's nuclear bomb." It's relatively cheap, potentially invisible (you may not even realize you've been attacked), and incredibly difficult to defend against (or to monitor in weapons agreements). The greatest danger may not be in what it will do to people, but in what it will do to crops.

Social and Environmental Impacts of Its Products

Increased use of biotech will result in economic displacement in agriculture. While BST may increase dairy production on individual farms as much as 20 percent, it's estimated that one-third of America's small dairy farmers will be bankrupted in the process. The dream of an ecologically sustainable agriculture will grow dim, as farmers become *more* dependent on high tech inputs. In addition, as certain strains become more popular, genetic variability in agriculture may narrow even further, increasing the risk that disease will wipe out ever-larger areas.

Stress (heat, salt or mineral) tolerant plants may encourage farming in the few remaining native habitats. These lands have often remained out of production because crops won't grow there. Biotech will solve that problem and produce pressures to farm on marginal lands.

Many plants are susceptible to the same pesticides as weeds that compete with them. By making the plants resistant to the pesticide, new markets may open up for certain chemicals. Some of the pesticides now being researched have polluted groundwater or otherwise contaminated the environment.

Social Consequences of This New Industry

The need for up to the minute technical expertise means that industry will seek to control that resource. As knowledge increasingly becomes a valuable commodity, the traditional independence of the university will erode.

The new biotechnologies raise a bewildering variety of profound ethical and moral issues. For example, scientists have successfully produced human growth hormone (HGH), which can be used to treat dwarfism. But there just aren't enough dwarfish people seeking treatment to make HGH profitable. Should we allow this product to be used by parents who simply want taller children?

Should giant corporations control the substances of life?

ACTION*

1. **Fight patenting of novel organisms.** By making it impossible to own genetic information, we take some of the edge off the profit lust, protect ourselves against control of precious resources of economic giants, and make it more practical to discuss what we really want from biotech. Congress has considered legislation and it will come up again. Write your Congressmember at the House of Representatives, Washington, DC 20525, and to your Senator at the US Senate, Washington, DC 20510. Ask your environmental organization to take a position against patenting of life forms.

2. **Campaign to keep irrational biotech products off the market.** We don't need more milk (we already pay to keep milk production down), so we don't need BST. Support state legislation to ban BST, to require labels, or organize consumer boycotts of BST milk. Similarly, we don't need herbicide tolerant plants. That's the wrong way to go. We need less pesticide use, and not more.

3. **Push for the adoption of local ordinances** requiring disclosure of releases, discharges or emissions if a biotech research or production company plans to move into your area. The City of Cambridge, Massachusetts, has adopted an ordinance that also requires certain levels of safety containment and monitoring for biotech facilities.

4. **Lobby for the adoption of a local ordinance** requiring a permit, disclosure of the release, monitoring, and liability insurance in each case that a company plans an intentional release of a GEO in your area.

5. **Organize forums and discussions** to help educate others about the potential problems biotech presents.

*Action section by Michael Picker

Renewable Energy

AMORY B. LOVINS AND KAREN C. BADALIAN

THE 1990'S—A NEW decade and final phase of the 20th century. In the United States we have come a long way towards using energy more sensibly. But we still have a long way to go. For example, energy intensity reductions have slashed this country's annual energy bill by an incredible $150 billion since 1973. But at the same time, the energy currently wasted in the US costs twice as much as the federal deficit and more than the entire $10,000-a-second military budget.

In spite of confusing federal policies and numerous market barriers, the transition to a sustainable energy system is happening much faster than was thought possible 10 years ago. Since 1979, the US has reaped more than seven times as much new energy from savings as from *all* net increases in energy supplies. Most of these new supplies have come from sun, wind, biomass, and flowing water. These renewable sources, which the glossy magazine ads from the nuclear industry say cannot provide much un-

til the next century, now supply more than a tenth of the nation's total energy. Nuclear power, after absorbing about $200 billion in public and private investments, now delivers to the US considerably less energy than wood.

During the 1970's, using such unsophisticated tools as caulk guns and duct tape, Americans managed to cut OPEC's market share in half. And most of the best energy-saving technologies now on the US market weren't available even one year ago. Wider scale use of these technologies could save twice as much electricity as could have been saved five years ago, and at only a third of the real cost.

While this technological revolution shows no signs of abating, smart US utilities are shifting their plans to accommodate a growing energy-efficiency market. By helping customers use energy more efficiently—through information, design services and financial incentives—utilities make saved electricity into a commodity. Utilities that

Amory Lovins, a physicist, has been an energy consultant for 15 years, advising governments, international organizations and corporations. He is the author of over a dozen books including the groundbreaking *Soft Energy Paths.* **Karen Badalian** is Publications Editor at the Rocky Mountain Institute.

Kolonia, Pohnpei, Micronesia. Students from various islands attend a program to teach South Seas islanders to implement appropriate technology such as methane-conversion, solar dryers, water heaters, water desalination devices and photovoltaic devices for various purposes (photovoltaic demonstration system shown). CHARLES CASE

sell both electricity and electrical savings shift their orientation from being vendors of a single product to being a service industry.

The shift is difficult for businesses that have operated for decades as monopolies. They must not only redefine their corporate missions, but also their employees' career goals and personal identities. Yet, the bottom line is clear: selling efficiency makes money. Because providing energy-efficient services is cheaper than running a power plant, the utility's costs will decrease more than its revenues. Revenues minus costs equals profits.

The money saved by energy efficiency and use of renewable resources is equaled if not surpassed in environmental bonuses. For example, a single 18-watt compact-fluorescent lamp, producing the same light as a 75-watt incandescent lamp for 13 times as long, will over its lifetime save about one-ten-millionth as much electricity as a huge (1,000 megawatt) power station generates in a year. That doesn't sound like much. But it means that this *single* lamp will avoid the emission from a typical US coal plant of a *ton* of carbon dioxide, which contributes to acid rain, plus nitrogen oxides, heavy metals and other pollutants. If it displaces a nuclear instead of a coal-fired power station, the same single lamp will avoid the production of half a curie of strontium-90 and cesium-137 (two major components of high-level waste), and 25 milligrams of plutonium-about equal in explosive power to 850 pounds of TNT, or to at least 2,000 cancer-causing doses of radioactivity.

By selling less electricity and more efficiency, utilities won't have to raise electric bills to pay for putting diapers on dirty coal plants to reduce acid-gas emissions. By helping customers acquire super-efficient lights, motors and appliances, utilities can instead burn less coal, emit less sulfur and use part of the money saved in operational costs to clean up their remaining power plants. Similar economic incentives could be applied to the more complex issues of abating nuclear proliferation, improving domestic energy security and reducing dependence on Middle Eastern oil.

Though progress is slower abroad, particularly in developing nations, economic incentives and environmental concerns are beginning to raise awareness about energy efficiency and renewable resources. After all, replacing an incandescent with a compact-fluorescent lamp will save 70-85 percent of the energy per unit of delivered light whether the lamp is used in Belgium or Bihar. Superwindows cut cooling loads by the same (or greater) percentage in Bangkok as in Bakersfield.

In Third World countries, the environmental stakes may be even higher than in modern nations. Consider, for example, a village in upland Nepal. Rolls of high-tech plastic sheeting could be combined with local building materials to install simple but very effective solar greenhouses on homes. The greenhouse provides heat in winter, reducing the need for firewood and thus reducing deforestation. This, in turn, reduces soil erosion, and thus helps alleviate flooding downstream in India. Ultimately, avoiding the flooding may prevent a famine that could otherwise kill several hundred million people.

It is fashionable now to pay less attention to energy issues than we did in the past. But environmentalists should continue to stress the necessity of using resources efficiently, as a path to the sort of sustainable development that will enable us to meet the needs of humankind while preserving the environment on which we all depend.

ACTION*

Consumer Action:

1. **Insulate your home.** Weatherstrip doors and windows, install stormwindows and plastic sheeting to keep the heat in and the cold out (or the reverse in summer). Wrap water heaters with insulating "blankets," insert a "bottom band" or rigid foam underneath and install water heater to the plumbing system.

2. **Change your light bulbs.** The best energy-efficient light bulbs on the market today use 75 percent less electricity and last 9 to 13 times longer than their conventional counterparts.

3. **Add more insulation** to the walls, floors, foundation and attic when building or remodeling your home, In a hot climate, add a "radiant barrier" of shiny foil in the attic to keep roof heat from radiating down the attic floor. Install "superwindows"—windows treated with low-emissivity coatings and special gases on and between the panes of glass—to add insulating power and save heating/cooling costs.

4. **Replace old or burned-out appliances** with efficient ones. Several models of refrigerators on the market use up to 50 percent less electricity than less effi-

*Action section by Amory Lovins, Karen Badalian (1-4) and Brad Erickson (5-9)

cient models. State-of-the-art natural gas heaters are now up to 97 percent efficient, and the best color TVs save up to four-fifths the energy of their counterparts. Tankless water heaters can reduce water heating costs by heating water only as needed, without storing it as conventional water heaters do.

These are just some examples of energy efficient technologies and techniques that are commercially available and eminently practical. A "Where-to-Get-It List of Technologies" is available for $5 from the Rocky Mountain Institute.

Political Action:

5. **Push Congress to legislate energy efficiency** in all consumer appliances and industrial equipment. Urge national subsidies for home insulation to conserve heating costs, and support urban tree planting to conserve cooling costs. Ask for sweeping legislation to prevent energy waste in lighting, heating, manufacturing, advertising and transportation. The consumer changes listed above need to be institutionalized. Utilities need to be forced to assist economically and technically.

6. **Stop nuclear power.** Insist that all nuclear waste be laid to rest within 3 miles of where it is generated and generators must pay for the disposal. Boycott and campaign against General Electric and Westinghouse. Contact INFACT (see Making War Obsolete Resource Section for boycott info).

7. **Cut a deal.** *No* discussions on nuclear waste dumps *anywhere* until agreement is reached on the phase-out and shutdown of all military and civilian applications of nuclear power and weapons. Waste dumps should be opposed by everyone, everywhere until this agreement is signed and sealed. The nation needs a planned transition to low energy use and renewable energy production. As we phase out nuclear power we need to plan alternatives for workers. The US government needs to make a commitment to increase solar power for new buildings and refit old ones. There needs to be massive energy efficiency conversions, including at military installations.

8. **Make local utilities community-owned.** Breakup big federal power authorities. Make the Nuclear Regulatory Commission accountable to a citizen board. Focus on target institutions like oil companies; break them up.

9. **Support the communities** resisting nuclear dumps in their environs.

RESOURCES

Organizations

Abalone Alliance
2940 16th Street, Room 310
San Francisco, CA 94103
(415) 861-0592

Promotes alternative, safe energy sources, moving away from nuclear dependency. They focus on the California nuclear reactors at Diablo Canyon and Rancho Seco, but their methods and message can help any group fighting for safe energy sources. They publish the Radiation and Alternatives Bulletin, *or RAD BULL $10/ year. Membership is $25/year, $15/low income.*

Alliance to Save Energy
1725 K Street NW, Suite 914
Washington, DC 20006
(202) 857-0666

A coalition of business, government and consumer leaders dedicated to conducting research and pilot projects to stimulate increased efficiency of energy use and investment in energy efficiency. They use these experiences to formulate policy initiatives and conduct education projects. Write or call for a publication list. Memberships are $25 for individuals, $1000 for foundations.

Center for Third World Organizing
3861 Martin Luther King, Jr. Way
Oakland, CA 94609

A national network of organizers, activists and scholars, CTWO trains community organizers, provides technical assistance and produces research and publications on issues affecting poor communities of color in the US. Their work includes toxics, health, immigration, housing and education.

Citizen's Clearinghouse for Hazardous Wastes
P.O. Box 926
Arlington, VA 22216
(703) 276-7070

Founded in 1981 by Love Canal leader Lois Gibbs, CCHW is the only national environmental organization started and led by grassroots activists. Provides information to individuals with legitimate toxic waste problems and questions on what to do. Publishes two quarterlies: Action Bulletin *and* Everyone's Backyard.

Citizens for a Better Environment
942 Market Street, Suite 505
San Francisco, CA 94102
(415) 788-0690

Works to reduce toxic pollution in the urban environment through a combination of technical research, litigation and advocacy. Publishes the CBE Environmental Review *quarterly. A membership with subscription is $20/year.*

Committee for Responsible Genetics
186 South Street, 4th Floor
Boston, MA 02111
(617) 423-0651

Started by Cambridge community leaders pushing for regulation of biotech research, CRG helps to organize state conferences on biotech, has organized scientists and researchers against biowarfare and is active on human and medical topics related to biotech. Publishes Genewatch.

Data Center
464 19th Street
Oakland, CA 94612
(415) 835-4692

A comprehensive informational re-source center that monitors toxics compa-nies as well as press coverage of hazardous waste dumping. Has published Toxic Night-mare, *a 5-volume collection of articles on hazardous dumping.*

Environmental Action
1525 New Hampshire NW
Washington, DC 20036
(202) 745-4870

Does environmental lobbying, research and citizen action on several aspects of glob-al warming. Established the Energy Conser-vation Coalition, which brought together 20 national groups to work together on clean air lobbying and recycling issues. Member-ship ($25/year for individuals) includes En-vironmental Action Magazine, *which cov-ers recycling and waste reduction. They also publish* Powerline, *on the economics of en-ergy conservation.*

Environmental Policy Institute-Oceanic Institute
1130 17th Street NW, #630
Washington, DC 20036
(202) 544-2600

Originally an advocacy organization, EPI merged with Friends of the Earth and the Oceanic Society in February 1989 with the intention of expanding their activities to incorporate lobbying and research, and to develop an international base of member-ship and activity. EPI has mobilized public education and citizen organizing on bio-technological issues, for the past seven years. They are lobbying on such issues as animal patenting, agricultural research pol-icy and hydroelectric dams. Recent activities include research on plutonium use in the US, and producing press packets on the Valdez disaster. One of their publications is Altered Harvest, *by Jack Doyle, the Director of Ag-riculture and Biotechnology at EPI.*

Foundation on Economic Trends
1130 17th Street NW, Suite 630
Washington, DC, 20036
(202) 466-2823

Led by writer and technology critic Jer-emy Rifkin, who has been at the forefront of almost every fight over biotech, pushing is-sues and asking questions for more than a decade.

Greenpeace USA
1436 U Street NW
Washington, DC 20009
(202) 462-1177

Among other environmental concerns, Greenpeace monitors toxic waste disposal and works to enforce corporate and govern-mental responsibility for toxic dumping through educational campaigns and direct actions. One of their periodicals, Interna-tional Waste Trade Update, *is a study of 115 shipments of toxic wastes sent from indus-trialized countries to Latin America and Af-rica over the last two years.*

International Alliance for Sustainable Agriculture
1701 University Avenue SE, Room 202
Minneapolis, MN 55414
(612) 331-1099

A support and information organiza-tion for the sustainable agriculture move-ment since 1983. Focuses on research and documentation, organizational support and network building, and education and infor-mation dissemination. Members receive the monthly Manna, *which reports on current agricultural policies and IASA actions.*

National Coalition Against the Misuse of Pesticides
530 7th Street SE
Washington, DC 20003
(202) 543-5450

Founded in 1981, NCAMP is a clearing-house of information on pesticides and pes-

ticide alternatives. They answer telephone calls and mail inquiries, hold an annual national forum (usually in March) and issue two newsletters, Pesticides and You *and* NCAMP Technical Report.

National Toxics Campaign
37 Temple Place, 4th Floor
Boston, MA 02111
(617) 482-1477

Through its nine regional offices nationwide, NTC provides information and technical assistance to local organizations fighting toxics in their communities. The quarterly Toxics Times *chronicles their work.*

Native Americans for a Clean Environment
307 So. Muskogee Avenue
Tahlequah, OK 74464
(918) 652-6298

Formed in 1985 in response to widespread concern over the use of radioactive materials at a nearby plant, NACE organizes against proposed hazardous waste sites on native land in Oklahoma. An excellent source for those seeking information on toxic wastes in Native American communities.

Natural Resources Defense Council
40 West 20th Street
New York, NY 10011
(212) 727-2700

Works to protect natural resources and to improve the quality of the human environment. Internationally recognized for their well-researched and well-publicized campaigns against toxics in the home, in food and in the workplace. Supports important litigation on many issues, including tropical rainforest preservation. A good resource for the toxic waste export issue.

Northwest Coalition for Alternatives to Pesticides
P.O. Box 1393
Eugene, OR 97440
(503) 344-5044

An information service providing resources for development of pesticide alternatives. They have a five-state coalition represented on their board of directors and a national and international membership. Their information packets include "Pesticide Exposure and the Role of the Physician," and "Avoiding Trouble Down the Road: Managing Roadside Vegetation."

Oxfam America
115 Broadway
Boston, MA 02116
(617) 482-1211

An international agency that funds self-help development and disaster relief projects in poor countries and raises funds on a grassroots level. Oxfam America is one of seven autonomous Oxfams worldwide. They are at work in Mozambique on clean water issues, in Ethiopia on sustainable agriculture development and in Cambodia on development of pesticide alternatives. They issue Oxfam-Am News *and an annual report.*

Pesticide Action Network
P.O. Box 610
San Francisco, CA 94101
(415) 541-9140

Publishes PAN North America Newsletter *and* The Dirty Dozen Campaigner, *the international newsletter of PAN's "Dirty Dozen" campaign. Provides educational materials and is the North American regional office for the international Pesticide Action Network.*

Public Citizen Critical Mass Energy Project
215 Pennsylvania Avenue SE
Washington, DC 20003
(202) 546-4996

A group founded by Ralph Nader. Opposes nuclear power until proven safe, and supports alternative energy programs. Publishes Public Citizen *magazine. Membership is $20/year.*

Rachel Carson Council, Inc.
8940 Jones Mill Road
Chevy Chase, MD 20815
(301) 652-1877

A pesticide information and education center helping individuals and groups who face serious pesticide problems and need educational guidance.

Rocky Mountain Institute
1739 Snowmass Creek Road
Snowmass, CO 81654-9199
(303) 927-3128

Publishes a list of more than 150 articles from periodicals around the world about the ongoing research at RMI. The guide includes a price list and form for ordering publications.

Rural Advancement Fund International
P.O. Box 1029
Pittsboro, NC 27312
(919) 542-5292

Works on North/South issues related to agriculture, and supports world efforts toward sustainable and appropriate agriculture. They publish communiqués and 4-page alerts on biotechnological products and their impact on the Third World.

Sierra Club Pesticide Management
   Coordinator
Terry Shistar
Rural Route 5, Box 163
Lawrence, KS 66046
(913) 748-0950

Terry is a Sierra Club volunteer who provides networking resources for pesticide management. She is also a member of the board of the National Coalition Against Misuse of Pesticides.

United Farm Workers of America
1741 South Harvard Boulevard
Los Angeles, CA 90006
(213) 734-8302

The UFW has three priorities, all of which they are working on primarily through the boycott of table grapes: the banning of the "Dirty Dozen" pesticides; education about testing for pesticide residue in produce; and collective worker negotiations in the farm produce industry. They address their grievances and demands to the farm produce industry rather than the government, choosing direct action over bureaucracy. The boycott is working—sales of table grapes have dropped—but continued support is needed if the three priorities are to be met. Their magazine, Food and Justice, *provides updates on their campaigns.*

Books

Altered Harvest: Agriculture, Genetics and the Fate of the World's Food Supply. Jack Doyle. New York: Penguin Books, 1985.

A classic. It's an engrossing and in-depth examination of agricultural biotechnology and all the implications of that new industry.

Alternatives to Land Disposal. Arlington, VA: Citizens Clearinghouse for Hazardous Wastes. (Available from CCHW.)

Biotechnology and the Environment. Margaret Mellon. Washington, DC: National Biotechnology Policy Center of the National Wildlife Federation, 1988.

Overview of potential environmental impacts of biotech. Readable, with good, simple explanation of the science underlying the technology. Available from NWF, 1400 16th Street NW, Washington, DC 20036.

Brittle Power: Energy Strategy for National Security. Amory B. Lovins and L. Hunter Lovins. Andover, MA: Brick House, 1982.

Broken Code: The Exploitation of DNA. Dr. Mark Lappé. San Francisco: Sierra Club Books, 1984.

Readable and informative, with background and an excellent overview of biotech issues. Especially good sections on biomedicine, the ethics of human genetic issues and priorities for the new technologies.

Gene Wars: Military Control Over the New Genetic Technologies. Charles Piller and Keith R. Yamamoto. New York: Beech Tree Books/William Morrow, 1988.

Piller is a science writer and Yamamoto is a professor of biochemistry and biophysics. Exhaustive investigation into military use of biotech research.

Hazardous Waste in America. Samuel Epstein. San Francisco: Sierra Club Books, 1982.

Describes toxic waste dumping, waste oil dumping, midnight dumping and the contamination of groundwater. Also includes sections on the technology of waste disposal, toxic waste law and suggestions for action.

It's in Your Power: The Concerned Energy Consumer's Survival Kit. Stuart Diamond and Paul S. Lorris. New York: Rawson Associates, 1978.

The New Politics of Science. David Dickson. New York: Pantheon Books, 1984.

Outlines the ways in which technology has become power in modern life, and how economic interests control the use of that power.

Pesticides: 44 Questions and Answers. Gretta Goldenman and Sarojini Rengam. San Francisco: Pesticide Action Network, 1989.

In a simple question and answer format, this booklet systematically addresses the pesticide issues most often discussed. Available for $4 from PAN (see listing, above).

Problem Pesticides, Pesticide Problems. by Gretta Goldenman and Sarojini Rengam. San Francisco: Pesticide Action Network, 1989.

A citizen's action guide to the international code of conduct on the distribution and use of pesticides. Also available in Spanish. $15 from PAN (see listing, above).

Resource Efficiency Housing Guide: A Select Annotated Bibliography and Directory for Helpful Organizations. Robert Sardinsky and John Klusmire. Snowmass, CO: Rocky Mountain Institute, 1987.

A comprehensive review of resources to help homeowners select the resource-efficient options most suitable to their own lifestyles. The guide lists periodicals, books, energy offices, schools, technical information services, alternative energy associations and other resources which offer the best advice and training available.

Silent Spring. Rachel Carson. New York: Oxford University Press, 1951.

A classic book about the decline in bird populations as a result of DDT and other pesticides. Includes recent information on the US sale of banned pesticides to foreign countries and on the recovery of DDT in the US food chain, as a by product of the still-legal pesticide DDE.

Toxic Nightmare—Environmental Perspectives. 3 volumes. Oakland, CA: Data Center.

Available from the Data Center (see listing, above).

Toxics and Minority Communities. Oakland, CA: Alternative Policy Institute/Center for Third World Organizing, 1986.

Available from CTWO (see listing, above).

Toxic Wastes and Race in the United States. New York: Commission for Racial Justice/United Church of Christ, 1987.

PART NINE

WATER

Oceans

JACQUES COUSTEAU

THE OCEANS OF THE WORLD ARE suffering from a dangerous decrease in vitality. Before 1977, we thought the bulk of the decline was due to chemical pollution. But after diving extensively, taking hundreds of measurements and hundreds of samples of water and sediment, we began to realize that the drop in animals—vertebrates and invertebrates—which feed upon the meadow that is the ocean was much bigger than could be explained by chemical pollution.

It became obvious to me that the decline was also due to what I call mechanical destruction. By that I mean dynamite fishing, fishing in spawning grounds, using nets with mesh so small that they take the little fish as well as the adults, diverting rivers, filling in marshes and other stupidities.

If all of this is not changed, we face a catastrophe in the long term. But those in power make only short-term decisions. They put a band-aid where there is a cancer. For them the only thing that counts is eco-nomic productivity during the next four or five years. When they are obliged by public opinion to do something, they cheat. They commit to something and don't do it or do it badly.

A good example is what has happened in the Mediterranean. After years of fighting and conferences, the 18 nations that border on that sea have signed a pact. It's a good document. But it is not yet implemented to the degree it is supposed to be. More than $15 billion are needed over the next 10 years. Where are they?

Still, overall, there is some hope. The rate of yearly damage inflicted on the oceans is decreasing. We cannot be satisfied with that. But it shows that results can be obtained if pressure is fully applied.

The main role of the ocean is so obvious that nobody talks about it—and that is to sustain life. It does so not by providing food or minerals but by providing water. Without water there is no life.

In looking at the oceans I cannot say

Jacques Cousteau is the world's best-known authority on the sea, an activist working to protect the seas for decades through advocacy and education. His underwater explorations have become familiar to people around the globe through televised documentaries and bestselling books.

that one is more or less healthy than another, because differences are temporary. Water moves. That's why pollutants like DDT are found in the livers of penguins in the Antarctic, where there's no pollution. To show how water moves: in 90 years there will not be one drop of water in the Mediterranean that is there today. The pollutants in that sea will finally come to pollute the rest of the oceans. The same is true for the Caribbean, the North Sea, the Gulf of Finland and so on. While rivers and enclosed or semi-enclosed seas are in worse shape today than the open ocean, that may not be true in 10 or 20 years.

A majority of ecologists have been accused—sometimes rightly so—of having a negative influence on progress. Every time there is a project to build a dam or a generating plant, they say: "No, no, no, no. You are going to pollute." Instead of simply being negative they need to offer constructive counter-proposals. That may sometimes add to costs, but it is feasible. They require a lot of imagination, but contribute to the protection and improvement of life in a constructive manner.

Within this framework, there are a lot of things I am concerned about. I want to contribute to avoiding the eradication of species. Each time we eradicate a species—and we are eradicating several hundred each day—we impoverish the planet for millions of years. Every time we suppress an animal forever, we lower the level of what we can teach our children.

ACTION*

Oceans cover 70 percent of the Earth's surface and contain the most biologically diverse community in the world. Oceans are the lungs of the planet: marine plankton are actually responsible for 80 to 90 percent of the photosynthetic (oxygen-producing) activity of the planet.

The most diverse ecosystem on Earth is the coral reef, which shares many attributes with the rainforest. Coral reefs are stable, climax tropical communities that are often thousands to millions of years old. These intricately complex systems actually contain more species than the rainforests. The oceans remain and do not "disappear" in the same way rainforests do when they are destroyed—which makes protection of the oceans so much more difficult. Their destruction—by overfishing, harvesting of marine mammals, dumping of nuclear, toxic and sewage wastes, and the run-off of agricultural pesticides—occurs "out of sight, out of mind." Further complicating the protection of oceans is that beyond coastal areas, they "belong" to no one, and international efforts to regulate their sustainable use are virtually nonexistent.

The issue of the loss of jobs and the need to feed the hungry masses surfaces often in discussions of limiting environmental destruction of the oceans. But it is actually ocean destruction that eliminates jobs and resources from hungry people. Giant factory ships are stealing limited resources from the 8 to 10 million traditional fishers who have sustainably harvested their coasts for thousands of years; the big ships overfish the resources with their high-tech equipment. The products of this high-tech fishing end up as expensive canned fish that people

*Action section by Todd Steiner

Fort Bragg protest of US Department of Interior's proposed offshore drilling schemes for Mendocino coastline. Nationwide expression of outrage led to cancellation of plans.
DAVID CROSS

from developing nations cannot afford. And as the recent 10-million-gallon oil spill in Alaska illustrates, the corporate profit motive leads to environmental destruction, with little care for the ocean environment or the fishermen who depend on its resources.

We must educate our fellow citizens to recognize that the oceans are vital to the life support system of the Earth. We cannot use them as our sewer and expect them to be forever bountiful.

1. Investigation:

Sign on as a crew member on a seaward ship with questionable motives and document what's happening. Contact some of the action-and research-oriented environmental groups for ideas. Bring your video camera along! The out-of-sight na-

ture of ocean destruction calls for heroic individual actions.

2. Direct action:

Participate in nonviolent direct action to expose and delay destructive ocean practices. Remember, although the destruction takes place far out at sea, the decisions and profiteering from the practices occur in corporate headquarters in our own communities. Don't let them off the hook!

3. Consumer Intervention:

Boycott all canned tuna products. The killing of over 100,000 dolphins by the international tuna industry is an unnecessary travesty. Nearly 95 percent of all tuna is harvested in ways that do not harm these highly evolved social mammals. Corporate greed is driving several species of dolphins toward extinction. The effect of the slaughter of these species on the ultimate health of the ecosystem is unknown.

Boycott Icelandic fish products. Iceland remains one of the last few countries to exploit endangered whale species. The organized boycott of their fish products is making them reconsider the economic benefits of continuing this ultimately unsustainable activity.

4. Education:

Form a grassroots Earth Island Center in your community, and work to make your neighborhood canned tuna and Icelandic fish free zones. Set up an environmental video and speaker series. Begin a tuna boycott and set up educational picket lines outside your supermarket. Enlarge your campaign to include your entire state! Along the Pacific coast, Gulf of Mexico and the Northern Atlantic, form or join efforts to oppose offshore oil drilling.

5. Letter Writing:

Write your Representatives and Senators and urge them to support the ratification of the Law of the Sea Treaty. Encourage them to support stricter implementation of the Marine Mammal Protection Act, and increase funding for the National Marine Sanctuary program. Demand stronger laws against ocean sewage disposal and open ocean dumping. Demand an end to offshore oil drilling, and high seas driftnets that are strip-mining the oceans.

Write to European Economic Community (Environmental Commissioner, European Commission, Rue de la Loi 200, B-1049 Brussels, Belgium) in support of an import ban on tuna caught by killing dolphins.

Write to the Ambassador of Iceland (2022 Massachusetts Avenue, NW, Washington, DC 20008) and demand that they end their so-called "research whaling."

Water Resources and
Water Rights

DAVID FULLERTON

A human being needs 80 litres of water to live reasonably per day. Consumption rates vary from 5.4 per person in Madagascar (enough to keep alive) to 500-plus litres in the US.

—UNITED NATIONS
ENVIRONMENT PROGRAMME

WATER DEVELOPMENT HAS been closely linked to economic development in both industrial and non-industrial nations. A desire to accommodate rising populations, and to spur industrial and agricultural production have all led to increased utilization of water resources for industry, power and irrigation, and for domestic use. Reservoirs, groundwater pumping and intricate distribution systems form the backbone of these systems. Most large-scale water development is now taking place in the developing world with the encouragement of the international lending agencies. Both China and Brazil are considering huge water development projects. Unfortunately, this increased draw upon natural water supplies has had severe effects.

Much of the potential water supply in industrialized nations has already been developed. It is there that we must look to examine the down side of water development.

Nowhere has water development been taken to a greater extreme than in California. There, thousands of miles of canals, tens of thousands of wells and 1,300 reservoirs impounding some 43,000,000 acre-feet of water, have enabled giant cities and the richest agricultural area in the world to flourish.

But these economic gains have come at great cost to the people and the environment of California:

David Fullerton is Chairman of the Sierra Club's Northern California Water Committee. He also coordinates the non-profit Bay-Delta Hearings Project, which seeks improved water quality standards for the San Francisco Estuary.

- Run-off from irrigated fields laced with toxic compounds, herbicides and pesticides has severely degraded water quality. Kesterson, where run-off containing selenium from just 8,000 acres of farmland led to widespread mortality among birds and other wildlife is just an extreme example. Over 17 million Californians drink water polluted by untreated agricultural run-off.

- Giant dams on all the major rivers of the Central Valley have blocked spawning routes for salmon and other anadromous fish species with a devastating effect upon natural spawning. Ninety-eight percent of the San Joaquin River is diverted at Fraint Dam.

- The few wetlands still remaining have great difficulty obtaining adequate water supplies as most of the water is already committed to urban and agricultural uses. What water is available is often polluted from agricultural run-off.

- Diversions amounting to 50 percent of average historical flows now threaten the San Francisco Estuary, the largest on the West Coast, and its unique community of fish, birds and other wildlife.

- Huge corporate farms dominate much of the Central and Imperial Valleys. Such areas produce sterile, stratified rural communities consisting of a few well-to-do managers and large numbers of impoverished and landless farm workers.

Much damage has been done, but some of the harm can still be reversed. More fresh water needs to be put into the rivers, wetlands and estuaries. Toxic run-off from farms should be reduced through better

A contaminated West Coast lagoon. Who benefits from water contamination? Who decides? RACHEL JOHNSON

water management and retirement of the worst land. Tax, research and political biases in favor of agribusiness need to be eliminated.

A reallocation of water to benefit people and the environment will not come easily or rapidly. Urban water conservation and reclamation need to be expanded. But the key is agriculture, which uses 85 percent of the developed water in the state. Irrigation techniques need to be improved. Cropping patterns need to shift away from such low-value, high-water crops as irrigated pasture, cotton, alfalfa and rice. The giant state and federal agricultural water subsidies, which allow waste and the planting of inappropriate crops, need to be reduced or eliminated.

There are several lessons to be learned from California's experience:

- There is a limit to the amount of water that can safely be diverted from the natural environment.

- Water subsidies lead to an artificially high demand for water and to calls for yet more water development.

- Water policies that give a priority to short-term economic gain inevitably shortchange the water needs of people and the environment.

- Agribusiness is anti-democratic. The social effect is a rural class structure. Politically, agribusiness strongly influences water policy to its own benefit. Water quality and the needs of the environment often suffer as a result.

- Informed public debate and representation of affected populations, including non-human ones, should be the cornerstone of future water policy.

*ACTION**

1. **Oppose unnecessary new water projects.** Insist on conservation, and nonstructural approaches to water supply such as purchase of water rights.

2. **Insist that environmental questions receive consideration equal to economic ones.** What are the conditions of lakes, creeks, rivers and deltas in your region? Is wildlife thriving or declining?

3. **Fight water subsidies.** Find out whether agriculture in your region is water-efficient or water-wasteful. Are water-intensive crops such as rice grown in a relatively dry area and thus overly dependent on irrigation?

4. **Learn where your water comes from.** Find out what dangers potentially threaten your water supply—agricultural or civic diversion, industrial contamination, or agro-chemical runoff. Alert your community if threats exist and organize to protect your water rights.

5. **Identify and challenge wasteful water use** in your region whether agricultural, industrial or urban. Refurbish water supply mains. Many cities like New York have tremendous leakage—some of the pipes are 100 years old. Cover canals to prevent evaporative loss. Saving water involves lots of jobs.

6. **Prevent contamination.** Insist on a prohibition of the use of lasting agricultural chemicals that can runoff into streams, rivers and lakes and seep into groundwater.

7. **Stop irrigating deserts.**

8. **Stop depleting aquifers** like Ogallala for short-term use.

9. **Keep remaining usable water usable.** Keep toxics out.

*Action Section by David Fullerton and Brad Erickson

RESOURCES

Organizations

California Department of Water Resources
P.O. Box 942836
Sacramento, CA 94236-0001
(916) 445-3157

Offers a catalogue of publications on numerous subjects for readers at all levels. Publication 160-87, California Water: Looking to the Future, is a good, if somewhat biased, introduction to water in California.

Clean Water Action Project
317 Pennsylvania Avenue SE
Washington, DC 20003
(202) 547-1196

A national citizens' lobbying organization dedicated to the preservation of clean groundwater. They engage in public education, referral services and fundraising, and focus on empowering local citizens to lobby and build coalitions. Successful actions include drafting the Clean Water Act of 1972 and organizing a national campaign on toxic hazards education. Their quarterly, Clean Water News, costs $24/year.

The Cousteau Society
930 West 21st Street
Norfolk, VA 23517

Jacques Cousteau, founder of the society that bears his name, has probably done more to educate the world on ocean conservation than any other individual. Membership in the Cousteau Society ($28/year per family) includes the Calypso and Dolphin Log, two full-color magazines.

Earth Island Institute
300 Broadway #28
San Francisco, CA 94133
(415) 788-3666

Has projects on marine mammals, sea turtles, offshore oil drilling and coral reef ecosystems. Earth Island is dedicated to providing activists with resources useful for local organizing on international and local issues. Membership ($25/year; $15 low-income) includes EI Journal, an international environmental news magazine, as well action alerts on projects of your interest.

Environmental Defense Fund
257 Park Avenue South
New York, NY 10010
(212) 505-2100

A national membership organization dedicated to developing and promoting creative solutions to environmental problems through a partnership of science and law. Active in finding solutions to water problems that benefit current water users and the environment, particularly water marketing approaches. They publish a bi-monthly newsletter, EDF Letter.

Friends of the River
Fort Mason Center
San Francisco, CA 94123
(415) 771-0400

The largest grassroots organization for river preservation in the nation. Through the work of its members, FOR has protected several rivers under the Federal Wild and Scenic Rivers Act. They are dedicated to the conservation of water and energy supplies. Their bi-monthly newsletter, Headwaters, reports on river use and preservation issues, including recreation, energy and clean water.

Greenpeace USA
1436 U Street NW
Washington, DC 20009
(202) 462-1177

An international organization working on various ocean issues, including marine mammals, nuclear proliferation on the oceans, sea turtles, offshore oil drilling, protection of Antarctica and ocean pollution. Greenpeace's well-known nonviolent direct actions to publicize ocean issues have been supplemented in recent years with a large research and lobbying staff. Membership ($25) includes their magazine, Greenpeace.

International Rivers Network
301 Broadway, Suite B
San Francisco, CA 94133
(415) 986-4694
An international membership organization dedicated to protecting the world's river systems from destructive development and supporting indigenous people's rights. They have mobilized public opinion against the damming of China's Yangtze River and the World Bank's $500 million loan to Brazil for construction of ecologically disastrous dams. IRN uses letter writing campaigns, cost-effectiveness studies and publishes the bi-monthly World Rivers Review *($25 a year).*

The Oceanic Society
1536 16th Street NW
Washington, DC 20036
(202) 328-0098
Works for the protection of the marine environment, and for all species that depend on its health for their survival. Has focused on such issues as ocean dumping, dredging, land-based sources of marine pollution, comprehensive coastal protection, and protection of marine biological diversity. Their periodical is Ocean Watch.

Books

Biological Oceanographic Processes (3rd edition). T. Parsons, M. Takahashi and B. Hargrave. Oxford, England: Pergamon Press, 1984.
The quintessential academic textbook on ocean ecology.

Cousteau Almanac. Jacques Cousteau. Garden City, NY: Doubleday, 1981.
A huge reference encyclopedia with inspiring quotations by the author and articles on water pollution, sound pollution, ocean ecosystems, fish diseases caused by pollution, endangered fish and turtles, oil spills, energy conservation in the home, space travel, grassroots organizing, the risks of nuclear war, attempts to preserve aboriginal cultures in places like Amazonia, and ancient but endangered species such as the baobab trees of Africa.

Mind in the Waters. Joan McIntyre. New York: Sierra Club Books/Scribner, 1974.
A collection of poems, stories, experiments, myths, paintings, photos and fantasies about whales and dolphins. Contains articles about whale and dolphin physiology, eating habits, intelligence, communication, patterns of reproduction and migration. Includes an account of a whale leading the author's boat through rocky reefs on a foggy night, as well as contributions by native peoples, and by Neruda, Merwin, McClure, and D.H. Lawrence.

The Sea Around Us. Rachel Carson. Boston: Houghton Mifflin, 1970.
An introduction to the ecology of the sea.

GLOSSARY

Tools, Terms and Tactics A-Z

BRAD ERICKSON, CLAIRE GREENSFELDER, JANE McALEVEY AND MIKE ROSELLE

Affinity Group An autonomous, consensus-based discussion and action group usually consisting of five to fifteen activists united by an issue, campaign, specific direct action, or a shared commitment to ongoing political dialogue. At large scale demonstrations affinity groups act as decentralized and independent mobile action units, maximizing diversity and creativity to help achieve the goals of the action. Affinity groups, or "AG's" have been central to the successes of the anti-nuclear power and weapons movements of the 1970's and early 1980's, and to the present anti-intervention movement.

Billboard doctoring The art of modifying offensive roadside billboards with paint, or with pre-painted paper panels and wheatpaste, to reflect a socially conscious message.

Blockade An obstruction put in the path of an advancing vehicle or person to prevent passage. An attempt to stop or delay an activity that is considered by the blockader to be immoral or illegal.

Boycott A campaign to enlist the public to refuse to condone an immoral or illegal action by not purchasing products, attending events, or otherwise participating in enterprises that support the offending party. The Montgomery bus boycott in Selma, Alabama was critical in catalyzing the civil rights and black power movements of the 50's and 60's.

Campaign Any organized activity through which a group of people seek to achieve a common goal. A campaign traditionally has a clear beginning, a concrete objective and an end.

Canvassing Raising awareness, financial support and/or identifying voters through the process of walking door to door, neighborhood by neighborhood, and talking to people about a specific issue that demands action or about a candidate for public office. Canvassing is also done on the telephone now, but with a more limited impact.

Civil Disobedience The act of deliberately disobeying a law in order to make a personal statement of protest against a specific law, or the institution that enforces the law.

Coalition An alliance of groups or organizations that are working together to achieve a common, specific goal. A coalition is usually temporary but can be ongoing.

Collective   A group of people who are working or living together in order to achieve a common goal through sharing resources and responsibilities. Collectives are voluntarily joined and egalitarian in that no one person has more or less power than another.

Consensus   A decision making model. An alternative to majority rule in which agreements are reached unanimously. Meetings are *facilitated* rather than chaired to insure equal opportunity for participation. One person may *block* consensus if she disagrees with the group. This sends the decision back to discussion either to reformulate the deci-

sion so that agreement is unanimous or for the group to decide to table the decision until later. Consensus has been used as an efficient model of decision making and has the added benefit of preventing relationships of domination that result in resentment and alienation.

Democracy   A process that reflects equal representation in decision making around issues that affect people's lives. Thomas Jefferson said "I know of no safe depository of the ultimate powers of the society but the people themselves; and if we think them not enlightened enough to exercise their control with a wholesome discretion, the remedy is not to take it from them, but to inform their discretion." See also vote.

Demonstration   An action that seeks to call public attention to an issue. It can be by an individual or by a large group of people, and can be either passive or confrontational, persuasive or coercive. Its purpose is to build support for the position taken by the participants and it is part of a larger campaign.

Direct Action   An action that is taken to achieve a specific result. It can be anything from signing a petition and writing a letter to physically intervening in an objectionable action. Direct action is result oriented, and often high profile.

Ecotage   From sabotage. Actions that seek to prevent ecologically destructive activities through direct intervention, and can involve either deliberate obstruction, the destruction of machinery or other illegal actions. See also Monkeywrenching.

Facilitation   Facilitation describes the process used to help a group of people reach a mutually acceptable resolution to a question or problem. Also a technique of running meetings with active listening, rather than Robert's Rules of Order.

Poster announcing demonstration against arms shipments to Central America.
Bob Thawley/David Solnit

Graffiti The writing of messages on the walls of buildings, subway cars, street signs, etc. In many communities this is an important form of political expression and a creative response to oppressive industrial architecture and design.

Guerrilla Product Labeling The act of relabeling a product in order to reveal its real contents or the real intentions or actions of its producer. Often done with mass-produced stickers put out as part of a larger campaign.

Guerilla Theater An action or demonstration that uses drama to illuminate or clarify an issue. It can involve satire or other types of humor, or graphic reenactments of events that are being protested. Examples: mock funerals for justice or "die-ins" where masses of people dramatize the effects of nuclear war or some reprehensible government policy by pretending to be its victims.

Hunger Strike Refusing food and/or water over a period of time to draw attention to an injustice and/or to directly demand a change in policy. The Veterans' Fast for Life in 1986 called for an end to US intervention in Nicaragua. Often used as a resistance tactic for inmates and prisoners—one of the few options left to them to register protest.

Internationalism Acting in solidarity with the global community. See Solidarity.

Investigative Journalism Seeking to research and publicize information about an issue, action or individual that has been willfully kept from the public eye; sometimes at personal risk to the journalist, and sometimes causing a change in public policy as when the Watergate cover-up was exposed.

Jail Solidarity Sticking together behind bars: a strategy for activists in custody. Demanding equal treatment under the law for all who were arrested and rejecting efforts to create favoritism, or to divide and conquer the group.

Letter campaigns Generating volumes of mail to an individual, corporation or other entity in order to express public opinion for or against a specific policy.

Literacy "A person is literate to the extent he or she is able to use language for social and political reconstruction . . . to be literate is to be present and active in the struggle for reclaiming one's voice, history, future. Literacy is the precondition for engaging in struggle around the relations to meaning and relations to power." —Paulo Freire

Litigation The process of seeking resolution to problems through using the courts and the legal system.

Love For many, the most important ingredient of activism. Che Guevara said of love, "Let me say, with the risk of appearing ridiculous, that the true revolutionary is guided by strong feelings of love. It is impossible to think of an authentic revolutionary without this quality."

Mailings Activist training school. The art of putting multiple pieces of paper in envelopes during the late hours of the evening. A group ritual also known as "the threes": stuffing, stamping and sealing. This is often done to get out a big mailing for a campaign.

Media Outreach Working with mainstream and/or alternative press (print, television, radio) to get the message out to the maximum number of people. Requires a basic knowledge of what information a reporter needs to cover a given story: who, what, when, where and why?

Monkeywrenching Throwing a spanner, or wrench, into the machine in order to halt

Anti-toxics protestors alter a road sign in Louisiana's chemical corridor during a march from Baton Rouge to New Orleans. SAM KITNER 1988, GREENPEACE

its progress. A term coined by author Edward Abbey and used to describe actions taken to protect nature and people from destructive machinery. Literally or figuratively, monkeywrenching stops the machinery that damages people and the Earth.

Necessity Defense   Sometimes referred to the *choice of evils* defense, a legal defense that seeks to justify an illegal action that was taken in order to prevent or intervene in the commission of a more serious or greater crime. The Plowshares peace activists who destroyed nuclear warheads because they believed the warheads violated international laws against the killing of civilians used the necessity defense. International law specifies that it is the duty of individual citizens to disrupt activities that violate human rights. See also Nuremberg Principles.

Non-cooperation   Gandhi said that "Non-cooperation with evil is a sacred duty." It can include strikes, nonpatronage or boycotts, giving up privileges awarded by an unjust government and disobedience of state authority. Through mass non-cooperation a people can render themselves ungovernable and hence, unconquerable. Gandhi wrote "So long as I lived under a system of government based on force and voluntarily partook of the many facilities and privileges it created for me, I was bound to help that government to the extent of my ability when it was engaged in a war, *unless I non-cooperated with that government and renounced to the best of my capacity the privileges it offered me.*"

Nonviolence   A philosophy and practice of resisting violence through nonviolent means, not only as a tactic to be abandoned when no longer convenient but as an unwavering commitment to end the use of force in governance, in settling disputes, and as the path to equal rights and true democracy. Martin Luther King, Jr., wrote "First it must be emphasized that nonviolent resistance is not a method for cowards; it does resist. If one uses this method because he is afraid or merely because he lacks the instruments of violence, he is not truly nonviolent."

Nonviolence Trainings Training workshops carried out widely in the civil disobedience movement in preparation for action of civil disobedience. Practical training includes practicing how to react nonviolently when confronted by violence.

Nuremberg Principles After World War II, the US adopted these principles at the Nazi War Crime Trials. These principles affirm that there is an international law that can be enforced to prosecute crimes carried out even though they were legal in the country in which they were committed. Violators can be prosecuted and sentenced in the courts of international justice and enforcement is possible through voluntary sanctions on offending nations by the world community. For activists there is potential in applying these principles to current violations of international law. See also Necessity Defense.

Occupation An act of civil disobedience in which the protestors physically occupy an office or facility such as a nuclear power plant or university administration building to disrupt and protest the activities of that office or facility.

Outreach Any act of contact with one's community or constituency that has the aim of educating, input gathering, and organizing. Mailings, canvassing, petition drives, lectures, special events and the use of media are some common forms of outreach.

Petitions An organizing tool whereby numerous individuals sign a statement or a demand. The gathering of signatures measures the support for a given position and can demonstrate a show of public support to government or industry.

Phonebank A group of people calling targeted lists of phone numbers to educate, build public support, gather opinions or raise money.

Phone trees An organizational tool whereby any size group can be quickly informed of an upcoming meeting or action. Usually, the lead person is responsible for calling 3 or more others who in turn each call 3 or more others who in turn call 3 or more people, etc.. Everyone shares the responsibility and the word gets out quickly.

Picketing To make a human fence in front of a business, organization or institution to prevent entrance and disrupt its activities. This form of protest is most often used by striking employees who are members of a labor union.

Publications Books, pamphlets, magazines and newsletters can all serve to help educate the public and help keep one's constituency abreast of new developments.

Public speaking Still one of the most powerful skills an activist can develop. From meetings to rallies to interviews and press conferences, spokespeople get the word out and legitimize a cause.

Questioning Authority A critical consciousness in which one examines and contrasts the words, actions and motivations of authority figures. Even the authorities in this book should be scrutinized. Engage in discussions with your friends, co-workers and fellow activists to develop your own positions.

Rallies Mass gatherings intended to arouse group enthusiasm and action and to summon strength and support, often as part of a larger campaign.

Rent Strikes A refusal by a group of tenants to pay rent, usually in protest of high rates, unsafe living conditions or delinquent building maintenance.

Revolution "Revolutions—that is, periods of accelerated rapid evolution and rapid changes—are as much in the nature of human society as the slow evolution which incessantly goes on now among the civilized races of humankind. And each time that such a period of accelerated evolution begins, civil war is liable to break out on a small or large scale. The question is, then, not so much how to avoid revolutions, as how to attain the greatest results with the most limited amount of civil war, the smallest amount of victims, and a minimum of mutual embitterment. For that end there is only one means; namely, that the oppressed part of society should obtain the clearest possible conception of what they intend to achieve, and how, and that they should be imbued with the enthusiasm which is necessary for that achievement."

—Peter Kropotkin

Sit-in The old fashioned sit-in is still an effective means of expressing one's personal opposition. In the Mayor's office, in the street, or just in the way, sit-ins demonstrate your commitment to reach a resolution to a problem at the risk of being arrested or otherwise physically evicted.

Solidarity Unity (as of a group or social class) that produces or is based on community of interests and objectives. Solidarism is the sociological theory maintaining that mutual interdependence of members of society establishes common ground for social organization based on commonality of interests. The Women's Movement, the Anti-Intervention Movement, the Labor Movement and others are internationally organized forms of solidarity.

Spokescouncils Used in large demonstrations or campaigns, spokescouncils are meetings attended by selected representatives of affinity groups to plan strategy. Representatives then return to their respective groups in order to discuss proposals, and return to develop a consensus for action. This process involves everyone in decision making while avoiding time consuming large group meetings. Sometimes called *steering committees*.

Strategy A plan developed for the purpose of achieving a specific goal. A good strategy is one that realistically assesses the situation and the potential for success. It relies on good information and clear thinking. Planning strategy is the key to achieving goals.

Strike To stop work in order to force an employer to comply with demands. A general strike is one in which all workers are called upon to strike in order to massively non-cooperate with an unacceptable government, halt its functioning and defy its authority over the populace.

Teach-in An extended and often nightlong meeting especially of college students and faculty members for lectures, debates and discussion on an important and often controversial topic such as US foreign policy.

Trespassing Unlawfully entering another's property. A form of civil disobedience that is sometimes a consequence of occupations and direct actions.

Unions Organizations of workers who are united to ensure fair working conditions, decent salaries, benefits—and in general to act as one united voice when negotiating with an employer. Unions often act or take a stand on broader social conditions beyond employment issues.

Vigil The act of keeping awake when sleep is customary. A period of watchfulness and wakefulness as in mourning the victims of war or state repression. Also to stand and watch before and/or during a demonstration or action.

Vote   A convention of democracy in which community members record their decision on paper and the resultant tally is upheld as representing the will of the people. How well voting embodies and preserves democratic principles depends upon fair and accurate election procedures, whether various parties and candidates have equal access to media and other means of communication with the voter, levels of voter participation and education, degree of public debate and voter confidence in the electoral process.

War Tax Resistance   Refusing to support a government that engages in activities that you believe to be immoral or illegal by withholding taxes, or by withholding an amount equal to the portion that would go for military or otherwise objectionable expenditures.

Witnessing   Or bearing witness, a tradition often used by the Quakers, where one demonstrates her/his opposition to an action by being present during its commission and expressing disapproval without intervening. The purpose is to awaken the conscience of the person, institution or community involved.

Workshops   Small group meetings held for the purpose of educating and organizing around specific issues.

Yell   A loud outcry. In certain situations when democracy has been subverted and dialogue refused, yelling may be the only possible means of being heard.

Zeitgeist   Literally, "spirit of the times." A trend of thought and feeling in a given period of history. All broad-based movements are based in an assessment, whether conscious or not, of the prevailing social climate.